Negotiating Opportunities

Negotiating Opportunities

How the Middle Class Secures Advantages in School

Jessica McCrory Calarco

OXFORD
UNIVERSITY PRESS

OXFORD

UNIVERSITY PRESS

Oxford University Press is a department of the University of Oxford. It furthers
the University's objective of excellence in research, scholarship, and education
by publishing worldwide. Oxford is a registered trade mark of Oxford University
Press in the UK and certain other countries.

Published in the United States of America by Oxford University Press
198 Madison Avenue, New York, NY 10016, United States of America.

CIP data is on file at the Library of Congress
ISBN 978–0–19–063444–5 (pbk.)
ISBN 978–0–19–063443–8 (hbk.)

CONTENTS

ACKNOWLEDGMENTS

This project has been with me through so many life changes—new jobs, new cities, new roles, new babies. At every turn, I have been lucky to find tireless companions to help me on that journey. This book would not have been possible without the support of mentors, colleagues, family, and friends. I am forever grateful to those who pushed me to do just a little bit more and those who reminded me to take time to breathe.

Annette Lareau, who graciously signed on as my dissertation advisor despite the project already being underway, deserves special thanks for her sage advice and constant encouragement. Annette read multiple drafts of the book manuscript, and her careful feedback helped me greatly improve the clarity of the writing and the ideas. Throughout the years, Annette has become so much more than just an advisor—she has been a tremendous advocate for me and my work and, especially in difficult moments, a dear friend.

Others at the University of Pennsylvania, especially my dissertation committee—Grace Kao, Melissa Wilde, Randall Collins, and Stanton Wortham—were also instrumental in helping me develop as a writer and a scholar. I rarely make it through a day without reflecting on some key piece of professional wisdom from Grace Kao, and I never start a new draft or chapter without a Melissa Wilde-inspired outline. Annette Lareau, Stanton Wortham, David Grazian, and Charles Bosk filled my ethnographic tool-kit; Randall Collins filled my head with theory and taught me to see the bigger resonance in everyday patterns. My first writing group—Elizabeth Lee, Keri Monteleone, and Laura Napolitano—read numerous drafts and kept me sane during the inevitable rough patches of ethnographic research. The Department of Sociology at the University of Pennsylvania and the Institute for Education Sciences provided financial support for my graduate studies, for which I am deeply grateful.

As I made my way from graduate student to assistant professor, I could not have asked for better colleagues than the ones I found at Indiana University. Brian Powell has been my most enthusiastic cheerleader and my go-to source of advice on teaching, research, writing, and everything in between. Brian read multiple drafts of the book manuscript and offered invaluable counsel in navigating reviews and revisions. Tim Hallett constantly reminded me of the value of ethnographic work and the importance of connecting that work to theory. Brian Steensland and Fabio Rojas shared useful insights regarding the book publishing process. Other senior colleagues—including Eliza Pavalko, Jane McLeod, Clem Brooks, Pam Jackson, and Peggy Thoits—helped me refine key ideas in the book. The members of the Junior Faculty Working Group ("Jeff-Wig")—including Jennifer Lee, Steve Benard, Youngjoo Cha, Cate Taylor, Weihua An, Keera Allendorf, Andy Halpern-Manners, and Elaine Hernandez—offered feedback on early drafts and moral support throughout the writing process.

This book would not have been possible without the support of the students, parents, teachers, and administrators at "Maplewood Elementary" and "Fair Hills Middle School." They welcomed me into their classrooms, their homes, and their conversations, and I am humbled by their generosity and their willingness to candidly share with me so many aspects of their daily lives. I hope that it is clear from the book how impressed I was and continue to be with the teachers' dedicated devotion to their students, with the students' seemingly endless enthusiasm for learning, and with the parents' deep commitment to their children's well-being.

I am grateful to Oxford University Press for supporting this project as it evolved into a full book manuscript. As editor, James Cook played a key role in guiding me through the publishing process. I especially appreciate that James was able to find reviewers to provide such detailed and thoughtful feedback. The reviewers' suggestions were instrumental, particularly for clarifying the book's theoretical contribution and for structuring the manuscript to show how students, parents, and teachers all play a role in creating inequalities in schools.

Moving to Indiana took me hundreds of miles from the support networks I had built in my early career, and I was immensely lucky to find in Bloomington not only wonderful colleagues but also a new family of friends—Jen Brass, Matt Baggetta, Elaine Hernandez, Andy Halpern-Manners, Cate Taylor, Amy Gonzales, Kim Rosvall, Rich Phillips, Steve Benard, Youngjoo Cha, Joanna Woronkowicz, Scot Ausborn, Keera Allendorf, Nikos Zirogiannis, and Tehanee Ratwatte. Our Sunday dinners, weekend play dates, and late-night chats have kept me sane, and I deeply value the chance I have had to learn and grow with them as scholars, parents, and friends.

Whether close by or far away, my actual family has never wavered in their support of me or my career. My parents, Anne and Duane McCrory, did not bat an eye when I asked to move back home for graduate school. They have always shown a keen interest in my research, and their love and generosity have carried me through many difficult times—for that I am eternally grateful. My siblings, Emily East and DJ McCrory, who were still in high school when I started graduate school, graciously (or maybe grudgingly) let me share their bathroom and provided much needed comedic relief from the daily grind of academia. They have grown alongside this book—Emily becoming a teacher and a mother and DJ pursuing his own PhD—and I treasure the (albeit too rare) conversations we get to have about my work and theirs.

Dan Calarco is my constant—my longest and most treasured companion on this journey. Through years of interstate commuting, late nights of field note writing, endless decisions to spend "just a few more days in the field," and even a cross-country move, Dan has supported me with patience, love, and admiration, often letting his own ambitions take a back seat to my lofty goals. Our children, Layla and Leo, bring so much joy and laughter to my life. They challenge me to find balance in each day; their spirit inspires me and gives me strength. Becoming a mother has made me more keenly aware of how difficult it is to parent in ways that promote equality for all children but has also helped me to realize more fully the imperative of doing so.

Negotiating Opportunities

Introduction

One sunny February morning, the students in Ms. Dunham's[1] fifth-grade class were taking a math test. The test included a number of questions involving the "distributive property" of multiplication (i.e., the idea that $a(b + c) = (a \times b) + (a \times c)$). Question 5, for example, read as follows:

> Susan has 3 boxes of pencils. Mark has 2 boxes of pencils. Each box contains 8 pencils. How many pencils do Susan and Mark have all together?

Jesse, a wiry-built, working-class, white student, wearing jeans and a striped T-shirt, was bent over his test. Jesse had a deep frown on his face, and he was tapping his pencil lightly on the desk. Ms. Dunham, meanwhile, weaved slowly around the room, glancing over students' shoulders. Ms. Dunham paused next to Jesse's desk. Sensing Jesse's frustration, she leaned down and whispered, "You okay?" Jesse looked up sheepishly. Pointing at Question 5, Jesse hesitated and then admitted quietly, "I don't get this one." Ms. Dunham nodded and gave Jesse a quick explanation, urging him to "add up the boxes and then use the distributive property." When Ms. Dunham finished explaining, Jesse was still frowning, but Ms. Dunham did not appear to notice.

Instead, Ms. Dunham was looking at Ellen, a tall, middle-class, white student wearing gray cotton pants and a purple sweater. Across the room, Ellen was waving her hand in the air and calling out in a loud whisper, "Ms. Dunham!" As Ms. Dunham moved toward her, Ellen let her shoulders fall in a dramatic slump, groaning "What does number five mean?"

Ms. Dunham gave Ellen the same brief answer she gave Jesse, but Ellen was not satisfied. Tilting her head thoughtfully, Ellen asked, "Wait, but does that mean we're supposed to multiply?" Hearing this, Ms. Dunham squatted beside Ellen. They began to whisper together, talking through a longer, more detailed explanation. Ms. Dunham watched as Ellen worked through the problem, nodding each time Ellen asked, "Is this right?" When Ellen finished the problem, Ms. Dunham gave her a big smile, saying "Looks good!"

From across the room, Jesse looked on as Ms. Dunham worked with Ellen. Sighing, he sank low in his chair. He continued to frown at his test. Eventually, Jesse skipped the problem and moved on. When time was up, Jesse turned in his test incomplete.

Let's unpack this example. Jesse and Ellen were both average students. They had similar scores on standardized tests. They were both placed in the same ability level for math. They were even struggling with the same math problem. And yet, their outcomes could not have been more different. Ellen, a middle-class student, got the question right. She finished the problem quickly and was able to move on to the rest of the test. Jesse, a working-class student, struggled with the question for a long time and eventually left it blank. He did not even get partial credit.

Situations such as this one were common at Maplewood Elementary, where I spent more than 2 years observing and interviewing middle-class and working-class students, their parents, and their teachers. In my fieldwork at Maplewood, I regularly saw middle-class students overcome problems that stymied their working-class peers.

Those patterns were not the patterns I set out to study—I was initially interested in cross-class friendships. And yet, I could not get those patterns, or the inequalities they produced, out of my head. Ultimately, then, I shifted my focus to ask: *How does the middle-class secure unequal advantages in school?*

RESEARCH GOALS

My goal in this book is to answer that question and to understand how children, parents, and teachers collectively generate advantages for middle-class children. At the theoretical level, I draw insights from prior research on cultural capital, teacher bias, children's agency, student resistance, and teachers' authority. Empirically, I focus on students' strategies for managing challenges in school, on parents' efforts to teach those strategies, on teachers' responses to those strategies, and on the processes that translate students' strategies into unequal profits.[2] Specifically, I use my fieldwork at Maplewood to answer the following research questions:

1. How do children deal with challenges in the classroom?
2. How (and why) do those efforts vary along social class lines?
3. How do teachers respond to those efforts?
4. How (and why) do those responses contribute to inequalities?

EXISTING THEORETICAL EXPLANATIONS

Existing research provides clear evidence of middle-class advantage. We know, for example, that parents' education and income are the best predictors of a child's school performance (Duncan et al. 1998; Guo and Harris 2000; Reardon 2011; Sirin 2005). Children from more privileged backgrounds typically receive higher grades and test scores, go further in school, find more stable jobs, and earn higher incomes than do those from less privileged families (Duncan and Brooks-Gunn 1997; Quillian 2012; Reardon 2011; Torche 2011; Walpole 2003).

Existing research also offers a number of theoretical reasons for that middle-class advantage. As I will discuss, however, those theories fall short of fully explaining the patterns I found.

Before delving into those theories, it is important to note that this is an ethnographic study—not a quantitative or experimental study. In the classroom, my goal was to observe real-life interactions (and their consequences) as they unfolded in context. That ethnographic approach has significant benefits, but it also has limitations. I could not, for example, subject middle-class and working-class students to the exact same challenges in the exact same situations and then compare their responses. Nor could I compare how a given teacher reacted to middle-class and working-class students exhibiting the exact same behavior in exactly the same circumstances. Finally, I could not hold constant teachers' treatment of students and then compare how those responses affected middle-class and working-class students over time. As a result, I cannot precisely estimate the effect of social class on student behaviors or tease apart the relative importance of different factors in explaining teachers' responses to those behaviors. Nevertheless, and as I hope my field notes and analyses make clear, an ethnographic approach is particularly useful for revealing the (often subtle and taken-for-granted) social processes that produce and maintain inequalities. Ethnography is also especially well-suited for linking those processes to larger social theories.

Cultural Capital and the Hidden Curriculum

Along those lines, cultural capital theory offers one possible explanation for how the middle class secures unequal advantages. Building on the work of Pierre Bourdieu (1977, 1984), scholars such as Annette Lareau (2000, 2011) have argued that middle-class advantages in our society result, in large part, from the alignment between middle-class culture and institutional culture.[3] From that perspective, children's home lives vary along social class lines, and those variations lead children to develop class-based beliefs, habits, and preferences (Hart and Risley 1995; Heath 1983; Lareau 2011). Schools, while open to students of all backgrounds, are not neutral fields (Bourdieu 1996). Rather, schools are middle-class institutions, and teachers expect students (and parents) to behave in "middle-class" ways (Lareau 2000; Stephens et al. 2012).[4] Those expectations, however, are not explicitly taught. Instead, they remain part of the "hidden curriculum" (Anyon 1980; Apple 1980; Wren 1999). As a result, middle-class students—who learn at home to follow the hidden standards—are better able to meet teachers' expectations and reap the rewards for doing so.

Let's consider the Jesse and Ellen example through the lens of cultural matching. From that perspective, we might assume that Jesse and Ellen dealt with their struggles differently because of the class cultures they learned at home. We might also assume that Ms. Dunham gave Ellen more help because Ellen's behavior more closely aligned with the school's middle-class expectations for how struggling students should behave.

These are important possibilities, but they cannot fully account for the patterns I observed at Maplewood. Teachers, for example, did not always expect students to proactively seek support when they were struggling. As I explain in Chapter 2, there were times when teachers wanted students to work through difficult problems on their own rather than ask for help, to complete their assignments on time rather than seek extensions, and to wait patiently with their hands raised rather than call out.[5] In those moments, we might expect middle-class students to adjust their behavior to meet teachers' expectations. In reality, they rarely did so. Instead, middle-class students persisted in calling out and seeking support. Those efforts were also successful. In most cases, teachers granted middle-class students' requests, even when those requests went beyond what teachers intended to provide.

Scholars who study cultural capital have found somewhat similar patterns among middle-class parents. Those parents secure advantages for their children, at least in part, by pushing back against institutional expectations (i.e., by requesting that their children be placed in advanced tracks or classes, even when they do not explicitly qualify; see Baker and Stevenson

1986; Lareau 2000, 2011; Lewis and Diamond 2015; Useem 1992). Less clear, however, is whether those parental efforts "count" as cultural capital and (as I discuss in more detail later) whether middle-class children engage in similar efforts with similar success.[6] Thus, although cultural capital theory—at least in terms of its emphasis on cultural alignment and compliance with institutional expectations—might explain some of the advantages that middle-class students were able to secure in the classroom, it cannot fully explain their success in securing advantages in excess of what teachers were initially willing to provide.

Bias in Student–Teacher Interactions

Research on teacher bias offers another explanation for middle-class advantage. From that perspective, stereotypes—including class, racial/ethnic, and gender stereotypes—influence how teachers perceive and interact with their students (Jussim and Harber 2005; Oakes 2005; Rist 1970).[7] Teachers, for example, systematically underestimate the capabilities of less privileged students (Kozlowski 2015; Oates 2003; Ready and Wright 2011), discipline them more harshly (Gregory, Skiba, and Noguera 2010; Kupchik 2009; Morris 2005), and provide them with fewer opportunities for high-quality learning (Eder 1981; Oakes 2005; Rist 1970).[8] Mismatches between teacher and student background characteristics typically exacerbate teachers' biases (Alexander, Entwisle, and Thompson 1987; Downey and Pribesh 2004; Ferguson 2003), and those biases have real consequences for students. Students internalize teachers' perceptions, and those evaluations then influence students' subsequent performance and thus become "self-fulfilling prophecies" (Brophy and Good 1972; Jussim and Harber 2005; Rosenthal and Jacobson 1968).[9]

Given such findings, let's now consider how teacher bias may have operated in the Jesse and Ellen example. From that perspective, we might assume that Ellen received more help because Ms. Dunham perceived her—consciously or subconsciously—as more deserving of support. We might also assume that Jesse was more reluctant to ask for help, at least in part, because of the way that Ms. Dunham and other teachers had treated him when he asked for support in the past.

These are key considerations, and it is certainly possible that subtle prejudices played some role in shaping interactions between students and teachers at Maplewood. However, I find reason to question the idea that teacher bias fully explains the advantages middle-class students were able to secure in school. For instance, when working-class students did seek support, teachers generally granted those requests. In the previous example, Ms. Dunham initially gave both Jesse and Ellen the same hint for Question 5.

It was only after Ellen pressed Ms. Dunham for more assistance that Ms. Dunham squatted beside Ellen and gave her more in-depth support. Furthermore, and as illustrated with Jesse and Ms. Dunham, many teachers went out of their way to provide unsolicited support to students who appeared to be struggling, even if those students did not actively seek help.

Thus, teacher bias might explain some of the advantages middle-class students were able to secure in the classroom, but it does not fully explain the patterns of support-seeking and support-giving I observed. At Maplewood, for example, teachers' responses to students seemed to vary more with students' behaviors than with students' background characteristics. Bias-based explanations for inequality cannot account for those patterns, as they rarely discuss how students' behaviors might prompt unequal responses from teachers.[10]

Children as Active Agents

Studies of cultural capital and studies of teacher bias are also limited by their view of stratification as a top-down process. Both traditions have focused on the inequalities that result from differences in the resources that parents and teachers provide to children. However, as childhood scholars have argued, that top-down view underestimates the importance of children's role in social life (Corsaro 2005; Corsaro and Eder 1990; Eder 1995; Thorne 1993). In particular, it ignores how children guide parents' and teachers' decisions about which resources to provide (Chin and Phillips 2004; Pugh 2009; Valentine 1997; Williams 2006; Zelizer 2002).

Research on cultural capital, for example, acknowledges the possibility of strategic advantage-seeking but does so only in the case of middle-class *adults*. Those studies show that middle-class parents regularly intervene at school to secure advantages for their children (Brantlinger 2003; Cucchiara 2013; Horvat, Weininger, and Lareau 2003; Lareau 2000, 2011; Nelson 2010). They do so by challenging educators' decisions and demanding accommodations (e.g., changes in course placement) that they perceive as better meeting their children's needs (Sui-Chu and Willms 1996; Useem 1992).[11] Those studies clearly show middle-class parents shifting opportunities toward themselves (or their families) and away from others. Much less has been said, however, about *children's* efforts to secure advantages for themselves—how they prompt parents' interventions, how they learn to use similar strategies, how they activate those strategies, or how that activation contributes to inequalities in school.

Research on teacher bias also takes an adult-focused view of stratification in school. From that perspective, teachers are arbitrarily and unfairly biased against less privileged students, and those biases shape the expectations and opportunities that teachers provide (Brophy and Good 1972; Jussim and Harber 2005; Ready and Wright 2011; Rist 1970). Children are treated merely as the passive victims or beneficiaries of teachers' biases. Although children's behaviors and orientations might shape teachers' treatment of and responses to them, such possibilities have gone largely unexplored.

By underestimating children's agency in interactions with parents and teachers, research on cultural capital and teacher bias falls short of explaining the patterns that I find. Closely examining the previously discussed situation, for example, we see that Jesse and Ellen dealt with their struggles in different ways. Jesse was reluctant to ask for help—he acknowledged that he was struggling only after Ms. Dunham asked if he was okay. Jesse also did not ask for further clarification—he just accepted Ms. Dunham's initial response even though, as he told me later in an interview, he "didn't even understand what she said." Ellen, on the other hand, was eager to ask for help—she waved her hand in the air and called out to announce that she was struggling. Ellen also continued to press for support in excess of what Ms. Dunham intended to provide. Rather than accept Ms. Dunham's initial answer ("add up the boxes and then use the distributive property"), Ellen kept asking follow-up questions ("Does that mean we're supposed to multiply?" and "Is this right?") until she was sure she had the correct answer. Ms. Dunham, meanwhile, initially gave Ellen the same brief explanation she gave Jesse. Over time, however, and as Ellen kept asking more questions, Ms. Dunham gave Ellen additional help, walking her through the problem and even confirming that her answer was correct. Such patterns suggest that understanding educational inequalities requires keen recognition of the complexity of social interaction and the agency that individuals—and even young children—have in those exchanges.

Student Resistance and Teacher Authority

Resistance theory does more to acknowledge children's (or at least adolescents') agency in the stratification process, but it is also limited in key ways. According to scholars such as Paul Willis (1981), Jay MacLeod (1995), and Julie Bettie (2014), working-class students, especially those struggling in school, come to view teachers and schools as full of false promises (see also McRobbie 2000). Repeated failures and frustrations lead them to reject the school's premise that success in life is determined by success in school. In doing so, working-class students also come to reject the authority of teachers and schools and to define success in alternative ways. Those findings are important, but they have only been tested in adolescent populations. With younger children, research has shown that positive feelings toward school run high, even among less privileged and minority students (Ford and Harris 1996; Tyson 2002). Classic work on social class and student resistance is also increasingly dated, predating the college-for-all era (Goyette 2008) and recent economic and social changes that have made it more difficult to achieve financial success without a college degree (Kalleberg 2011). Moreover, the recent work that has been done on student resistance raises questions about the idea that resistance is reserved for the working class (Diehl and McFarland 2012; McFarland 2001; Pace 2003; Pace and Hemmings 2006).[12] In a study of student–teacher interactions in high school, for example, McFarland (2001) found that the major challenges to teachers' authority came from popular middle-class students (often boys), who challenged teachers as a way to elicit laughter and approval from friends.

Resistance theory also falls short of fully explaining the patterns I observed. At Maplewood, the working-class students did not reject the authority structure of the school. Jesse, for example, loved school and loved his teachers. Most mornings he would sneak out of the cafeteria early so he could be the first one in the classroom, giving him an extra minute or two to tell Ms. Dunham stories about games he had made up with his cousins or things he had seen on TV the night before. As discussed in Chapter 1, working-class students such as Jesse did not always define success in purely academic terms, but they still viewed respect for the teacher's authority as a central part of that success. Furthermore, I found that when elementary students engaged in resistance, it was usually the middle-class students who did so—not the working-class students, as scholars such as Willis, MacLeod, and Bettie might predict. At Maplewood, middle-class students saw through a different facade of classroom life—that following teachers' rules and expectations is the only path to success. In doing so, those students seemed to recognize that by rejecting the authority structure of the classroom and pushing back against teachers' rules and expectations, they could actually improve their chances at success in school.

Overall, then, research on cultural capital, teacher bias, children's agency, and student resistance represents a useful tool for understanding some aspects of classroom inequality. At the same time, those traditions have limitations that make them incapable of independently explaining how middle-class students secured unequal advantages in school.

SUMMARY OF FINDINGS AND CONTRIBUTIONS

Building on the previously discussed findings, I argue that the middle-class advantage is, at least in part, a *negotiated advantage*. Middle-class students succeeded not just because they complied with teachers' expectations, and not just because they were perceived as more deserving of support, but also because they requested assistance, accommodations, and attention in excess of what was fair or required and because they pressured teachers to grant those requests, even when teachers were inclined to say "no." Fairness is a tricky concept because students differ in their individual needs, abilities, and circumstances. Legally, some students are entitled to more support than others (Shifrer, Muller, and Callahan 2011). Thus, in calling some of the middle-class students' requests "unfair," I mean that those requests would, if granted, provide advantages that could not reasonably be justified by the circumstances at hand.

Such negotiated advantages are the result of a complex chain of interactions that begins with parents and children at home and culminates with children and teachers at school. The working-class parents taught their children to take responsibility for their own success in school and to avoid burdening teachers with requests for support. As a result, working-class students at Maplewood tried to deal with problems on their own. Although they were sometimes successful in doing so, they often spent more time struggling, got more problems wrong, and got more frustrated in the process. The middle-class parents, on the other hand, taught their children that it was the teachers' job to help them succeed. As a result, middle-class students asked, asked loudly, and kept asking until they got the support they desired. Teachers, meanwhile, could have denied those requests. As in the case with Ms. Dunham, however, they rarely said "no," even when saying "yes" meant granting requests in excess of what was fair or required. As a result, middle-class students typically got more support from teachers and were better able to overcome challenges in school.

These findings are important because they expand and clarify our understanding of the processes that produce inequalities in school. With respect to cultural capital theory, at least as it is most commonly applied, these patterns support the idea of cultural matching but also suggest that the middle class can negotiate advantages beyond those that teachers intend to provide.[13] With respect to research on teacher bias, these patterns confirm that schools are not neutral institutions, but they also highlight the importance of considering both sides of teacher–student interactions and acknowledging the role that children's behaviors and orientations might play in prompting teachers to respond in unequal ways. Similarly, and with respect to resistance theory, these patterns suggest that overt resistance to teacher authority is not limited to the working class. Rather, challenges to teachers' authority are central to middle-class students' and parents' efforts to negotiate additional advantages in school.

That is not to say, however, that working-class students or working-class parents should be blamed for failing to secure their own negotiated advantages. Compared to their more privileged peers, less privileged families have limited resources to use for leverage in their interactions with schools (Bennett, Lutz, and Jayaram 2012; Horvat et al. 2003). As a result, schools often treat less privileged families as second-class citizens, and they can be easily swayed to meet the interests of more privileged families at the expense of their working-class peers (Cucchiara 2013; Lareau and Horvat 1999; Lewis and Diamond 2015; Lewis-McCoy 2014).[14] Given those patterns, it seems reasonable for working-class parents and children to distrust institutions and to assume that schools may not be responsive to their needs. It also seems unfair to expect working-class students to achieve equality by demonstrating a set of skills that they are not explicitly taught in school. Even teaching those skills more explicitly—as Knowledge Is Power Program (KIPP) charter schools and programs such as Prep for Prep have tried to do (Lack 2009; Tough 2012)—may not be enough to help working-class students catch up to their middle-class peers. By virtue of their intimate familiarity with the system (as cultural capital research has shown) and their power and status in society (as research on bias and stereotypes has shown), middle-class students (and their parents) will likely just find new ways to stay one step ahead.

Thus, as I argue in the Conclusion, a better solution would put responsibility for equality in the hands of educators, middle-class parents, and middle-class students—those who have the authority and the resources to make real change. If we really want a more level playing field for students, we need middle-class families to be mindful of the consequences of wielding their privilege, and we need teachers to say "no" and deny the requests that exceed what is fair or required.

DIFFICULT CHOICES

I base the previously presented arguments on a longitudinal, ethnographic study of middle-class and working-class students in one suburban, public elementary school. Before describing the study in detail, it is important to recognize that ethnography, like all research methods, involves difficult choices. I had to choose which school (or schools) to study, who to observe, when to observe, and what to include in my field notes.[15] I had to decide what to wear, what to say, and how to build trust in the field. Those choices have consequences, and I did not take them lightly.

Design Decisions

Much of the research on social class and schooling compares middle-class students in middle-class schools to working-class students in working-class schools (Heath 1983; Lareau 2000, 2011; Nelson and Schutz 2007; Pugh 2009).[16] That approach, however, has a number of limitations. Research suggests, for example, that school composition is correlated both with teachers' instructional practice (Anyon 1981; Camburn and Han 2011; Gamoran, Secada, and Marrett 2000) and with teachers' treatment of students (Oakes 2005; Ready and Wright 2011). As a result, comparing middle-class students in middle-class schools to working-class students in working-class schools would make it difficult to determine whether inequalities in students' experiences result from differences at the school level or from differences in the resources, experiences, and skills students bring from home.[17] To avoid those pitfalls, and to better understand how students' own class backgrounds matter at school, I wanted a research site that would allow me to compare middle-class students and working-class students as they interacted in the same classrooms and with the same teachers and peers.

Although I designed this study to focus on social class, I recognize that class is not the only cause of classroom inequalities. Rather, gender, race, and ethnicity intersect with class in important ways and also matter independently for students and their outcomes.

With respect to gender, we know that despite men's historical advantages, female students now outperform male students on most measures of educational achievement and attainment (Buchmann and DiPrete 2013; Buchmann, DiPrete, and McDaniel 2008). Those differences appear to stem, at least in part, from gender differences in behavior. Boys are generally louder and more disruptive (Younger, Warrington, and Williams 1999); they may even pride themselves on their lack of effort and achievement (Morris 2008; Willis 1981). Given those differences, teachers set higher expectations for girls, rate their behavior more favorably, and punish them less harshly than they do boys (Bertrand and Pan 2011; Jones and Myhill 2004; Morris 2005).

Despite these differences, there is also reason to believe that gender is not always so salient in school. Gender differences in student behavior and achievement, for example, are less pronounced in elementary school than in the later grades (Buchmann et al. 2008; Willingham and Cole 1997). Gender also seems to matter less for students from more privileged backgrounds (Entwisle, Alexander, and Olson 2007). That may be, in part, because boys are more sensitive than girls to peer attitudes regarding academics. Research shows that when boys attend schools with stronger cultures of achievement (common in more privileged schools), their attitudes, behaviors, and achievement levels are more on par with those of girls (Legewie and DiPrete 2012).

With respect to race and ethnicity, we know that the face of education is changing[18] and that non-white students face real challenges in school (Kao and Thompson 2003; Roscigno and Ainsworth-Darnell 1999). Black and Latino students, for example, benefit tremendously from teacher support, but they often struggle to form close connections to educators (Crosnoe, Johnson, and Elder 2004; Stanton-Salazar 2001). Teachers also rate black and Latino students as less well behaved than their white and Asian American peers (McGrady and Reynolds 2013; Riegle-Crumb and Humphries 2012).[19]

The previously mentioned differences are clearly important, but there is also reason to question whether race alone can explain inequalities in schooling. In terms of home lives, middle-class black students are often more similar to middle-class white students than they are to working-class black students (Hardie 2015; Lareau 2011; Tyson 2002). This similarity extends to schooling as well, where middle-class black students report attitudes toward schooling that are similar to those of their middle-class white peers (Hardie 2015; Tyson 2002). Middle-class black students may also face lower levels of teacher bias than do poor and working-class black students, especially if they attend whiter and more affluent schools (Ready and Wright 2011).

The "perfect" research site would allow me to explore those racial/ethnic and gender differences and their intersections with social class. Unfortunately, such a field site proved extremely difficult to find. In this case, the perfect field site would have had even number of middle-class and working-class students, and those groups would have been equally divided not only by gender but also across different racial and ethnic groups (e.g., ⅛ white working-class students, ⅛ white middle-class students, ⅛ black working-class students, ⅛ black middle-class students, ⅛ Latino working-class students, ⅛ Latino middle-class students, ⅛ Asian American working-class students, and ⅛ Asian American middle-class students). Unfortunately, because schools and neighborhoods are highly segregated by class and race/ethnicity (Logan, Minca, and Adar 2012), that "perfect" school did not exist. Thus, because I wanted to strategically compare students from different social class back-grounds in the same school setting, I opted to prioritize class diversity and work with the "natural" racial/ethnic composition of the school.

Research Site and Participants

The decisions I made in designing this study ultimately led me to Maplewood Elementary. Maplewood is a public elementary school (not a charter or magnet school)[20] in Fair Hills, a suburb of a large, Eastern city. The low brick building sits back from the road, surrounded by trees and playing fields and a large playground with swings, slides, monkey bars, and other playground equipment. The long, brightly lit hallways are adorned with inspirational posters and colorful displays showcasing students' projects and artwork. Teachers generally arrive early and stay late, and the school is often buzzing with activities—band concerts, craft fairs, carnivals, bake sales, PTA meetings, and so on—well into the evening.

With respect to academics, Maplewood is not the highest performing school in the region, but it does have a strong focus on achievement. The students score well above state averages on standardized tests. Teachers are required to participate in continuing education classes (many have master's degrees), and turnover is very low. Parents also praise Maplewood—in interviews and on public web forums such as GreatSchools.org—for the quality instruction their children receive.

Demographically, Maplewood serves approximately 500 students in Kindergarten through fifth grade. The school population is predominantly white (82%), but it includes a growing number of (middle-class) Asian American students (6%) and (poor and working-class) Latino students (9%). Although the majority of Maplewood's families are middle class, a substantial minority are from working-class backgrounds.

That socioeconomic diversity is possible because of Maplewood's suburban location.[21] The school draws students from a variety of neighborhoods across a large geographic area. Some students walk to school; others ride the bus for 30 minutes or more. Some students live in mobile home communities or rented apartments. Others live in modest one- or two-story tract homes built in the 1940s and 1950s. Still others live in million-dollar homes with sprawling lawns in fancy, new housing developments.

Social class is a taboo term in American society and one that has countless meanings and definitions (Lareau and Conley 2008). Building on prior research on social class, families, and schools, I opted to identify students' social class backgrounds based on their parents' educational and occupational status (Condron 2009; Lareau 2000, 2011; Quinn 2015). I initially planned to compare four groups: poor, working class, middle class, and upper middle class. My observations revealed, however, that although some aspects of family life varied across those four groups,[22] the primary differences in problem-solving and student–teacher interactions were between students from middle- and upper-middle-class families, on the one hand, and those from poor and working-class families, on the other hand. Thus, in the interest of clarity and brevity, and consistent with prior research on social class and family life (Lareau 2011), I condensed the four categories into two, which I label "middle class" and "working class."

Using those labels, middle-class families all had at least one parent with a 4-year college degree and at least one parent employed in a professional or managerial occupation. Middle-class parents worked as teachers, lawyers, computer engineers, office managers, and in other similar occupations; almost all of the mothers had college degrees, although many stayed home or worked only part-time. Parents in working-class families typically had only a high school diploma, although some were high school dropouts and others had completed some post-secondary education (often at a community college or trade school). In most working-class families, both parents worked full-time, often as food service workers, store clerks, day-care providers, transportation workers, or in other similar jobs. The working-class families at Maplewood were similar to the "settled-living" working-class families that Rubin (1976) and Edwards (2004) describe: Most parents had steady jobs and stable relationships, and they provided neat, clean homes for their children. There were a few single-parent families in both class groups.

Not surprisingly, the middle-class and working-class families at Maplewood also differed in terms of income and wealth. Middle-class families had household incomes averaging $120,000 per year.[23] The vast majority of the middle-class families also owned their own homes, with an average home value of roughly $475,000.[24] Working-class families earned, on average, $35,000 per year. Most rented mobile homes, apartments, or townhouses. The few families that owned their homes lived in houses with an average value of roughly $300,000.

However, there were financial outliers. A few working-class parents had union jobs or successful small businesses and, as a result, earned relatively high wages ($60,000 or more per year). Two middle-class parents lost their high-paying jobs during the course of the project and, as a result, found themselves scrambling to get by. Thus, although income and wealth are known to be important predictors of educational success (Reardon 2011), I opted to focus on education and occupation because they were more stable over time and also appeared to be more closely connected to the styles and strategies that families used in interacting with schools and other institutions (Lamont 1992, 2009; Lubrano 2004; Rivera 2012; Streib 2015).[25]

At Maplewood, the project involved one cohort of students—those who were in the same grade and who progressed from one grade to the next together—their teachers, and their parents. In terms of demographics, the participants reflected the makeup of the school and the community in general. My observations included 46 white middle-class students, 17 white working-class students, 7 Asian American middle-class students, 7 Latino working-class students, 1 Latino middle-class student, 1 mixed-race (black/white) middle-class student, and 1 mixed-race (black/white) working-class student.[26] The various social class and racial/ethnic groups were roughly divided along gender lines (43 boys and 37 girls in total). Of those students, 65 also took part in follow-up observations in middle school; the other 15 (7 working-class and 8 middle-class students) moved away before seventh grade. The 17 teachers with whom I worked at Maplewood were predominantly white and female, although the observations did include 1 black female teacher and 5 white male teachers (3 regular classroom teachers and 2 teachers of "enrichment" classes such as art, gym, and music). At Fair Hills Middle School, all 10 of the seventh-grade teachers were white; the group included 4 men and 6 women.

DATA COLLECTION AND METHODS

The Appendix provides a detailed description of the fieldwork and the choices and challenges it involved, including my efforts to obtain permission for the study, negotiate access to the field site, recruit participants, and manage relations in the field. In addition, I also provide key details here to help ground the chapters that follow.

Observations and Interviews

At the start of the project, the students were in third grade, spread across four classrooms. I followed these same students to fourth grade and through the completion of their fifth-grade year. I then observed them again in seventh grade at Fair Hills Middle School.

Initially, I was interested in understanding how social class mattered in students' peer interactions and especially how cross-class friendships might help alleviate inequalities in school. Over time, however, my observations revealed that social class was particularly salient in student–teacher interactions. Thus, as is common in qualitative research (Hammersley and Atkinson 1995; Luker 2010), and as I explain in more detail in the Appendix, I opted to shift my focus to student problem-solving instead.

During the more than 2 years I spent at Maplewood, I regularly observed students in their "homeroom" classes, in their ability-grouped math classes, during enrichment classes such as gym and art, at lunch, on the playground, and during other school activities (assemblies, field days, parties, etc.). From March 2008 to June 2010, I visited the school at least twice a week, spending approximately 3 hours observing during each visit. Because there were four different classes in each grade, I divided my observations equally between them.[27] I also rotated the days and times I observed each class so as to observe students interacting in a variety of settings and activities.

In order to determine students' social class status and achievement levels, I conducted parent surveys and collected data from students' school records. During the fall of the students' fourth- and fifth-grade school years, I sent home surveys with questions about students' home lives, family backgrounds, school achievement, friendships, and extracurricular activities. After receiving the completed surveys, I entered the information into an Excel file. During the spring of the students' fifth-grade year, I spent nearly 40 hours combing through stacks of paper files, adding information to the Excel file (by hand) about each student's marking period grades, standardized test scores, teacher comments and behavior ratings, and records of contact between parents and the school.[28]

I also conducted in-depth interviews with students, parents, and teachers, and I used those interviews to deepen my understanding of the patterns I observed. Of the 80 students I observed at Maplewood, 21 participated in interviews, which I conducted during the summer after the students completed fifth grade. The parents of those students (N = 24) participated in interviews as well, as did all 12 of the third-, fourth-, and fifth-grade teachers at Maplewood. The audio-recorded interviews included open-ended questions about a range of topics.[29] With teachers, I asked about teaching styles, students, parents, and common classroom challenges.[30] With children and parents, I asked about home lives and activities; experiences at school; friendships; and interactions with teachers, family members, and peers. I spoke separately with children and their parents, but I asked similar questions. Parent interviews generally took place at home and lasted 90–150 minutes. Student interviews all took place at home and lasted 30–90 minutes.

In addition to standard interview-type questions, student and parent interviews also included four vignettes describing common classroom challenges (e.g., "Jason is struggling to understand the directions on a test"). After reading each vignette aloud, I asked interviewees how they thought the fictional student would handle the situation (e.g., "What do you think Jason will do?"). I then asked parent interviewees if they (or their child) had encountered similar challenges and, if so, what happened. Comparing interviewees' answers to those questions allowed me to search for patterns both within families and across different social class groups.

With the follow-up research at Fair Hills Middle School, my goal was to understand how the patterns of interactions I observed at Maplewood persisted or changed over time. From March 2012 to June 2012, I conducted regular observations in the seventh-grade classrooms at Fair Hills.

I interviewed 10 seventh-grade teachers at Fair Hills and conducted follow-up interviews with 13 students I had previously interviewed after fifth grade.

In addition to those formal interviews, I also had countless informal conversations with teachers, students, parents, and administrators at both Maplewood and Fair Hills. Those conversations typically took place in between activities, during lunch and recess, and before and after school.

Those conversations were useful, but I tried to spend most of my time just observing classroom life as it unfolded. During lessons and activities, I would walk around quietly or sit in empty seats. While observing, I also kept brief jottings in a notebook. The jottings included timelines of events, diagrams, descriptions of people and interactions, and snippets of dialogue. Students would often peek over my shoulders, so I quickly got into the habit of jotting in cryptic short-hand and substituting pseudonyms for all real names.

At the end of each observation session, I spent an additional 6–12 hours expanding my jottings into detailed, typed field notes. I also password-protected all of the project files and substituted pseudonyms for any remaining real names. Although all of the people described in this book are real, I sometimes changed particularly identifying characteristics to protect their anonymity.

As a part of my observation efforts at Maplewood, I also conducted strategic counts of specific classroom behaviors.[31] My initial observations suggested that social class was particularly salient in certain types of student–teacher interactions. To further clarify those patterns, and during the last 6 months of observations at Maplewood, I chose 16 observation periods (four hour-long sessions in each of the four fifth-grade classrooms)[32] during which to count students' requests for help from teachers.[33] During the count sessions, I used charts to track all the requests for assistance, clarification, information, and checking of work that teachers received.[34] I then compared how the types and frequency of requests varied by social class. As I discuss in Chapter 3, some situations resulted in more requests than others, but the overall patterns were very similar.

Field Relations

In an era of accountability, teachers, parents, and students are subject to considerable scrutiny.[35] It was not surprising, then, that some in the Maplewood community were initially wary of my presence. Students regularly inquired about me, the project, and its goals. They asked how long I would be hanging around, whether I was training to be a teacher, and whether I would "tell on" them if they did something wrong. Questions about my age (mid-twenties), marital status (I got married halfway through the project), whether I had kids of my own (not at the time), and what I liked to do in my spare time (running and reading) were also common, particularly when students invited me to sit with them at lunch. The parents and the teachers also had questions and guarded concerns, but they were rarely so blunt in raising them.

In my interactions at Maplewood, I worked hard to assuage any fears about the project or my presence in the school. With the teachers, I stressed that I was there to learn from them and not to evaluate them. Those messages seemed to help. After a few weeks in the classroom, teachers would regularly turn to me—often the only other adult in the room—to vent and share their frustrations about parents or students or new mandates from the school. They also gradually let their guard down, reprimanding and joking with students in front of me without hesitation.

With the students, I stressed that my goal was not to get them in trouble and that I would not share anything that they said or did—at least by name—with their parents, their teachers, or their peers. These were 8-, 9-, and 10-year-olds, so of course they were loath to take an adult at her word. A few students even tried to test the veracity of my claims while we were walking to gym class. Ted, Brian, and Ethan, all middle-class boys, were at the back of the line, and I was following behind them:

As we pass the custodial closet, Brian looks around furtively, then ducks quickly inside before immediately coming back out again and rejoining the line. Ted then follows suit, jumping in and out of the closet right after Brian does it. When they are both back out in the hall, they grin at each other with nervous excitement. Ethan, meanwhile, turns and looks at me wide-eyed, as if waiting for a reprimand. Seeing Ethan's worried expression, I chuckle and explain quietly that "I'm just here to observe. I'm not here to tell on you or get you in trouble." Ethan nods, but Ted's eyes light up with sudden curiosity. Interjecting, he asks eagerly: "Even if we did something *really* bad? I shake my head, explaining: "Only if someone's life was in danger." Hearing this, Brian jumps into the conversation. Readying his fist in the air, he asks playfully, challenging me: "So . . . if I punched Ted in the face right now, and the sub didn't see, you wouldn't tell?" I shrug, smiling coyly. Brian looks at me, pulls his fist back further, then turns his gaze to Ted, who cringes with anticipation. Brian looks back at me, at Ted, and back at me again, then drops his fist, grinning sheepishly. All three boys then devolve into giggles and dash off after the rest of their class down the hall.

I had decided early on that winning students' trust would be key if I did not want my presence to affect their behavior. As I reminded the boys in the hallway, that meant telling on students only if someone's life was in danger—something I thankfully never had to do. It also meant playing up my own student status. Although I dressed for my observations in the "office casual" style typical of most of the teachers at Maplewood, I always carried a backpack (which students often stopped to admire) and I usually ate lunch with the students rather than in the teachers' lounge.

Data Analysis

My observations and interviews and record-culling efforts yielded a veritable mountain of data to be analyzed. I tackled that mountain of data in two different, yet complementary, ways. The first step was more inductive. I read and re-read the field notes and interview transcripts and then spent time reflecting on what I had found, often while running or during the many hours I spent commuting between home, graduate school, and my field site. I also wrote (or sometimes audio recorded) analytic memos (Hammersley and Atkinson 1995; Lareau 2000), which I used to identify emerging patterns in the data, to discuss those patterns in relation to the existing literature, and to determine next steps in the data collection process. As the patterns—including social class differences in the nature of students' requests from teachers, in their style of interacting with teachers, and in parents' messages to their children at home—became clearer, I also developed a series of data matrices (Miles and Huberman 1994) to help me identify disconfirming evidence and test alternative explanations for the patterns I saw.[36]

The second step in the analysis was more deductive, involving a formal coding of the transcribed interviews, field notes, and other data. I used the themes from my analytic memos to develop a coding scheme. I then applied that coding scheme to my qualitative data using Atlas.ti software. The coding process allowed me to identify and trace patterns in the data and to examine how themes occurred and related to one another and to attributes of situations and participants in them. During the coding process, I also expanded and revised the coding scheme to fit more closely with the data.

A NOTE ON CLASS, RACE, AND GENDER

Class is an important dimension of inequality in its own right. Much of the research on inequalities in education has concentrated on less privileged students (Bettie 2014; Carter 2003; MacLeod 1995; McRobbie 2000; Stanton-Salazar 1997; Willis 1981). Those studies are important, but they make it difficult to tease apart the relative importance of race and class in shaping students' experiences and outcomes. Furthermore, we know that American society is deeply and increasingly divided along socioeconomic lines (Lacy 2015) and that those differences—in income, wealth, educational attainment, and occupational status—have real and lasting consequences for children and their families (Duncan and Brooks-Gunn 1997; Quillian 2012; Reardon 2011; Torche 2011; Walpole 2003). Given those patterns, my goal in this analysis is to understand how class matters in students' efforts to solve problems in school and how those efforts (and teachers' responses to them) contribute to larger patterns of class-based inequality.

I focused my analyses on differences by social class, but I also considered how gender, race, and ethnicity might intersect with class to shape students' experiences in school. In doing so, and as I explain in more detail in Chapter 7, I found that although gender and race and ethnicity did matter in some aspects of classroom interaction, the class-based patterns of problem-solving I observed at Maplewood were largely consistent across gender and racial/ethnic lines.[37] Within particular class groups, for example, boys and girls and white and non-white students made similar numbers and types of requests for support. The content of those requests sometimes varied, but students approached those interactions in relatively similar ways.

Brian and Cody provide a useful illustration of these patterns with respect to race. Both boys were mixed race: They had black fathers and were being raised by white single mothers. Both boys had wavy hair and olive skin; they both loved sports and video games and cracking jokes. Despite those similarities, however, the boys had starkly different lives. Brian's mother had a master's degree and worked in a high-paying job as a corporate manager. Brian spent most of his after-school time in organized activities with middle-class white peers. He had a cell phone. He had been to Disney World twice. Cody's mother had only a high school diploma and worked in retail. Cody spent his time hanging out with cousins and with other kids who lived in his mobile home neighborhood. Those differences extended to the classroom as well. In school, Brian's behavior was largely indistinguishable from that of his middle-class white friends. He regularly asked his teachers for assistance and accommodations and attention, and he appeared to do so comfortably and confidently. Cody's interactions with teachers, meanwhile, closely mirrored those of his working-class white peers. He typically tried to deal with problems on his own. Or, if he did seek support, he did so warily and only after his middle-class peers had successfully done the same.

Mandy and Ethan, both high-achieving, middle-class white students, provide another useful illustration of the patterns I found with respect to gender. Both Mandy and Ethan were heavily involved in extracurricular activities, including martial arts and scouts. Both were also "teacher's pet" types—they regularly volunteered to help with classroom tasks, relished praise, and looked for opportunities to demonstrate their smarts. Mandy and Ethan did differ in some important ways. Like the other boys, for example, Ethan placed a high priority on humor. Unfortunately, Ethan was not as naturally funny as some of his peers, and his jokes were sometimes met with eye rolls from classmates or even admonishment from teachers (such as when he started saying "Konichiwa" to his friends, thinking he was saying a "curse word in Japanese"). Mandy, in turn, and like many of the other girls (especially the high-achieving ones), focused less on being funny than on being a leader (i.e., taking charge in group activities and keeping everyone else on task). Whether with friends on the playgrounds or with partners in class, Mandy was always directing others, even when doing so put her relationships in jeopardy (such as when one friend stopped playing with her because she was "too bossy"). Despite those differences, however, Ethan and Mandy were remarkably similar in their interactions with (and especially their requests from) teachers. They were both proactive in seeking support and in pushing back when they did not get the assistance, accommodations, or attention they desired.

That is not to say, however, that non-class differences between students were inconsequential. Kal and Rajeev, for example, were both middle-class Indian American students. Both were also smart and high-achieving and took pride in those successes. They differed in the fact that Kal was born in the United States, whereas Rajeev was born in India and had only recently immigrated. Rajeev had learned English before arriving, but he spoke with a thick accent and sometimes stumbled over phrases. Those differences also seemed to have real ramifications. Kal had mostly middle-class, white, male friends; like them, he focused on being funny and athletic. With teachers, Kal was also boisterous and demanding. As I explain in more detail in Chapter 7, Kal's fifth-grade teacher, Mr. Fischer, even noted that Kal asked more questions than "any other student" he had ever had. Meanwhile, Rajeev kept mostly to himself. He was painfully quiet and shy with his classmates, and he only rarely approached his teachers with questions and requests. Although I cannot state with confidence that those differences were a reflection of the boys' national origins, they suggest that language, nationality, and immigrant experiences could introduce variations into the patterns I observed.

Despite those differences, the overall patterns suggested that social class was particularly salient in shaping students' efforts to solve problems in school and especially their reliance on teachers to support them in that process. Those findings, although possibly surprising to some, were also consistent with prior research. As noted previously, it is known that gender differences in children's behavior and achievement (Buchmann, DiPrete, and McDaniel 2008; Morris 2008; Willis 1981; Younger et al. 1999) are less pronounced in more privileged schools—such as Maplewood—where students are surrounded by more academically focused peers (Legewie and DiPrete 2012). Similarly, research suggests that class matters as much for racial minority students as it does for their white peers (Ainsworth-Darnell and Downey 1998; Carter 2003; Hardie 2015; Jack 2014; Lareau 2011; Tyson 2002).

Given such findings, this book focuses on social class. I describe how students' problem-solving strategies varied along social class lines and how those variations contributed to inequalities in school. In doing so, however, I also note places where gender and racial/ethnic differences emerged, and I discuss those differences in more detail in Chapter 7.

OVERVIEW

This book challenges standard assumptions about the processes that advantage middle-class families over their working-class peers. It reveals that the middle-class advantage is, at least in part, a *negotiated advantage*. Essentially, that means that middle-class individuals secure advantages not just by complying with institutional expectations, or by being perceived as more deserving, but also by negotiating for extra advantages and by pressuring institutions to grant those requests, even when those institutions might prefer to say "no."

These analyses are based on an ethnographic analysis of social class differences in students' problem-solving strategies. Drawing on observations and interviews with students, parents, and teachers in one socioeconomically diverse school, I show how children learned strategies for managing challenges in school, how they activated those strategies in the classroom, how teachers responded to those strategies, and how those responses contributed to larger patterns of inequality. In doing so, I find that negotiated advantages are the result of a complex chain of interactions that begins with parents and children at home and culminates with children and teachers at school.

Chapter 1 focuses on the first end of that chain. Drawing on interviews with parents and children, it describes how parents coached their children to manage problems in class-based ways and how children came to internalize (albeit gradually and with some pushback) those lessons. Middle-class parents, I found, felt a deep sense of responsibility for their children's academic success. As a result, they taught children to practice strategies of *influence*. Essentially, middle-class children learned that when they encounter problems at school, they should use their teachers as resources, avoid consequences, and be assertive in seeking support. Working-class parents, on the other hand, felt primarily responsible for their children's character development. Reflecting back on their own experience in school, they worried that teachers might punish students who complain or ask for special favors. Thus, working-class parents taught their children to practice strategies of *deference* instead. As a result, working-class students learned to treat teachers with respect, take responsibility for their actions, and tackle problems on their own.

Chapter 2 moves further along the chain, examining the link between home and school. Using interviews with teachers and observations of elementary school classrooms, it reveals the alignment (or lack thereof) between what parents taught children at home and what teachers expected from students at school. Drawing on interviews with children, this chapter also discusses how children viewed teachers' expectations and how they decided what counts as an "appropriate" response. I found that teachers did not have consistent expectations for student problem-solving. Instead, those expectations varied from activity to activity and even from moment to moment. There were times when teachers wanted students to acknowledge their struggles and proactively seek support (favoring middle-class strategies of influence), but there were also times when teachers wanted students to work through difficult problems on their own, times when they did not want to give extra credit or extra time, and times when they wanted students to wait patiently with their hands raised rather than approach them with requests (favoring working-class strategies of deference). Despite those frequent variations, however, teachers rarely made their expectations explicit. That ambiguity left students to decode what teachers wanted in a given moment, and that decoding process led students to rely even more heavily on the class-based lessons they learned at home.

Chapters 3–5 discuss the consequences of children's reliance on parents' class-based coaching for managing problems in school. Each chapter focuses on a different problem-solving strategy (assistance-seeking, accommodation-seeking, and attention-seeking). In these chapters, I analyze how children's use of those strategies varied along social class lines and how those variations contributed to inequalities in the classroom. I observed similar class-based patterns in third, fourth, and fifth grade. Those patterns, however, became more pronounced over time as children gradually internalized the lessons described in Chapter 1. As a result, most of the examples presented in Chapters 3–5 derive from fourth-grade and especially fifth-grade classrooms.

Chapter 3 highlights social class differences in children's efforts to seek *assistance* from teachers. When confronting academic or social challenges, most middle-class children readily sought assistance from teachers. They were also proactive and persistent in making requests. Working-class children instead tried to deal with problems on their own. Although they occasionally asked for help from teachers, they did so only when it was apparent that requests were welcome and would not result in reprimand (e.g., when teachers approached them to offer assistance). Working-class students were also less insistent in making requests. They raised their hands rather than call out or approach teachers directly, and they rarely asked follow-up questions, even when they were still confused or struggling. Those differences in assistance-seeking also had real consequences. Middle-class students received more help than did their working-class peers. As a result, they were often able to complete their work more quickly and more accurately.

Chapter 4 describes social class differences in children's efforts to seek *accommodations* from teachers. During the school day, classroom rules, procedures, and expectations sometimes conflicted with students' individual needs or desires. In those situations, middle-class children often treated rules as flexible—they tried to negotiate changes and exemptions. Furthermore, when middle-class children were caught breaking rules, they would offer impassioned excuses for their actions, and they were generally able to avoid punishment by doing so. Working-class children, on the other hand, almost never tried to negotiate changes to or exemptions from rules, expectations, and procedures. Instead, they treated rules as fixed and adjusted their behavior accordingly. Furthermore, when working-class students were caught misbehaving, they rarely offered excuses; they simply endured their punishment without complaint. Those contrasting approaches to rules and expectations also contributed to inequalities. Because teachers generally said "yes," middle-class students had more opportunities to express their creativity, experienced less discomfort and fewer inconveniences at school, and even avoided consequences for misbehavior.

Chapter 5 examines social class differences in children's efforts to seek *attention* from teachers. Regardless of social class, students wanted—even craved—attention. They wanted to talk about their interests, experiences, knowledge, and lives outside of school. They wanted praise and recognition for a job well done. Middle-class and working-class students differed, however, in the types of behaviors for which they sought attention and the strategies they used to catch a teacher's eye. Specifically, middle-class students sought attention for their unique talents, skills, and experiences, and they did so in overt ways. Working-class students instead sought attention primarily for their commonalities with and helpfulness to others. They also did so in more oblique ways and only when it was clear that teachers had time to provide attention. Those class differences in attention-seeking had meaningful consequences. Through their more frequent and more difficult-to-ignore bids for attention, and through their success in persuading teachers to grant those requests, middle-class students had more opportunities to share stories with, receive validation from, and make personal connections with their teachers.

Whereas Chapters 3–5 focus primarily on students, Chapter 6 completes the chain by revealing why and how teachers translated class-based problem-solving strategies into unequal opportunities in school. Teachers almost always rewarded middle-class students' strategies of influence. They did so by providing assistance, accommodations, and attention in excess of what was fair or required and by creating conditions in which middle-class students (but not working-class students) felt comfortable making requests for support. That privileging of middle-class students, however, did not seem intentional. Teachers tried to support working-class students, but time and accountability pressures made it difficult for them to recognize students' tacit struggles, forcing teachers to rely on students to voice their own needs. Teachers also seemed compelled to grant middle-class students' requests, even in situations where they might have preferred to say "no." In those moments, teachers relented because they wanted their students to feel supported and, more problematically, because it was often easier and less time-consuming (at least in the face of persistent pushback) to say "yes" and much riskier to say "no."

Chapter 7 adds nuance and context to these findings. This study as a whole is useful for understanding how social class matters in the classroom. That focus on social class is important, but it does leave unanswered a number of questions. Chapter 7 turns to those lingering questions. Specifically, and drawing both on my own data and on insights from prior research, I discuss the significance of class-based strategies and how they change as students move through school. I describe how gender, race, and ethnicity might matter in shaping students' interactions with teachers. I explore how class-based patterns might vary across schools with different types of characteristics, and I also consider the extent to which students might learn class-based behaviors from their peers.

The book concludes with a summary of key findings and a discussion of implications for research, policy, and practice. Specifically, I argue that the middle-class advantage is a negotiated advantage that results from a complex chain of interactions involving students, parents, and teachers. Engaging with existing research, I discuss how these findings highlight the importance of cultural capital, teacher bias, student resistance, and teacher authority while also revealing the limits of existing theoretical models for explaining class-based inequalities in school. Although this book is not intended as an evaluation of best practices, the Conclusion does include suggestions for educators, parents, and policymakers. First, I describe how sensitivity to social class differences can help teachers connect with working-class students; recognize their struggles; and support them with assistance, accommodations, and attention. I also discuss the challenges—including large class sizes, intense accountability pressures, and high levels of need—that make it difficult for teachers to assess and respond to students' individual needs. Second, using research on KIPP schools, individualized instruction, and cognitive–behavioral therapy, I argue that although it is possible to teach "middle-class" skills to less privileged students, such efforts are likely to fall short of fully eliminating inequalities, and they might create even more problems than they solve. As this book clearly shows, middle-class families are skilled at securing new resources and teaching their children to do the same. They gain advantages not only by following rules and expectations but also by negotiating changes to and exemptions from them. They also use their power and influence to ensure that schools feel compelled to grant those requests. Thus, even if schools teach working-class students to act like middle-class students, middle-class families will likely find new ways to maintain their negotiated advantages. In terms of solutions, that means that the problem of class-based inequalities has to be tackled (at least in part) at its source—the middle-class families who seek support in excess of what is fair or required and the educators who feel compelled to grant those requests. Convincing middle-class families not to negotiate for extra advantages will almost certainly be an uphill battle. Given those challenges, it will likely be up to educators to deny those requests, and they will likely face backlash in doing so. Without those denials, however, middle-class children will always stay one step ahead.

CHAPTER 1

Coached for the Classroom

For the fifth graders at Maplewood Elementary, Rocket Day was one of the most highly anticipated events of the year. In May, as part of a month-long unit covering both astronomy and the history of space exploration, the students all built and decorated plastic "rockets." On Rocket Day, teachers and parent volunteers set up "launching stations" on the field behind the school. Almost 100 students then paraded outside with their rockets past their parents, who had all been invited to attend. Four at a time, students launched their rockets, chased them approximately 100 yards across the playground, and then ran back to rejoin the line, reload their rockets, and launch again.

A few minutes into the event, Amelia Graham, a working-class, white student whose long bangs brushed the top of her glasses, had just finished her first launch. At the far end of the field, Amelia bent down and picked up her rocket from the ground. She frowned, took a few steps, and then bent down again to retrieve the rocket's parachute, which had landed approximately 10 feet away. The strings connecting the rocket to the parachute had broken during the flight. As Amelia jogged slowly back toward the launching stations, she held the rocket in one hand and the parachute in the other. Rather than rejoin the line, however, Amelia sat down in the grass by herself, approximately 10 yards from where the other students were waiting, close to where the parents were standing to watch. Although there were many parents in attendance, Amelia Graham's parents had to work and could not attend Rocket Day. Her face set tight with concentration, Amelia inspected the broken strings and then began to knot the broken ends back together. Because the strings were so thin and frayed, it took a number of tries to get the knots to hold. After approximately 10 minutes, having triple knotted each side and tugged the strings to check, Amelia got up from the grass and went to the back of the line.

Meanwhile, Ted Peters, a middle-class, white student wearing nylon track pants and a soccer T-shirt, had just retrieved his rocket and was running back toward the launching stations. Rather than rejoin the line, however, Ted turned and ran toward his mother, who was watching with the other parents on the sidelines:

> As Ted approaches, Ms. Peters smiles broadly and praises Ted for a "great flight." Frowning, Ted holds out his rocket and explains that the string attaching the rocket's parachute has broken. After inspecting the broken string, Ms. Peters says encouragingly, "Go ask Mr. Fischer for a new string. I'm sure he'll be able to help." Ted's grim expression brightens. He turns and dashes off to show the broken string to Mr. Fischer, who retrieves an extra string from a supply bin and helps Ted reattach the parachute. The whole exchange takes less than a minute. Ted then immediately rejoins the line to launch his rocket again.

Like Amelia, Ted could have tried to fix the broken string on his own. Instead, Ted turned to his mother for help. Ms. Peters then used that request as a teachable moment, coaching Ted to use Mr. Fischer as a resource to solve the problem for him.

Unlike Ms. Peters, Amelia's parents were not there for Rocket Day—they could not skip work for school events. Despite their absence, however, there is reason to suspect that their voices likely played at least some role in guiding Amelia's actions that day. In third grade, for example, Amelia came home confused about her report card. Amelia had earned an A in math for the marking period, but the teacher also included a comment noting that Amelia "doesn't seem to put enough effort into class." Amelia told her father that the comment "didn't make sense"—she was one of the top-performing students in the class. Amelia's father, however, discouraged Amelia from asking about it because he worried that she might get in trouble for doing so. Even 2 years after that event, Mr. Graham could recall the incident vividly. In an interview during the summer after Amelia's fifth-grade year, Mr. Graham explained,

> I told Amelia not to ask about it, cuz the teacher probably wouldn't be too happy. I just want my kids to be respectful and responsible. My kids, I always told 'em. "Look, if you've gotta give somebody a hard time, give it to me. Don't give it to your teachers. Don't give it to other parents." And I've never had a teacher complain. Or, if my kids go and play at somebody else's house, I've never had a parent say: "Your child can't come back." You know? My kids are good for the teachers and for other parents.

Mr. Graham seemed to believe that it was disrespectful for students to complain or bother teachers with requests. Mr. Graham also stressed those views to his children at home. In doing so, he may have prompted Amelia not to ask Mr. Fischer for help wither broken string.

Ultimately, both Ted and Amelia fixed their rockets, but it took Amelia much longer. Furthermore, whereas Amelia went to the back of the line to wait, Ted took his rocket and stepped in behind the friend who had gone before him in the first round. Because of those choices, Ted got to launch his rocket four times, whereas Amelia got to launch hers only twice.

OVERVIEW

The contrast between Ms. Peters' advice and Mr. Graham's advice was part of a larger pattern of social class differences in parental coaching at Maplewood. Specifically, middle-class parents taught their children to manage problems at school using *strategies of influence*. That meant treating teachers as resources, being assertive in making requests for support, and actively avoiding consequences for missteps. Working-class parents, on the other hand, coached their children to manage problems at school using *strategies of deference*. That meant treating teachers with respect, tackling problems on their own, and taking responsibility for their actions.

That class-based coaching also had real consequences for students and for their understanding of how best to manage problems in school. Like Ted and Amelia, students at Maplewood gradually adopted (albeit to varying degrees and with some pushback) their parents' class-based strategies and internalized parents' messages about the importance of using those class-based strategies when managing problems at school. Evidence of that gradual internalization could be seen in interviews conducted after fifth grade, wherein parents and children expressed similar ideas about managing classroom problems and told similar stories about how children's goals, beliefs, and behaviors changed over time. It could also be seen in the fact that social class differences in students' interactions with teachers became more pronounced from third grade to fifth grade.

Of course, such patterns were not perfect. Some parents (including those in upwardly mobile families) were less vigilant than others about teaching class-based strategies, and some children (including shy and high-achieving middle-class children) were less willing and able to follow their parents' lead. Despite those variations, however, parents' class-based coaching still seemed to play a critical role in shaping the class-based patterns of problem-solving that I observed at Maplewood and that I describe in more detail in Chapters 3–5.

COACHING IN CONTEXT

As demonstrated by Jesse and Ellen in the classroom and Ted and Amelia on Rocket Day, the middle-class and working-class children at Maplewood often dealt with problems in contrasting ways. Those patterns were consistent with a larger body of research highlighting social class differences in children's interactions at home (Calarco 2014a; Hart and Risley 1995; Heath 1983; Lareau 2011) and at school (Calarco 2011; Jennings and DiPrete 2010; Lubienski 2000; McLeod and Kaiser 2004; Nelson and Schutz 2007; Streib 2011; Tach and Farkas 2006). Less clear, however, is how children learn to behave in class-based ways.

Scholars of socialization typically imply that those class-based behaviors are a natural and automatic outgrowth of social class differences in children's home lives (Bourdieu 1977; Bronfenbrenner 1958). A number of studies highlight parallels in the class-based skills, beliefs, and values espoused by parents and their children (Heath 2012; Hitlin and Piliavin 2004). Lareau (2011), for example, finds that, like their parents, middle-class children exhibit an "emerging sense of entitlement," whereas working-class children demonstrate an "emerging sense of constraint." Lareau concludes that those differences are likely the product of social class differences in parenting styles. Specifically, she finds that whereas middle-class parents carefully organize their children's lives, encourage them to voice their opinions, and regularly intervene for them when problems arise in school or other institutional settings (see also Chin and Phillips 2004; Cucchiara 2013; Hays 1996; Horvat, Weininger, and Lareau 2003; Nelson 2010; Sui-Chu and Willms 1996), working-class parents instead grant their children ample time for free play, guide their behavior through directives rather than negotiation, and defer to authorities (see also Calarco 2014a; Edwards 2004; Streib 2015).

Scholars of class-based socialization have revealed a number of important findings, but their research is also limited in two key ways. First, the conclusion drawn by many of these scholars—that class-based socialization is an automatic and implicit process—ignores evidence that culture can be passed from parents to children in more active ways (Elder 1974; Pugh 2009; Thorne 1993). We know that parenting is often strategic and goal-oriented.[1] Middle-class parents, for example, intervene for their children at school (Brantlinger 2003; Hays 1996; Lareau 2000; Nelson 2010), and working-class parents try to manage how their families are perceived by others (Edwards 2004). However, because scholars pay little attention to the logics of action that guide child-rearing decisions, it is unclear whether or how parents deliberately try to equip children to manage their own challenges.[2] Research even suggests that children can be strategic actors as well. It is known, for example, that children some-times contest the choices that their parents make about what they should eat or buy or how they should spend their time (Chin and Phillips 2004; Pugh 2009; Zelizer 2002). Less clear, however, is how children respond to ongoing socialization efforts—how they come to accept and utilize the class-based strategies that parents teach them at home. Lareau (2011), for example, does not interview children or observe them without their parents present. Thus, she cannot say how children make sense of the par-enting they experience or how they act on those messages when parents are not there to direct them.

Second, existing research has done little to show how class-based socialization contributes to larger patterns of inequality. Certainly, some studies have shown that the class-based behaviors children dem-onstrate in school are correlated with learning and achievement out-comes (Carneiro and Heckman 2003; Farkas 2003; Heckman and Rubinstein 2001; Heckman, Stixrud, and Urzua 2006). Those studies, however, rarely model the full socialization process, tracing children's classroom behaviors from their origins at home to their consequences at school. Lareau (2011), for example, assumes that social class differ-ences in parenting matter for inequalities, but she does not actually show the profits (or losses) that children get from demonstrating their sense of entitlement or constraint. One notable exception to this trend is Hart and Risley's (1995) study, which links social class differences in parents' language use to children's emerging vocabularies and to their subsequent achievement in school. Hart and Risley cannot state, how-ever, how children actually use their language skills or how they learn to do so from their parents at home.

In summary, social class matters both at home and in the classroom, shaping the parenting that children receive, the behaviors that children demonstrate, and the success that children achieve. Less clear, however, are the mechanisms that produce these patterns and link them to larger inequalities. It is not known, for example, whether the transmission of class cultures is an active process or a passive one. Nor is it known how the lessons that children learn at home ultimately translate into inequali-ties in school or what role parents, children, and teachers play in that process.

This chapter examines these possibilities. First, I consider how parents teach their children to behave in class-based ways. Next, I explore the extent to which children internalize those lessons. In doing so, I also set the stage for subsequent chapters, which will explore how children activate class-based behaviors in school and how those actions contribute to larger patterns of inequality.

MIDDLE-CLASS PARENTS: COACHING INFLUENCE

The middle-class parenting that I observed was in many ways consistent with patterns found in prior research. Among the middle-class parents at Maplewood, for example, ensuring children's academic success was widely viewed as a primary responsibility of parenting (see also Brantlinger 2003; Lareau 2000, 2011; Nelson 2010). That sense of responsibility also led middle-class parents to carefully monitor their children's progress in school and to intervene when problems arose (see also Cucchiara 2013; Horvat et al. 2003; Sui-Chu and Willms 1996; Useem 1992).[3]

Those efforts, however, also had limits. During the school day, for example, middle-class parents could not always be there to step in and ensure their children's success. Given those limits, middle-class parents taught their children that they could ensure their own success by practicing strategies of influence. Those strategies included using teachers as resources, being assertive in making requests for support, and avoiding consequences for missteps.

Teaching Resourcefulness

Looking back on their own experiences in school and in the workforce, middle-class parents viewed support-seeking as a tremendously beneficial skill. Ms. Matthews, for example, is a kindergarten teacher and a married mother of three children. Her husband has a bachelor's degree and works as a regional manager for a communications company. In my interview with Ms. Matthews, conducted after her son Tyler's fifth-grade year, she talked about how important it is for children to feel comfortable advocating for themselves:

> I really feel like they need to have those skills . . . to be able to talk to [the] teacher to understand and to work through those problems. I tell my kids: "This is a place where you go every day. You talk to this teacher every day. He's invested in your interests. He likes you. You couldn't be any safer unless you were at my house." [I tell them:] "It's okay to ask questions in that setting." And once they learn to overcome that hurtle, it becomes easier to then deal with asking for [other things]. When you get into a boss situation, your mom doesn't call and say, "Sorry my son doesn't understand what he's supposed to come and do today at work." You know, you need to learn how to do that! And if you don't start at this stage, it makes it more difficult and then you get fired!

Middle-class parents expected that children's requests would result in rewards, not reprimands. They also worried that not seeking support could result in serious negative consequences—even getting fired.

Thus, when middle-class children encountered problems in school, their parents encouraged them to use their teachers as "resources" to support them in overcoming the challenges they faced. Ms. Giordano, for example, is a married mother of three children. She has a college degree and a job as a midlevel manager at a health care company. Her husband has a bachelor's degree and works in graphic design. Ms. Giordano's daughter, Gina, is bubbly and outgoing; she often got in trouble for talking in class. In fourth grade, Gina's grades began slipping from A's and B's to B's and C's. Ms. Giordano was worried. Rather than intervene, however, Ms. Giordano encouraged Gina to "use her resources" and go to her teacher for help:

> It's like I encourage Gina: "Go to the source. That's who your resource is, your teacher." We always tell her, "You go up and you talk to the teacher. You don't use your friends. You go to the teacher and find out." Like, Gina was [struggling with math homework] . . . and I told her, "Well, go ask your teacher what that means. That's your resource."

At Maplewood, teachers would often encourage students to "ask three before me"—to try to get help from classmates before approaching the teacher with questions. Like Ms. Giordano, however, middle-class parents believed that it was best for students to use the teacher as their primary resource because other students might also be confused and might give incorrect information. Middle-class parents recognized that teachers alone knew what would be "on the test." As a result, middle-class parents coached their children to turn to teachers—and not to peers—for support in overcoming challenges at school.

Teaching Assertiveness

Middle-class parents also explicitly coached their children to be assertive in interactions with authorities and especially when asking for support in managing challenges at school. Ms. Bell is a married mother of four. She has a bachelor's degree and works part-time as a physical therapist. Her husband is a corporate lawyer. Ms. Bell is bubbly and outgoing, and she expects all her children to be comfortable asserting themselves in interactions with others. Describing her son Aidan, a fifth grader at Maplewood, Ms. Bell noted,

> Well, Aidan's shy. He's really very shy. We're still working on eye contact, that kind of stuff. So, anyhow, we got him a book on male etiquette, and how you do things. And one of the things in it was how to shake hands. Well, we're sitting there reading it in the car and belly-laughing, you know: "You give three pumps. No more than three pumps."

Ms. Bell laughed as she explained this. She seemed to recognize that there was a bit of absurdity in teaching a 10-year-old to have a firm, professional handshake. However, she also stressed that such lessons were important for Aidan, and she coached him to be assertive in his interactions with teachers as well. In an interview conducted during the summer after Aidan's fifth-grade year, Ms. Bell recalled how Aidan struggled regularly with assignments in fourth grade. She also recounted in detail how she had encouraged Aidan to ask his teacher for help:

> And I go: "Aidan, why don't you ask Ms. Nelson for help?" And he goes: "I did, and she tells me to ask my neighbor. But all of them needed help." And I said: "You need to tell her that. You really just have to keep pushing. This is a lesson. You're gonna like some teachers, you're not gonna not like some. You're gonna have a boss you like, and a boss you don't like. You have to not let her take away your dream. You have to keep your attitude positive, and you're gonna learn from this. You're gonna think back on this: 'I made it through this, I can make it through this now.' So you really just have to keep pushing."

Like Ms. Bell, middle-class parents would often coach their children to "keep pushing" with their requests. A few middle-class parents (mostly those who were upwardly mobile) did worry that teachers might be frustrated if students made too many requests. However, even those parents still encouraged their children to feel comfortable voicing their needs. In doing so, and like middle-class parents more generally, they recognized teachers as key "resources," and they taught their children to be assertive in using those resources to manage problems at school.

Teaching Consequence Avoidance

Middle-class parents also taught their children (seemingly more inadvertent) messages about the importance of avoiding consequences for missteps. When middle-class children forgot their homework, for example, their parents would often drive the forgotten homework to school, despite the fact that Maplewood policy explicitly discouraged parents from doing so. Other parents would e-mail the teacher with excuses (e.g., "It was a really crazy morning" or "We were out late last night at his brother's soccer game") and ask that their child be excused from any punishment.

Middle-class messages about avoiding consequences were particularly common with respect to homework, but they also extended to larger issues as well. Christian Shore, for example, is a smart and high-achieving middle-class student, but he would often lash out at teachers and classmates with mean or sarcastic remarks. One morning in fifth grade, Ms. Hudson had her students write short essays describing their favorite place "in as much detail as possible." When they finished, Ms. Hudson had the students edit their stories with a partner, and then she cold-called a few students to read their essays aloud. Christian's essay about his bedroom was short and vague, just listing a few things such as "good books," "video games," and a "television." After Christian finished reading the essay, Ms. Hudson chided him for not including more detail. That response prompted a tirade from Christian:

> Christian leans forward in his chair and protests loudly: "But I did do that and Lizbeth [my partner] told me it was bad!" Ms. Hudson takes a step backward and blinks as though unsure what to say in response. Lizbeth pipes up to defend herself. Shaking her head, Lizbeth sneers: "He wrote about an outlet!" She explains dismissively that Christian's original (longer) essay was "silly"—it was about the electrical outlet that powers all his favorite gadgets. As Lizbeth reveals all of this, Christian shrinks in his chair, sliding lower and lower. His face is a deep crimson color.

Flustered, Ms. Hudson tried to move on, calling on another student to share. Meanwhile, Christian just glared at Lizbeth from across the table where they were both sitting:

> As the other student reads aloud, Christian sits up suddenly and begins to pound on his desk with his fist, growling through gritted teeth. He continues like this for just a few seconds—though it feels like much longer—and then slumps back in his chair again. Christian finishes his tirade just as the other student concludes her story. A few students clap politely for the speaker, but most are looking warily at Christian. Christian, meanwhile, sits up tall in his seat and begins to clap with false enthusiasm. He smacks both hands together loud and slow. Rather than look at the speaker, however, Christian glares at Lizbeth with a deep scowl on his face.

Later, Ms. Hudson took Christian aside to talk with him privately about his behavior. She also wrote an e-mail to Ms. Shore, letting her know about the outburst. Rather than thanking the teacher and indicating that she would correct her son, the mother defended him. As Ms. Shore explained in an interview after Christian's fifth-grade year,

> His behavior has only improved over time. I've always been comfortable saying it's harder for a little boy to sit still all day. And in first and second grade [before his gluten sensitivity was diagnosed], his food allergies could have been making him agitated. And he's very bright. And he has a lot of energy. But he's learned to manage it, and he's not having any negative impact on the class.

Like Ms. Shore, middle-class parents were quick to justify their children's missteps. They would also try to protect their children from consequences. As discussed in subsequent sections, that leniency seemed to teach middle-class children that their well-being should be ensured and that they should feel comfortable relying on others to accommodate their needs.

Middle-Class Parents' Competing Priorities

Middle-class parents believed that coaching their children to use strategies of influence would promote academic success. Such success was a priority for middle-class families. Thus, while middle-class parents sometimes taught their children about responsibility and other aspects of good character, those lessons often took a back seat to academic priorities.

In some cases, parents had to decide whether to prioritize hard work or good grades. Ms. Corsaro, for example, is a former teacher and stay-at-home mother of three children. In an interview conducted after fifth grade, Ms. Corsaro recalled how, in third grade, her daughter Julie was placed in the advanced math class. For the first time, Julie started having trouble with homework. As Ms. Corsaro explained,

> Julie's used to being good at things. And for math, for example, when they first started placing them, and she was on a higher-level math, and she really had to work for it, she wasn't used to that. She was used to things just coming easily to her. And she was discouraged. And I hate to see that in her, because I want to instill a good work ethic. I want her to realize, like, not everything is just handed to you. But she struggles with that. And it was a battle every night when she was doing her homework. "I don't understand this" and "It's so hard." And math is definitely my weakest subject, so I wasn't much help there. And there was one time, in fourth grade, I was helping her with it, and I was like: "Oh! It's all coming back to me." And then she went in, and she got everything wrong. And I said: "I am not helping you with math anymore. You have to go and see Ms. Phillips and tell her that you need help." And Ms. Phillips was wonderful and gave her some extra help. And it just clicked.

Ms. Corsaro wanted Julie to develop a "good work ethic," but she was also reluctant to let her struggle on her own. Instead, Ms. Corsaro tried to help Julie herself, and when it became clear that such assistance would not be enough to ensure that Julie got the answers correct, Ms. Corsaro coached her daughter to go to the teacher for help instead.

The tension between school success and good character was also apparent in situations in which parents had to decide whether to teach their children to take responsibility for their own actions or to avoid consequences for misbehavior. Later in her interview, Ms. Corsaro described, her voice breaking as though she was holding back tears, the hand-holding she had done for her children and her conflicted stance on not holding them more accountable:

> I think I've done a disservice to my kids by being so involved in school. Like, they forget things. And I get a phone call [from school, asking to bring in a missing item], and generally I'm there almost every day, so I do drop things off. And so there's no consequence. . . . I mean, I really do think it's a valuable lesson [to face consequences], that that's the best way to learn. But I don't want them to suffer.

Like Ms. Corsaro, middle-class parents at Maplewood wanted their children to learn habits such as work ethic and personal responsibility, but they also did not want their children to "suffer," either academically or emotionally. At least in most cases, then, middle-class parents' desire to ensure their children's school success ultimately trumped their concerns about developing good character.

WORKING-CLASS PARENTS: COACHING DEFERENCE

Like working-class parents in other studies, the working-class parents at Maplewood viewed character development as one of their primary parenting responsibilities. They seemed keenly aware of negative stereotypes portraying less privileged people as "lazy" and "rude." Given that awareness, working-class parents actively tried to distance themselves and their children from such negative labels and from the kinds of sanctions that might result from them (Edwards 2004).

With their children, working-class parents stressed the importance of demonstrating good character, particularly in situations (e.g., at school) in which parents could not be there to guide and direct them. Specifically, working-class parents coached their children to use strategies of deference when interacting with teachers and managing problems at school. Those strategies included treating teachers with respect, tackling problems on their own, and taking responsibility for their actions.

Teaching Respect

Like Mr. Graham in the opening example, working-class parents wanted to raise children who were, first and foremost, good people. Ms. Trumble, for example, is a married mother of five children. She did not finish high school and is not formally employed, but she earns a little money by babysitting friends' and relatives' children during work hours. Mr. Trumble went to a vocational high school and has a full-time job as a maintenance worker. In an interview conducted after her son Jeremy's fifth-grade year, Ms. Trumble described her goals for her children:

> I think the teacher's role is to, you know, *teach* 'em. Teach 'em their education, what they need to know. Like, the education part. I don't expect them to teach my kids their morals and stuff like that. I believe we teach them that at home. I'm not very religious, so it's not like that. I just want 'em to be raised to be good, decent people. To learn to respect other people, and to be nice. I think just having respect for other people. And respect for themselves. Treat people the way you want to be treated.

Like other working-class parents, Ms. Trumble wanted her children to do well in school. When her son Jeremy struggled with learning to read, Ms. Trumble fretted about how it might affect him long term, and she was tremendously grateful when Jeremy's teacher offered to provide him with extra support. At the same time, however, and also like other working-class parents, Ms. Trumble focused her own coaching efforts on teaching her children to be "good, decent people."

Working-class parents also cautioned their children that a lack of respect—particularly for teachers and other authorities—could have serious, negative consequences. Looking back on their own experiences in school, working-class parents assumed that students who complained or asked for help would be perceived as disrespectful and might even be reprimanded by their teachers. Mr. Graham, for example, recalled in his interview a story he had told his own children about a time when one of his teachers yelled at him for "challenging her" about a test question. He noted,

> The teacher gave us a test and none of us understood. We were like, "What are you talking about?" I mean, it was like she thought she explained it clear as day. And we read it, but it just didn't jive. [And] she was upset because we asked her about it. She yelled at us, cuz she just didn't understand why we didn't get it! That was a rough little time in school. I mean, a number of us were upset about it, crying upset about it. I think I probably took the brunt of it, cuz I was the one that challenged her.

Like Mr. Graham, working-class parents believed that children's requests— even well-meaning ones—might be perceived as disrespectful and might result in reprimand. Thus, working-class parents stressed that children should be "good for the teachers" by not burdening them with questions or requests.

Teaching Work Ethic

For working-class parents, respect was not the only element of character that might be undermined by an overreliance on support from others. Rather, working-class parents believed that such support would also undermine children's developing work ethic. Thus, when problems arose, working-class parents coached their children to manage on their own. Ms. Webb, for example, has a GED, and her husband is a high school graduate; they both work as convenience store clerks. During the summer after her daughter Sadie's fifth-grade year, Ms. Webb and I sat at the kitchen table in their mobile home. Ms. Webb's daughter Sadie, who had been watching television in the next room, came into the kitchen to get a drink. As I wrote in my field notes,

> Sadie opens a kitchen cabinet and pulls out a plastic cup. Turning to her mother, Sadie asks politely: "Can you help me get the iced tea?" Ms. Webb raises her eyebrow skeptically and laughs: "Get it yourself! What're you asking me for?" Sadie nods sheepishly and pulls a chair out from the kitchen table, using it to climb up and retrieve the can of iced tea mix from the cabinet above the refrigerator. As Sadie does this, Ms. Webb turns to me and says playfully: "She's a spoiled brat. Not gonna make it in the real world." I smile awkwardly, asking: "Whadda you mean?" Ms. Webb continues: "Sadie's a handful. She has a whining problem. I don't know if you've noticed it at school, but she has a whining problem at home."

Ms. Webb viewed Sadie's request for help as "whining," something only a "spoiled brat" would do. Like other working-class parents, Ms. Webb discouraged that kind of reliance on others and instructed her children to deal with problems on their own instead.

Like Ms. Webb, working-class parents at Maplewood were not shy about criticizing their children for a lack of hard work. Ms. Compton, for example, is a single mother of two children. She has completed some community college and works part-time in retail. In conversations with her children, Ms. Compton stressed that it was "lazy" to rely on others for support. During an interview conducted after her son Jesse's fifth-grade year, Ms. Compton explained that those conversations often took place while working with her Jesse on homework:[4]

> Jesse can be lazy. He's very, "I can't do it. I don't know what I'm doing." But he just needs a push to do it on his own. I just tell him, "You can do it. I know you can do it. I've seen you do this. I want you to try." Then he gets his confidence up and he snaps out of that low moment.

Like many working-class parents, Ms. Compton felt a responsibility to oversee homework but not to assist in its completion. She worried that assistance would promote "laziness" and thus pushed Jesse to "do it on his own" instead.

Teaching Personal Responsibility

Working-class parents also coached deference by holding children accountable for their actions and by stressing the importance of personal responsibility. With homework, for example, none of the working-class parents recalled driving back to school to drop off or pick up forgotten items. Working-class parents were also highly critical of the kinds of parents who would fail to hold their own children accountable for missteps. Ms. Campitello, for example, is a married mother of three children. She is a high school graduate and works part-time in the school cafeteria. Her husband is also a high school graduate and works as a plumber. Ms. Campitello appreciated the quality of the education her children received at Maplewood, but she spoke with disdain about the kinds of character traits commonly displayed by students and parents at the school. Comparing Maplewood to the working-class school her children previously attended, Ms. Campitello sneered,

> Parents here don't make their kids accountable or responsible for anything. They do everything for their kids. Everything. It's ridiculous. They don't make their kids responsible for anything. They're not responsible for their actions. And being a cafeteria worker, it's a perfect example. A kid left their cell phone in the cafeteria, and the parent called asking me to find it for them. Are you kidding me? In the olden days, it's like, you left your cell phone in the cafeteria? Well, you better hope it's still there tomorrow.

Like Ms. Campitello, working-class parents believed that letting children avoid consequences and rely on adults to solve problems for them would undermine their sense of responsibility.

That emphasis on personal responsibility was particularly apparent with homework and other small items, but it extended to larger issues as well. Ms. Webb, for example, recalled being distraught when she learned that her older daughter, Suzie, was taking things from her first-grade classmates:

> Initially, they told me it was an issue with "borrowing." But a month later, it came out that she was stealing. They said: "You know, hey. Suzie's taking stuff from other kids. She's not asking."

Ms. Webb was horrified at Suzie's behavior, so she took matters into her own hands:

> I resolved it at home. Suzie stole a Chap Stick, so I made her hold it. If she was watching TV, she held it. If she was eating dinner, she held it. If she was playing outside, she held it. She hasn't stolen since. But apparently that's excessive discipline. According to the school, that's abuse and they called Social Services, who came out and said: "Yeah, I understand what you're saying. She hasn't done it since, so next time just limit it [the punishment] to an hour."

The school found out about Ms. Webb's punishment when Suzie continued holding the Chap Stick all through class, prompting them to contact "Social Services." Such visits were not the norm for working-class families at Maplewood. However, working-class parents did let their children suffer consequences, including consequences that teachers deemed too severe. In doing so, working-class parents taught their children to accept responsibility for their actions and not to ask for reprieve.

Working-Class Parents' Competing Priorities

This is not to say that working-class parents viewed character development as their only responsibility as parents. On the contrary, the working-class parents at Maplewood cared deeply about their children's academic success. They wanted their children to do well in school, and some had even moved to Maplewood specifically to give their children a "high-quality" education. Like working-class parents in other studies (Horvat et al. 2003; Lareau 2000; Useem 1992), however, the working-class parents at Maplewood often felt less than confident in their own school-based knowledge and skills. As a result, they viewed teachers as "experts" who would know what was best for their children academically, and they generally deferred to their children's teachers on school-related matters.

Thus, even when working-class parents were skeptical of teachers' actions or advice, and even when their children's academic success was on the line, they rarely spoke up; they believed it would be rude to challenge the teachers' authority and might result in reprimands. Ms. Higgins, for example, is a stay-at-home mother of two children. She has a high school diploma. Her husband is also a high school graduate, and he works as a truck driver. In an interview conducted after her daughter Shannon's fifth-grade year, Ms. Higgins recalled being worried about Shannon (her younger daughter) when she started school:

> We knew that there was something a little off with Shannon, academically. Being home 100% with them, and you're not supposed to compare children, but I knew that it wasn't just the personality difference, there was something off.

When Shannon started kindergarten (at a predominantly working-class school approximately 10 miles from Maplewood), Ms. Higgins let the school administrators know about her concerns. The school tested Shannon for learning disabilities and found that she had speech and processing delays. Ms. Higgins was thrilled that Shannon would be getting help, recalling, "So, in kindergarten, I thought, "Okay, this is gonna be great." By January, however, the school had not provided any of the academic support to which Shannon was entitled. Ms. Higgins continued to wait, hoping for the best. She waited until the end of kindergarten and all through first grade. I asked Ms. Higgins if she talked to the school administrators, and she sighed, explaining,

> I was told that there was nobody to cover the services [Shannon needed]. And she was lost because she wasn't understanding. But I'm very easy-going as far as recommendations and suggestions. I don't tell the teachers what she needs—because teachers are with her in that sense. [They] know what's in her best interest. And I feel that they're not going to direct me in a way that's going to be harmful or hurt her in any way.

Ms. Higgins waited for 2 full years, but the school never provided Shannon with the support to which she was entitled. At the end of first grade, when the family moved to Maplewood, Shannon was barely performing at a kindergarten level—unable to read or write or even recognize letters and numbers. The teachers at Maplewood jumped into action immediately: By the end of Shannon's second week of second grade, she was receiving daily learning support, and by the end of fifth grade, she was less than half a year below grade level. And yet, such problems could have been avoided—and Shannon could have caught up more quickly—if someone had acted sooner.

The point here is not to blame Ms. Higgins or the teachers at Shannon's old school. The point is that working-class parents such as Ms. Higgins experienced a real tension between demonstrating good character and ensuring their children's success in school. In those moments, and driven by real fears about reprimand and social judgment, they prioritized respect, hard work, and personal responsibility.

COACHING'S CONSEQUENCES

In light of their parents' coaching, children generally came to internalize the messages they learned at home. That process was not an automatic one. However, over time, most students adopted their parents' beliefs about good grades and good character and also learned to practice the strategies that their parents taught them for managing problems at school.

Internalizing Messages About Influence and Deference

Children's internalization of parents' class-based coaching could be seen, in part, through parallels in parents' and children's responses to interview vignettes. During (separate) interviews with children and parents (conducted during the summer after the child's fifth-grade year), I read aloud brief, fictional stories about common classroom challenges. I then asked open-ended questions such as "What do you think Jason should do?" and "What do you think Kelly's mother will say?" Although the answers varied, I was able to identify the primary theme of each response and compare the prevalence of themes by age and social class. Responses to the vignette questions followed clear class-based patterns, with children's responses closely mirroring those of their parents.

Table 1.1, for example, reveals cross-generational similarities in beliefs about the appropriateness of using teachers as resources to overcome problems in school. The table describes parents' and children's responses to a vignette about "Jason," a student struggling to understand a test question. All of the interviewed middle-class parents said that Jason should go to the teacher to ask for help, and all but two of the middle-class children responded similarly. Those two students both said that Jason should probably go to the teacher for help but added the caveat that it depends

Table 1.1 SUMMARY OF OPEN-ENDED RESPONSES TO VIGNETTE 1
BY SOCIAL CLASS[a]

Vignette 1: *Mr. Patrick's fifth-grade class is working on a science test. Mr. Patrick is at his desk, grading papers. Jason, one of the students, gets to the third question and reads it silently to himself. It says: "Make a chart comparing the atmospheres on the earth and on the moon." Jason is confused—he isn't sure how to answer the question, or what to include in the chart.*

Prompt: *What do you think Jason should do?*

Response by Primary Theme	Middle-Class		Working-Class	
	Parents	Children	Parents	Children
Jason should go to the teacher for help	12	10	0	2
Jason should try his best	0	0	5	4
It depends on the teacher's rules	0	2	2	2
Jason should wait; the teacher will likely notice him struggling and offer help	0	0	2	1
Total	12	12	9	9

[a]Responses to vignettes were open-ended. I coded responses into themes to highlight patterns. Coded responses are presented here for ease of comparison.

on the teacher's rules. Working-class responses to this vignette were more varied, but there were often marked similarities between parents' answers and those given by their children. The most frequent response for both working-class parents and working-class children was that Jason should just try his best to answer the question on his own. Others indicated that Jason should wait because the teacher would likely notice that he is struggling and offer assistance. Still others said that it depends on the teacher's rules. None of the working-class parents said that Jason should go to the teacher for help, but two of the working-class students did suggest such a response. In both of those cases, however, the students later talked about how they were often reluctant to ask for help themselves out of concern that their requests might result in reprimand. They worried, for example, that if they asked for help, teachers would assume they did not read the test directions or that they were off-task when the material was presented in class. Those working-class students also worried about being perceived as disrespectful if they disrupted others by talking to the teacher during a test.

Class-based parallels between parents and children could also be seen in attitudes about whether it is better to trust or question teachers' judgment. Table 1.2 describes parents' and children's responses to a vignette about "Brian," who came home complaining about being "bored" in math class. All of the middle-class parents and almost all of the middle-class children

---

Table 1.2 SUMMARY OF OPEN-ENDED RESPONSES TO VIGNETTE 2 BY SOCIAL CLASS[a]

Vignette 2: *Brian, a fifth grader, usually gets good grades in math and does well on tests. Brian comes home from school one day and tells his mom that he is often bored during math class.* **Prompt:** *What do you think should happen with Brian?*

	Middle-Class		Working-Class	
Response by Primary Theme	Parents	Children	Parents	Children
Brian's mother should ask the teacher to move him up or give him extra work	9	5	2	0
Brian should ask the teacher to give him extra work	3	4	0	0
Brian's mother should ask for the teacher's advice at conferences	0	0	2	0
If it's really an issue, the teacher would notice and help Brian	0	0	3	1
Brian just needs to be more focused	0	2	2	5
Brian just does not like the material	0	1	0	3
Total	12	12	9	9

[a]Responses to vignettes were open-ended. I coded responses into themes to highlight patterns. Coded responses are presented here for ease of comparison.

assumed that Brian was bored because he was not being challenged enough. They also suggested that Brian should receive accommodations (e.g., moving up a math level or receiving supplementary work to complete) and that he should obtain such accommodations either by having his mother contact the teacher or by talking to the teacher directly. Again, working-class responses were more varied. However, compared to their middle-class peers, both working-class parents and their children seemed to see less of a need for requesting accommodations. Instead, they typically suggested that Brian just needs to be more focused in class or that if Brian's boredom was really an issue, the teacher would notice and offer to help.

Children also seemed to have adopted their parents' class-based beliefs about accountability. Table 1.3 describes parents' and children's responses to a vignette about "Kelly," who left a homework packet at school. The vast majority of middle-class respondents believed that Kelly should not have to suffer any penalty. Instead, both middle-class parents and their children suggested either that Kelly's parent should drive her back to school to retrieve the homework or that Kelly should be allowed to call a friend

Table 1.3 SUMMARY OF OPEN-ENDED RESPONSES TO VIGNETTE 3 BY SOCIAL CLASS[a]

Vignette 3: *Kelly gets home from school and opens her backpack to get out her homework. Reaching inside, Kelly realizes that she forgot to bring home the Social Studies packet that she is supposed to finish for tomorrow.*

Prompt: *What do you think should happen with Kelly?*

Response by Primary Theme	Middle-Class		Working-Class	
	Parents	Children	Parents	Children
Kelly should be driven back to school to retrieve the homework packet	5	5	0	0
Kelly should call a friend to copy the questions	6	4	3	4
Kelly should have to suffer the consequences	1	0	6	2
Kelly should tell the teacher and hope that she will be allowed to turn in the homework late without penalty[b]	0	3	0	3
Total	12	12	9	9

[a]Responses to vignettes were open-ended. I coded responses into themes to highlight patterns. Coded responses are presented here for ease of comparison.
[b]The wording of responses in this category varied somewhat between middle-class and working-class students. Middle-class students tended to suggest that Kelly should try to convince the teacher to allow her to turn in the homework late. As one middle-class student explained, "She should try to explain to her teacher because sometimes it's hard when this happens to you. The teacher might just think she's making an excuse, but she should try her best to explain. And the teacher should understand." Working -class students tended to view Kelly's fate as resting more with the teacher. As a working-class student explained, "She should go back and ask the teacher nicely if she can do it the next day. And maybe she'll get an extra day, but the teacher might just say: 'Well, I'm sorry but it was due today, so you have to stay in for recess.'"

(either to borrow and photocopy the packet or to write down the questions over the phone). Working-class respondents were instead inclined to believe that Kelly should be held responsible for her actions. Whereas a few respondents suggested the phone-a-friend option, none believed that Kelly should be driven back to school, and most suggested that Kelly should just suffer the consequences (although working-class children were more likely than their parents to hold out hope for reprieve).

Practicing Influence and Deference

Children's internalization of parents' coaching could also be seen in the way that they thought about and navigated classroom challenges. As noted previously, however, that process was far from automatic, with some children taking longer to follow their parents' lead.

Middle-Class Children: Practicing Influence at School

Consistent with their parents' coaching, middle-class students treated their teachers as resources. However, whereas some middle-class students readily adopted such strategies, others, including very high-achieving students, took more coaxing. Mr. and Ms. Dobrin both have advanced degrees and work full-time as computer engineers. Their oldest son, Ethan, excels in school, earning almost all A's and scoring extremely high on standardized tests. Ethan was very comfortable with certain kinds of requests—for example, asking for extra recesses or more time to study before a test or to demonstrate a new karate move. At the same time, Ethan was hesitant to admit when he was confused or struggling because he worried that it might make him seem "dumb." Given that reluctance, the Dobrins tried to stress to Ethan the importance of voicing his needs. Ms. Dobrin described that coaching in an interview that took place after Ethan's fifth-grade year:

> Ethan's teacher evaluations always said, "He's a joy. He's bright. He's making great grades, but he needs to ask for help sometimes." Now, I don't think asking for help is comfortable for Ethan, but what we try to impress on him is, "Think about how important it is that you get that information. If you need that information to do the job correctly, then you need to ask the teacher."

Chiming in, Mr. Dobrin added brightly,

> Having to admit that he can't do something is hard for Ethan. But you just have to do that sometimes. And he did it. Like, we've coached him into, when he hasn't understood

something, to e-mail his teacher and get the information. And [Ethan] would push back at first, but eventually he'd either send the teacher an e-mail, or tell him the next day, and the teacher would help him figure it out.

Like other middle-class parents, the Dobrins viewed help-seeking as a critical skill and one that would have direct benefits in terms of academic achievement. They also encouraged Ethan to perceive such requests in a similar way and to be willing to "flag a teacher down, or get up and go talk to the teacher during a test."

Those efforts seemed to hit their mark. As Ethan explained in an interview after fifth grade, he drew on his parents' coaching to seek support in school:

> Like, one time I was working on a research project, on the brain. And I couldn't find anything on the Internet to answer my questions, so I kept searching, and after three hours, my mom and dad started doing the research for me, and we still couldn't figure out some of it, so they told me to ask Mr. Fischer. And so I went in the next day and I said: "I couldn't figure it out. I couldn't find it on the Internet. Can you help me find it?" And Mr. Fischer got me to the right website that actually showed me the right information.

Essentially, Ethan seemed to have internalized his parents' lessons about the benefits of using teachers as resources in school.

Over time, high-achieving students such as Ethan gradually became more comfortable voicing their struggles. By the time Ethan finished fifth grade, he regularly called out with questions, as he did during a math test in Mr. Fischer's class:

> The room is quiet as the students work on their tests. Ethan looks up and taps his pencil eraser lightly against his cheek, frowning. As Mr. Fischer circles past, Ethan calls out quietly but hopefully, "Mr. Fischer?" Mr. Fischer immediately stops and turns toward Ethan, asking with genuine concern: "You okay?" Ethan shrugs and admits that he is not sure if he is interpreting a question correctly. Squatting down, Mr. Fischer does not give Ethan the answer, but helps him recognize his mistake. Ethan nods, quickly finishing the problem correctly.

In my interview with Ethan after fifth grade, I asked why he went to the teacher with questions. Wide-eyed he explained:

> I didn't want to guess and risk getting it wrong. I don't want to get it wrong, because then I won't get as high a grade as I should have gotten. So it's just better to go up and ask the teacher. And then normally I would get it right.

Although Ethan was initially reluctant to ask for support, his parents' persistent messaging eventually convinced him that it was better to ask than to "risk getting it wrong."

In light of the lessons about support-seeking that they learned at home, middle-class students were generally assertive in making requests. That assertiveness, however, did not always come easily. Rather, and particularly in the case of very shy children, middle-class parents had to step up their game. Ms. Long, for example, was a divorced mother of two children who worked full-time as a public relations specialist and was in the process of completing a master's degree. Ms. Long's daughter, Keri, was painfully shy. As a result, Keri was reluctant to ask her teacher for help when she started having trouble with math in third grade. Ms. Long recounted the following exchange:

> Keri was doing well in third grade. She had straight A's until this one math test.... [Before the test, she came to me] and said, "I'm confused about this." And I said, "Go talk to your teacher about it! You need to tell your teacher this is what you need help with."

Ms. Long was very direct in encouraging Keri to ask for help. Keri, however, was reluctant to take her mother's advice, and she did not ask for help before the test. Shaking her head disappointedly, Ms. Long continued her story:

> She didn't have the power in her to do it. To say: "I need help." And that brought her grade down! She got a C on the test and it brought her down. Which, to me, was very upsetting, because I told her, "Go! Get help!" And she just ... I dunno. Keri's very timid, very shy. I'm trying to teach her to look up and shake hands. That adults aren't scary and that the teachers are there to help her. It's getting better, but it's taken her a really long time.

Ms. Long was frustrated and disappointed by Keri's reluctance, but she was not deterred. Instead, and like other middle-class parents of shy children, Ms. Long continued encouraging Keri to voice her needs.

That persistence also paid off. Keri never overcame her shyness entirely, but she gradually became more comfortable asserting herself in interactions with teachers. During a social studies test in fifth grade, Keri readily acknowledged that she was struggling with one of the short-essay questions. The question read: "Identify one main event in the Civil War and describe its significance."

> Before setting the students to work, Ms. Dunham calls out "Use your resources. But it's open book, not open neighbor!" After working for a few minutes, Keri picks up her textbook and carries it with her as she approaches Ms. Dunham's desk. Pointing at a passage in the book, she asks quietly, "Does this count as a main event?" After glancing

at the book, Ms. Dunham explains, "This is a good event, but you probably want to look for something larger." Ms. Dunham then helps Keri recall some significant events they discussed in class.

In third grade, I rarely saw Keri ask for help. She did so only when teachers approached her to offer assistance or when she could "piggyback" on requests made by friends or classmates. By fifth grade, on the other hand, Keri regularly went to her teachers with questions and requests, although, like other shy students, she was still more timid in those interactions than were most of her middle-class peers.

Keri also linked her increasing comfort interacting with teachers to her mother's encouragement. I interviewed Keri during the summer after fifth grade. She sat curled in a ball on a living room chair, playing with the digital voice recorder I was using to record the interview. Throughout the interview, Keri's voice barely went above a whisper, and she made eye contact with me only rarely. However, when I asked Keri to tell me about fifth grade, Keri looked up and smiled broadly, saying, "It was good. I liked my teacher. She was nice. Like, she'd only call on you if you raised your hand first. And she was just nice." Similarly, when I asked Keri what students should do if they are confused or struggling in school, Keri responded emphatically, "Ask for help. My mom tells me that I should do it. And so I usually go and ask Ms. Dunham." Through their parents' ongoing efforts, shy middle-class students such as Keri eventually learned to feel comfortable (or at least more comfortable) asserting their needs and desires, and they reaped the rewards for doing so.

Given their parents' reluctance to hold them accountable, middle-class children were generally very comfortable avoiding (or at least trying to avoid) consequences for their missteps. In an interview after fifth grade, I showed Christian Shore the Kelly vignette about forgotten homework. Responding to the vignette, he stressed that if students "go up right away and explain," teachers will usually respond with lenience. He noted,

> This has happened to me a couple of times and it's annoying when it happens, but what I think [Kelly] should do is try to explain to her teacher. I'd go up in the beginning of the day and not wait until the last second. If you wait, they might think you're making excuses. If you go up right away and explain, you could say that you'll get it done tonight and bring it in tomorrow. I think the teacher would probably understand. They'd probably just tell you to do it tonight. No problem. They usually understand. It's not your fault if they don't.

Like other middle-class students, Christian had internalized the idea that teachers could be persuaded to reduce or eliminate standard punishments (e.g., grade penalties for missing assignments), and he was generally very comfortable seeking such reprieves.

Working-Class Children: Practicing Deference at School

Consistent with their parents' coaching, working-class students were careful to be respectful of their teachers. Jared Carson, for example, is a high-achieving, athletic, and popular working-class student. At recess, everyone wanted to be on his team, and as one teacher noted, "Jared is one of the most likeable kids in the class." Like most of the other boys in the grade, Jared also loved making jokes, but he was careful to avoid upsetting the teacher in the process. In an interview after fifth grade, Jared compared his approach to humor with that of Christian Shore, the middle-class student whose comments and outbursts in class often got him into trouble:

> Christian's like, the funniest kid in the grade, but he's funny because he gets in trouble and does funny stuff. And he's not afraid to get in trouble. But I don't do actions that are really disrespectful or something. I usually just like, make jokes. Like, I poke, I don't stab. So I really don't do anything to make fun of someone, or to make them feel bad. And I wouldn't do it if [the teacher] was in a bad mood, or if Christian just got in trouble.

Like Jared, working-class students were often keenly attuned to the needs and temperaments of those around them. Even when seeking attention (i.e., by making jokes), they calibrated their actions to avoid disrespecting teachers or eliciting a negative response.

In light of what their parents taught them about the importance of a strong work ethic, working-class students generally tried to work through problems on their own rather than burden teachers with requests. In an interview during the summer after fifth grade, Shannon Higgins explained what students need to do if they want to do well in school:

> You need to work hard and learn things. Like, teachers give you homework to learn things. And then if you get help from your mom and dad, you're not learning that stuff. And if you get it from a calculator, you still don't learn it.

When talking about challenges in school and about success more generally, working-class students often echoed their parents' sentiments about the drawbacks of relying on others, stressing that it was better to hide a problem or fix it themselves.

Following their parents' lessons about personal responsibility, working-class students rarely tried to avoid consequences for their missteps. I interviewed Ms. Trumble during the summer after her son Jeremy's fifth-grade year. During the interview, Ms. Trumble noted that her son Jeremy "sometimes forgets stuff." She went on to describe her response in those situations:

> I'll say, "You have to tell your teacher that you forgot it, and stay in for recess and get it done then." And that's what he ends up doing. Because I tell him, "There's nothing I can do. You forgot your homework. I don't know what it was."

Like other working-class parents, Ms. Trumble held her son accountable for his missteps. That expectation of personal responsibility stuck with Jeremy, as evidenced in fourth grade when he left his book report at home:

> Slumping into his seat next to Tory (middle-class, white), Jeremy laments, "I finally finished my book report last night, and then I left it at home." Tory looks at Jeremy and asks, puzzled, "Can't your mom bring it for you?" Jeremy shakes his head. "She has to work, so if I forget things, she says it's my responsibility." Tory blinks, bewildered. Later, when Ms. Burns checks homework, Jeremy apologizes and admits that he does not have his project. Ms. Burns says disappointedly: "You'll have to stay in for recess." Jeremy nods and does not protest.

Working-class students such as Jeremy had internalized their parents' coaching. They held themselves accountable for their missteps, even when their parents were not there to guide them in doing so.

Because working-class parents expected obedience to authority (see also Lareau 2011), working-class children's resistance to parents' coaching was less overt. However, working-class children did not always want to do as they were told. As we saw with Ms. Webb and the iced tea, for example, working-class parents were not always pleased with their children's level of respect, work ethic, and personal responsibility. A number of working-class parents (and especially working-class parents of lower-achieving boys) also reported frequent struggles over homework. They expected children to complete homework "on their own." In reality, however, children often needed prompting and assistance to get it done. Over time, however, and in light of parents' persistent messages, even some of the most reluctant working-class children (e.g., Zach and Jesse) did become more independent with homework or, at the very least, stopped asking their parents for help.

OUTLIER CASES: MANAGING MOBILITY

It is important to note that there were variations in the frequency and fervor of parents' coaching. Some of that variation stemmed from the challenges of getting shy and high-achieving middle-class students to feel comfortable seeking support. Other variations seemed to stem from the fact that social class is not always a fixed position. Upwardly mobile parents, for example, seemed to experience the tension between academic success and good character more acutely than did other parents. As a result, they were more ambivalent about the messages they conveyed to their children. That ambivalence, in turn, led children in upwardly mobile families to be more flexible in using strategies of influence and deference as well. These patterns can be seen in examples from two different upwardly mobile families—one middle class and one working class.

Upwardly Mobile Middle-Class Families

The upwardly mobile Healey family had a cautious attitude toward support-seeking and other strategies of influence. Both Healey parents grew up in working-class families and were first-generation college students. Both work full-time in finance. In their joint interview, conducted after their oldest son Ben's fifth-grade year, Mr. Healey explained that Ben is a high-achieving but shy student. Mr. Healey recalled how Ben's fifth-grade teacher, Mr. Potter, wanted Ben to be more comfortable seeking help:

> Mr. Potter kept saying: "Ben needs to come to me for help." He thought that was really important for Ben, but I don't really know. Mr. Potter wanted Ben to open up: "When he needs help, come to me for help." He said that in every conference we had with him. But Ben wasn't struggling. I probably helped him with homework three times in six years. And I guess Mr. Potter's theory was: "This kid's eventually gonna need to come to somebody for help, and he needs to learn how to do that." But I don't think Ben actually needed to do that in Mr. Potter's class. So I didn't quite get it.

In light of Mr. Potter's repeated encouragement, the Healeys did talk to Ben about help-seeking. As Ms. Healey explained,

> We did talk to Ben, a couple times. We said: "It's gonna get harder, and if there's anything you're in doubt about, you can talk to Mr. Potter." We told him several times throughout the year: "Listen, that's not a sign of weakness, it's a sign of strength. Everybody has weaknesses, everybody needs help, and you need to know when you need it." And Ben was like: "Yeah, I know."

At school, Ben would go to his teachers with clarifying questions (e.g., "Are we supposed to show our work?"), but he was more reluctant than most of his middle-class peers to admit when he was having trouble understanding the material. Toward the end of fifth grade, Ben—a straight-A student—began to struggle in his advanced math class. Despite those struggles, Ben remained reluctant to ask for help, and he ultimately earned a B in math for his last marking period.

Ben's hesitance in those situations seemed to reflect his parents' ambivalent attitude toward help-seeking. Like the other middle-class parents at Maplewood, the Healeys did recognize that support could be useful, and they did (occasionally) encourage their son to approach teachers with requests. However, compared to other middle-class parents, the Healeys—especially Mr. Healey—were less adamant in their coaching efforts. The Healeys were also more skeptical of the potential benefits of help-seeking, even when not asking ultimately resulted in a lower grade.

Given their parents' ambivalence, children in upwardly mobile families had more nuanced attitudes about the relative benefits of influence and deference. Compared to other middle-class students, for example, Ben Healey seemed more cautious about relying on teachers for support and being assertive in making requests. In our interview after fifth grade, Ben explained that he preferred to "go to my friends for help" and to use teachers as a "last resort." He noted that he would often ask his friend Steve (middle class, Asian American) because "he's the smartest probably." Ben went on to describe how, if Steve could not help him, Steve would usually go to the teacher and then report back to Ben with the answer. In class, I sometimes saw them go up to the teacher together, and Steve would usually lead the way.

That reluctance to make requests seemed to reflect Ben's ambivalence about the benefits and drawbacks of such behaviors. In our interview, Ben spoke disdainfully about classmates who asked teachers to check their work on tests or projects (a standard practice among middle-class students that I discuss further in Chapter 3). Ben noted,

> I never really did that. Because I think that's kind of like asking someone to do it for you. But they want to get a good grade, I guess. And I want to [do that too], but I think it's kind of cheap. Like, it's your work, you have to do it. Instead of having the teacher check it to see if it's wrong. And so I've definitely gotten a lot wrong.

As demonstrated in the previous examples, Ben's parents (especially his father) were skeptical of the benefits of support-seeking, and Ben seemed to have internalized that ambivalence. Like his middle-class peers, Ben clearly recognized a link between success in school and support from teachers. Unlike his middle-class friends, however, Ben was reluctant to exploit that opportunity for his own gain. Instead, he preferred to deal with problems on his own or rely on his friends for help, even when he got "a lot wrong" as a result.

Upwardly Mobile Working-Class Families

The upwardly mobile Carson family also had a complicated relationship to class-based parenting styles. Neither Mr. Carson nor Ms. Carson went to college, but they started a successful small business, and the income from the store allowed the Carsons to live very comfortably. They bought a house in a middle-class neighborhood. They took multiple vacations to the beach each summer. They enrolled their children in costly travel sports leagues. Except during trips to visit cousins out of state, their children interacted almost exclusively with middle-class friends.[5] Ms. Carson was also the only working-class parent who reported regularly checking her children's grades using the school district's online system. She explained,

> I love the fact that you can go on the computer [to see the grades], and actually, believe it or not, Jared goes on the computer almost as soon as he gets home from school, to check and see what his grade is. He'll be like: "An A–, what?" or "A 95? I thought I got 100!" Most of his grades are in the 90s. But every once in a while I'll come home and I'll be like: "An 82? What was that?" And Jared goes "I don't know. I was really tired. It was a hard test." It's like he's giving me the key that something's not working right for him. So that's when I'll, like, cut back on something, or talk to him to see if he's [having problems with friends]. I'll be like: "You're not sleeping [enough], or you're tired, or too much activity this week or something like that."

Unlike most of her working-class peers, Ms. Carson had also intervened at school with special requests. Those interventions resulted from the encouragement of her middle-class friends. Jared played baseball, basketball, and football, and during games and practices, the moms would often sit for hours and chit-chat. During one baseball game, a group of middle-class mothers instructed Ms. Carson to write a letter to the principal requesting that Jared not be placed in a particular teacher's class in fifth grade. Those same moms also encouraged Ms. Carson to ask Jared's teacher during conferences to move Jared up to the "next level" in spelling so that he would "always be challenged" (see also Lareau and Calarco 2012).

Despite those interventions, however, Ms. Carson was also different from her middle-class peers. Even in elementary school, for example, many of Jared's friends' parents were keenly focused on preparing their children for admission to "elite" colleges. Some had even considered switching to private school for middle and high school to improve their children's chances. Ms. Carson, on the other hand, expected that Jared would go to college, but she believed it would be best for him to start at a community college and then transition to a local 4-year school. She explained,

> Kristy [my oldest] did local first, community college, and then transferred to [a local four-year school]. So I'm hoping that unless Jared gets scholarships to go somewhere else, I'm hoping that he does at least one or two years local, here. Because I think it's hard when kids move away and go to school. Because I think it's hard to focus on being out in the world with all that, at the same time as trying to be growing up and going to school, because you're doing it all yourself. And I think that, this way if he lives at home and still goes to classes, he can just take his time a little bit with it. I think it would just be easier for him to just go to the local community college, take the regular courses that he's going to have to take anyway. Especially in the first two years, it's all the same. And hopefully it'll be something that can be transferred. And then get him a little job, so that you know, you gotta get your car, and everything else. It's just such a hard world. And for him to run right out and start having to do his laundry, and go get his own food, and then still meet the classes. I think he doesn't have to do that right away. But if he wants to [go further away], it's fine. I just think that it would be nice if he went slower.

Jared was one of the top achievers in the grade, athletically talented, socially savvy, and potentially an ideal candidate for an elite college. However, Ms. Carson wanted him to take the "slower" track, going to community college first and then on to a 4-year degree.

Ms. Carson also differed from middle-class parents at Maplewood in the emphasis she placed on good character traits such as respect, responsibility, and hard work. As she explained in an interview after Jared's fifth-grade year,

> Jared has always been more of an adult kid. And that's why all his teachers like him a lot. Because he knows when the teacher's annoyed, and he'll, like, he'll know when business is business. He'll get up and move himself out of a situation [when other kids are acting out], and then the [other] kids will come over and [start acting out again] and he's like: "No, look—she's not in the mood for this kind of stuff. I don't want to get in trouble." And he'll get up and move himself again and be like: "I'm gonna do my work."

Ms. Carson expected her son to respect his teachers and avoid situations where he might get in trouble. Unlike her middle-class peers, Ms. Carson also did not openly encourage Jared to use his teachers as resources or to try to advocate for himself at school:

> I try to have [my kids] rely on their classmates for questions and help with stuff, because they're in class with you, hearing the same thing you are. Turn to the friends, and ask the friends about the writing project, or the homework for that night, or whatever.

Like other working-class parents, Ms. Carson wanted Jared to respect his teachers and to tackle problems on his own, or at least rely on friends—and not teachers—as his primary resource.

Ms. Carson's mix of middle-class and working-class parenting styles seemed to leave Jared with a flexible attitude toward both strategies of influence and strategies of deference. He recognized that support-seeking had both benefits and drawbacks. During a math lesson, for example, the students had just learned a new set of geometry formulas, and they were supposed to be working independently on practice problems. Many of the students were struggling, and a few, including Jared's best friend Aidan (middle-class, white), got up to ask for help:

> Aidan pushes his chair back hard away from his desk. Grabbing his math notebook, Aidan marches up to Mr. Potter's desk. Aidan explains that he is confused about one of the problems. Mr. Potter nods and moves toward the chalkboard at the front of the room, motioning for Aidan to follow. As Aidan and Mr. Potter work through the practice problem together on the board, Jared glances up from his own notebook. Jared sits silently for a moment, watching Aidan and Mr. Potter. Then, slowly and quietly, Jared gets up from his seat, picks up his math notebook and his pencil, and tiptoes up toward the front of the room. Rather than go up to Aidan and Mr. Potter, however, Jared hangs back, about ten feet behind them. Jared listens intently as Mr. Potter explains the practice problems to Aidan and diagrams them on the board. Jared also copies their work into his own notebook. Then, before Mr. Potter and Aidan even notice that he has gotten up, Jared tiptoes back to his desk, slides into his chair, and continues with the rest of the problems.

Compared to other working-class students, Jared often seemed more comfortable interacting with teachers and voicing his needs. At the same time, and as this example highlights, Jared seemed to retain a working-class wariness of the potential drawbacks of seeking support in the wrong way.

Unlike his middle-class friends, Jared also viewed overreliance on teachers as antithetical to hard work, respect, and personal responsibility. During another math class, for example, Jared even went so far as to poke fun at middle-class students who were anxiously asking questions about a challenging word problem on a test. The problem read

> Elise is shopping at the store. She has one $20 bill, one $10 bill, and three $1 bills. Make an organized list that shows all of the different amounts that Elise could pay and receive no change.

That problem created significant consternation for the students. During the test, 12 of the 17 middle-class students raised their hands, called out, or went over to Mr. Potter (in some cases repeatedly) with questions. Neither of the 2 working-class students (Jared and Amelia) did so. Eventually, Mr. Potter stopped the test, called for everyone's attention, and explained the "shopping" problem aloud. Despite that explanation, however, a number of middle-class students were still confused:

> Josh (middle-class, white) calls out loudly: "So you don't need to use all the bills?" Mr. Potter nods quickly, pointing at Josh and saying: "Right!" Alan (middle-class, Asian American) then jumps, asking: "So, how many combinations do we have to make?" Mr. Potter laughs: "That's what you have to tell me!" Hearing that, Aidan (middle-class, white) follows up: "Do we tell you the number of combinations, or which ones?" Mr. Potter sighs and glances at the clock, as though he is growing impatient. He taps on the test sheet in his hands, indicating the instructions, as he explains: "Which ones, in an organized list." Finally, Julie (middle-class, white) pipes up, calling out: "Can we, like, use half the ten?" Mr. Potter scoffs, almost incredulous: "No!" Julie lets out a dramatic sigh. Jared, meanwhile, hears this and sits up eagerly, a sly grin on his face. He turns to Ben (middle-class, white), who is sitting next to him, and asks with a sarcastic sneer: "Can we, like, cross out the ten and write five instead?" Jared says this loud enough for the whole class to hear. Mr. Potter and a few of the students (including Julie) giggle appreciatively at Jared's joke.

Jared seemed to recognize that Mr. Potter was growing tired of the stream of questions. With his quick comedic timing, Jared also sensed that mocking the absurdity of Julie's question would be sure to get a laugh. On a deeper level, Jared's joke also seemed to reveal a skepticism of or even a disdain for his middle-class classmates' constant requests.

SUMMARY AND CONCLUSIONS

This chapter describes how the parents at Maplewood coached their children to manage problems in class-based ways.[6] In general, middle-class parents taught their children to practice strategies of influence—using teachers as resources, being assertive in making requests, and avoiding consequences for missteps. Working-class parents, on the other hand, taught their children to practice strategies of deference—respecting authority, working hard to overcome problems on their own, and taking responsibility for their actions. Of course, there were variations. Some middle-class parents, especially the parents of shy and high-achieving students, had to be more dogged in their efforts to get children to use strategies of influence. Other parents, especially those who were upwardly mobile, took a more ambivalent approach.

This chapter also describes how the children at Maplewood came to internalize the lessons their parents taught them at home. Interviews conducted at the end of fifth grade revealed marked similarities between parents and children in their response to hypothetical classroom challenges. In those same interviews, children were also able to recall numerous incidents in which they had used their parents' coaching to guide them in managing problems at school. Taken together, such findings suggest that parents' messages were indeed getting through. That internalization process, however, was far from automatic. In some cases, particularly with shy and high-achieving middle-class students, children resisted their parents' lessons, prompting frustration and often further coaching on the part of parents. Furthermore, and even without such overt pushback, it often took time and repeated coaching for children to gradually adopt the strategies their parents taught them at home. When it came to children's classroom behavior, for example, and as discussed in more detail in Chapters 3–5, patterns of influence and deference were more pronounced in fourth and fifth grade than they were in third grade.

The findings in this chapter add nuance to our understanding of the relationship between culture and inequality. Research on cultural capital often treats stratification as the product of cultural matching (Bourdieu 1996; Lareau and Weininger 2003; Stephens et al. 2012).[7] From that perspective, the middle class gains advantages by complying with the expectations of dominant institutions. Given that premise, we might assume that middle-class parents would teach their children to comply with teachers' expectations in school. However, that was not what I found. At Maplewood, it was the working-class parents who placed the larger emphasis on compliance (deference). The middle-class parents taught their children to expect teachers to comply with their requests, including those exceeding what was fair or required (influence). Rather than align themselves with institutional standards, it seems that middle-class children tried—and learned at a very young age—to set the standards instead. Although subsequent chapters explore the success of those efforts, this chapter provides compelling evidence of the strategies linking middle-class culture to larger patterns of inequality. By teaching strategies of influence, middle-class parents may help their children learn to negotiate additional advantages in school.[8]

By showing how those strategies are passed from one generation to the next, this chapter also deepens our understanding of the processes that link socialization and stratification. We know that middle-class parents frequently intervene on their children's behalf (Brantlinger 2003; Cucchiara 2013; Horvat et al. 2003; Lareau 2000, 2011; Lewis and Diamond 2015; Useem 1992). Those interventions can create real advantages for children, but unless middle-class parents also teach their children to create their own advantages, the cycle stops there. As demonstrated in this chapter, the middle-class parents at Maplewood did just that—they taught their children the strategies of influence that (they hoped, at least) would lead to success in school.

That is not to say, however, that working-class parents were unconcerned about their children's success or that they were taking a hands-off approach to parenting. On the contrary, the working-class parents at Maplewood worked diligently and deliberately to provide advantages for their children—even moving to Maplewood specifically to give their children access to better schools—and to help their children create advantages for themselves. They just did so in a very different way, one based on different priorities—good character over good grades—and different assumptions about the kinds of skills and strategies—deference over influence—needed to achieve their goal of success in the "real world."[9]

The point of this chapter is not to explain why middle-class and working-class parents coached their children to manage problems in different ways. However, existing research does offer some tentative evidence in that regard. Parents' lessons, for example, might reflect social class differences in their experiences interacting with teachers, employers, and other institutional authorities. It is known, for example, that schools often treat working-class families as second-class citizens (Cucchiara 2013; Lareau and Horvat 1999; Lewis and Diamond 2015) and that such treatment influences parents' educational orientations (Lewis-McCoy 2014). It is also known that middle- and working-class jobs offer workers different levels of status and authority (Lamont 1992, 2009; Rivera 2010) and that those differences are closely linked to parents' values for their children (Bourdieu 1990; Bronfenbrenner 1958; Kohn 1969). Those differences in parents' experiences may also have led parents to prioritize different goals in coaching their children to manage challenges in school. According to resistance theory, for example, working-class families reject the dominant culture's emphasis on academic success (and define success in terms of character instead) as a way to protect their own self-worth from the possibility of failure (Bettie 2014; MacLeod 1995; McRobbie 2000; Willis 1977).

Consistent with those possibilities, I found at least some evidence that parents were drawing on their own class-based experiences to shape their parenting decisions. Middle-class parents, for example, often recalled how strategies of influence benefitted them in college and in the workplace—recall Ms. Matthews' comment that if an employee is confused about an assignment and fails to ask for clarification, he or she will likely get fired. Interestingly, I found that working-class parents were more likely to refer back to experiences in elementary or secondary school rather than in the workforce—recall Mr. Graham's comment about how the teacher yelled at him and made him cry for "challenging her" by asking a question. That may have reflected the fact that working-class parents had experienced more negative treatment from teachers when they were in school and thus anticipated that their children would experience the same. Another possibility, however, is that working-class parents spent less time at Maplewood than did middle-class parents, and they were thus less able to see how schools and teachers and their expectations had changed over time. Future research should explore these possibilities in more depth, but my evidence seems to provide at least tentative support for the latter. In line with that view, I found that middle-class parents could all readily describe actual incidents in which asking for help or clarification or reprieve had benefitted their child. Working-class parents, meanwhile, had difficulty recalling incidents, at least at Maplewood, in which seeking support from the school led to a negative outcome. Furthermore, the few working-class parents who had sought such support (e.g., Ms. Higgins and Ms. Carson) generally had very positive things to say about that experience. In summary, it seems that although parents' class-based coaching may have reflected differences in the treatment that parents received from teachers and other institutional authorities, it did not appear to result from differences in how teachers at Maplewood responded to middle-class and working-class parents who approached them with requests for support.

Teachers did, however, play a critical role in determining whether strategies of influence and deference generated the outcomes that children and parents desired. As Chapter 2 demonstrates, teachers had expectations for student problem-solving, and those expectations shaped how teachers responded to students' problem-solving strategies. Those expectations, however, and in contrast to what research on cultural capital and the hidden curriculum might predict, were not fixed. Rather, teachers' expectations for student problem-solving varied from activity to activity and even moment to moment throughout the school day. Those ambiguities led children to rely on their parents' coaching in deciding how best to proceed. Thus, as discussed in Chapter 2, teachers were instrumental both in prompting children to activate the class-based strategies they learned at home and in determining whether those strategies resulted in reprimands or rewards.

CHAPTER 2

The Inconsistent Curriculum

M r. Cherlin's fourth graders had recently finished a unit on astronomy. After lunch, as the students settled back into their seats, Mr. Cherlin reminded them to clear their desks and take out a pencil for their end-of-unit test. After passing out the tests, Mr. Cherlin read the directions out loud, going through each section (definitions, multiple choice, and short answer) one by one. After each section, he paused and asked the students if there were "any questions." The students just stared back at him silently— no one called out or raised their hand.

During the test, however, a number of students became confused about what they were supposed to do. Mr. Cherlin was circling around and glancing over students' shoulders as they worked. As he did so, a few students (all middle class) asked for clarification about specific questions on the test. Middle-class student Jamie, for example, looked up at Mr. Cherlin as he passed and whispered, "Do we need to draw the moon phases or just write what they're called?" Mr. Cherlin patiently answered these questions, smiling and calmly reassuring students about how to proceed. After approximately 5 minutes of circling around, Mr. Cherlin returned to his desk, where he began typing on his laptop. The students, meanwhile, continued to work silently on their own.

When the students finished their tests, they were supposed to drop their tests in the "inbox" and pick up a worksheet with science-themed riddles. The riddles, however, were not easy, prompting some students (again, all middle class) to call out for help:

About half of the students are still working on the test. A few of the students who are finished start calling out to Mr. Cherlin with questions about the riddle worksheet. Liam (middle-class, white) declares loudly: "I don't get this!" Michelle (middle-class, white), meanwhile, dashes up to Mr. Cherlin's desk, calling out: "What's this one mean?" Mr. Cherlin hears the shouted questions and stands up behind his desk. Folding his arms, he says sternly: "Guys! Some people are still working and you're not being respectful if you're asking questions. You guys can figure these [riddles] out on your own."

The room immediately fell silently. A few students let their mouths hang open—seemingly surprised at Mr. Cherlin's sudden outburst—but no one tried to protest.

A minute later, however, Mr. Cherlin seemed to feel bad about getting gruff with the students and chastising them for seeking help:

Mr. Cherlin stands up behind his desk. He calls for the students' attention, but does so softer this time, more sorrowfully. His shoulders are rounded and his head is hanging low. As the students look up, Mr. Cherlin shakes his head, saying slowly: "I'm sorry. I probably shouldn't have given you that worksheet without explaining." Mr. Cherlin then goes on to explain that the riddles are just supposed to be a "fun" activity—a chance to practice their science vocabulary.

Mr. Cherlin then paused again. When he continued, his voice was firmer and more serious but still gentle. He reminded the students that their class-mates were still working on the test, that there "shouldn't be any talking," and that they should complete the riddles on their own. A few students nodded, and the room again fell silent as the class continued to work.

During the course of just a few minutes, Mr. Cherlin's stance on help-seeking changed dramatically. Before and even during the test, he readily answered clarifying questions about the assignment and helped guide stu-dents in figuring out what they were supposed to do. When students began calling out with questions about the riddle worksheet, on the other hand, Mr. Cherlin suddenly declared that asking for help was "not being respect-ful." Moments later, however, Mr. Cherlin backpedaled slightly, apologiz-ing for not giving students better directions about the riddle worksheet but continuing to insist (albeit more calmly and gently) that the students com-plete the worksheet silently on their own.

OVERVIEW

Subtle shifts in expectations, such as that just described, were common-place at Maplewood Elementary. With respect to problem-solving, for example, teachers' expectations were rarely consistent. Instead, they adjusted their expectations from activity to activity and even from moment to moment depending on the situation at hand. Teachers' expectations sometimes favored middle-class strategies of influence. That included situations in which teachers wanted students to seek support if they were struggling and situations in which it was okay to call out or approach the teachers directly with questions. In other moments, teachers' expectations favored working-class strategies of deference. That included times when teachers wanted students to work through difficult problems on their own, times when they did not want to give extra credit or extra time, and times when they wanted students to wait patiently with their hands raised.

That lack of consistency in teachers' expectations was made even more complicated by the fact that teachers rarely made their expectations explicit. In most cases, teachers' preferences about problem-solving strategies were apparent only in teachers' responses to particular strategies (i.e., answering students' questions or chastising them for asking). Of course, teachers did sometimes make statements such as "If you really need me, I'm up here." Even in those moments, however, it was not entirely clear how struggling students should proceed. How long should students work through a problem on their own before seeking help? If students do decide to ask for help, should they raise their hand and wait for the teacher to notice them or get up and approach the teacher instead?

Unfortunately, teachers' inconsistent and ambiguous expectations had real consequences for students. One consequence was that students could not be certain whether a given strategy would yield the outcome they desired. In the classroom, students could choose which strategies to use when managing problems. The success or failure of those strategies, however, often depended on teachers' responses to them. When teachers' expectations varied, a strategy that generated rewards in one situation could generate reprimands in another. Furthermore, when teachers' expectations were not made explicit, students were often left wondering which of those outcomes would occur.

Because of that uncertainty, teachers' inconsistent and ambiguous expectations also had a second consequence for students. Specifically, they prompted students to rely more heavily on the class-based coaching they received at home. When teachers made their expectations explicit, middle-class and working-class students used more similar strategies to manage problems at school. When those expectations remained vague, students had to decide for themselves how best to proceed, and they often used their parents' class-based coaching as a guide. Specifically, and in those ambiguous moments, middle-class students anticipated that strategies of influence would result in *rewards*, whereas working-class students presumed that those same behaviors would result in *reprimands*.

EXPECTATIONS IN CONTEXT

Although the primary focus of this book is on students and their efforts to manage challenges in school, it is important to situate those efforts in the classroom contexts in which they occurred. We know from research on classroom interactions that those contexts are co-constructed by teachers and students (Diehl and McFarland 2012; McFarland 2001). Thus, before considering how students acted on the lessons they learned at home, we must first consider the role that teachers played in (1) prompting children to activate particular problem-solving strategies and (2) determining whether those strategies were successful. Existing research sheds some light on these possibilities.

Scholars of classroom authority tell us that teachers wield considerable power over students (Buzzelli and Johnston 2002; Diehl and McFarland 2012; Metz 1978; Pace 2003; Swidler 1979). Officially, at least, teachers determine where students should be, what they should be doing, and whether their actions will result in reprimands or rewards. Given that authority, it seems reasonable to assume that assistance, accommodations, and attention will be meted out at the teachers' discretion. What that means, in turn, is that students' problem-solving strategies will not—and cannot—generate profits on their own. Rather, students seeking support are dependent on teachers' willingness to grant such requests (see also Calarco 2014b).

That willingness to grant students' requests is likely to hinge, at least in part, on teachers' expectations. Research on cultural capital, for example, often suggests that teachers reward those who comply with school standards (Lareau 2000; Lareau and Weininger 2003).[1] Those standards, meanwhile, are neither explicit (Bernstein 1958; Delpit 2006; Heath 1983) nor neutral (Bourdieu 1996). Rather, behavioral standards are often relegated to the "hidden curriculum" of schooling (Anyon 1980; Apple 1980; Wren 1999). From that perspective, schools expect students to follow certain codes of conduct, but they rarely teach students how to follow those codes. Moreover, because school standards are thought to be closely aligned with middle-class culture (Lareau 2000; Nelson and Schutz 2007; Stephens et al. 2012), middle-class students should have an advantage in complying with teachers' expectations, even when those expectations are not explicitly taught at school.

At the same time, there is reason to suspect that teachers' expectations are not as consistent as research on cultural capital and the hidden curriculum presumes them to be (Calarco 2014b). Although we typically think of schools as being highly regimented and rule-governed (Boostrom 1991; Jackson 1990), the reality is more complex. Research on classroom interactions, for example, finds that teachers use flexible standards (rather than fixed rules) as a way to balance competing classroom priorities (e.g., the need to educate, the need to keep order, the need to be responsive to situational constraints, and even the need to maintain positive relationships with students) (Buzzelli and Johnston 2002; Diehl and McFarland 2012; Metz 1978; Mullooly and Varenne 2006; Pace and Hemmings 2006; Swidler 1979). However, although those flexible standards may be useful for teachers, they also make teachers' expectations for students more ambiguous (Pace 2003; Thornberg 2007).

Those ambiguities create both challenges (Mehan 1980; Thornberg 2007) and opportunities (Halstead and Xiao 2010; McFarland 2001) for students. In the context of ambiguous expectations, success depends on students' ability to decode what teachers want (Arnot and Reay 2007; Ballenger 1992; Bernstein 1990) and adjust their behavior accordingly (Davidson 1996; Halstead and Xiao 2010; Hemmings 2003; Levinson 2001). At the same time, ambiguities in teachers' expectations create openings for students to challenge teacher authority and assert their own interpretations (Halstead and Xiao 2010; McFarland 2001; Pace and Hemmings 2006; Willis 1977).

Although we do not know precisely how students will respond to ambiguities in teachers' expectations for problem-solving, it seems possible that they will prompt students to rely more heavily on the class-based coaching they receive at home. We know from research in social psychology, for example, that explicit rules prompt individuals to behave in uniform ways (McPherson and Sauder 2013). When rules are instead ambiguous or inconsistently enforced, individuals have to think more about what is expected of them, and that interpretive process leads to more unpredictable behavior (Pescosolido 1992). Given the importance of culture—especially social class-based culture—in shaping how individuals perceive themselves and their surroundings (DiMaggio 1997; DiMaggio and Markus 2010; Kohn 1969; Markus and Kitayama 1991), it seems likely that middle-class and working-class students will interpret teachers' ambiguous expectations (and respond to those expectations) in different ways.

This chapter explores those possibilities. First, I examine teachers' expectations for student problem-solving, how they varied across situations, and how they aligned with strategies of influence and deference. Second, I describe how students responded to teachers' expectations and how those responses varied along social class lines. In doing so, I also set the stage for subsequent chapters, showing how ambiguity in teachers' expectations prompted students to rely more heavily on the class-based coaching they received from their parents at home and how teachers' responses to student problem-solving ultimately determined whether those strategies resulted in rewards or reprimands.

AMBIGUOUS EXPECTATIONS

At Maplewood, teachers' expectations varied from moment to moment depending on the nature of the activity and the situation at hand. Those expectations, however, were generally left unstated. As a result, it was often unclear whether teachers wanted students to practice strategies of influence or strategies of deference when managing problems at school.

Expecting Influence

In some instances, teachers seemed to prefer that students practice middle-class strategies of influence—using teachers as resources in managing problems and being assertive in making requests. Those preferences were particularly common in situations in which teachers faced numerous demands on their time and attention. They each had 25 students to teach and track and help. They had parents e-mailing constantly with requests. They had piles of paperwork to complete and meetings to attend. They had lunch money to collect, scraped knees to bandage, squabbles to settle, lesson plans to write, and new curricula to learn. They had state assessment tests and accountability pressures constantly looming on the horizon. Those tasks and distractions made it difficult for teachers to notice when students were struggling silently on their own and left them with limited time to check in with students one-on-one. One morning, on the way to lunch, Mr. Potter told me how horrible he felt after realizing that one of his students (working-class student Shannon) had been sitting with her hand raised, waiting to ask a question, for almost 10 minutes. Shaking his head, he lamented, "It's not that we don't care. It's just that we've got our heads down trying to get things done."

Given the numerous demands on their time and attention, teachers often relied on students to voice their own needs. When introducing a new timeline project in Social Studies, for example, Mr. Fischer told his fifth graders that they would be expected to type the descriptions of each event and also find pictures online to illustrate each event:

> Raising both hands reassuringly, Mr. Fischer says quickly: "But if you don't have a computer at home, let me know." He explains that students who need help are welcome to "come in and have lunch" with him, during which time he will work with them on getting the descriptions typed and finding images for their timelines. Pausing, Mr. Fischer adds in his trademark sarcastic deadpan: "You have to let me know, though. I can't read minds." Mr. Fischer chuckles at his own joke, and a few students giggle and nod approvingly.

As Chapter 5 explains, the teachers at Maplewood tried hard to get to know their students and connect with them one-on-one. However, with 25 students in a class, teachers rarely had time to figure out which students were up late because of their brother's soccer game, which students did not have time for breakfast, which students had parents going through a divorce, and which students did not have a computer at home. Thus, in many cases, teachers relied on students to acknowledge those struggles and voice their own needs.

At times, teachers made that reliance explicit, actively encouraging students to seek assistance and accommodations and attention. One morning, for example, Mr. Cherlin gave his fourth graders a "math vocabulary" worksheet to help them prepare for the upcoming State assessment tests.[2] Mr. Cherlin gave the students time to review the worksheet and identify any unfamiliar terms. After approximately 3 minutes, Mr. Cherlin called for the students' attention again:

> Lifting his eyebrows, Mr. Cherlin asks encouragingly: "Are there any questions about this? Or anything that we're doing for the State assessments?" Mr. Cherlin continues, adding: "It's important to ask, because if you don't understand something now, you'll probably see it again on the State assessments." At this point, a number of students raise their hands with questions about concepts like "multiples," "diameters," and "obtuse angles." Mr. Cherlin patiently answers the questions, using the Smart Board to illustrate key concepts.

Like Mr. Cherlin, teachers often relied on students to voice their needs. Some teachers—especially older teachers and those raised in working-class families themselves[3]—spent less class time soliciting and answering students' questions. However, even those more hands-off teachers viewed support-seeking as an important skill. They recognized, for example, that assignments and test questions were not always clear and that teachers alone had the information students needed to work through those challenges.[4]

Although teachers were sometimes explicit in stating their expectations, teachers' willingness to provide support and accommodations often became apparent only when they granted students' requests. In fifth grade, for example, Ms. Hudson's class was reading the novel *Maniac Magee*. During language arts, Ms. Hudson instructed the students to take out their books and "read Chapter 7 silently":

> Hunter, a middle-class student, sits at his desk, reading to himself. After a few minutes, he stops, leans in, and peers down at the pages of his book. He narrows his eyes in a puzzled expression. Using his finger to hold the page he was reading, Hunter closes the book. Taking the book with him, he pushes back his chair and scampers up to Ms. Hudson's desk. As he approaches, Hunter calls out in a loud whisper: "Ms. Hudson!"

Ms. Hudson looked up from her computer, raising one eyebrow questioningly:

> Hunter holds out his book with one hand, points at it with the other, and asks expectantly: "What's *this* mean?" Ms. Hudson slides her chair closer to Hunter, craning her neck to see. She pauses a moment, pursing her lips together pensively, and then explains: "Disheveled . . . it's like . . . a *mess*." Hunter grins and says "Thanks!" Ms. Hudson nods and gives Hunter a warm smile.

Given that Ms. Hudson told the students to read "silently," and given that she never offered to answer questions, we might have expected her to respond to Hudson's request by telling him to figure it out on his own (i.e., by using a dictionary). Instead, Ms. Hudson readily answered Hudson's question and did so with a smile. Thus, it seems that Ms. Hudson was, at least in that situation, happy to provide support. Like most teachers, however, she made that willingness apparent only obliquely and after-the-fact.

Expecting Deference

There were also times when teachers seemed to prefer that students practice working-class strategies of deference—treating teachers with respect and tackling problems on their own. Those preferences were less predictable than teachers' preferences for strategies of influence. In some cases, those preferences reflected teachers' explicit desire to teach lessons about hard work, respect, and personal responsibility. During the spring of the students' fifth-grade year, all the classes at Maplewood attended a presentation by a visiting scientist who had set up an inflatable planetarium in the gym. While waiting for their turn to climb through the tunnel into the blow-up dome, Ms. Hudson reminded her class that they were to be on their "best behavior" during the presentation:

> With her arms crossed and her voice low and stern, Ms. Hudson instructs her students to listen carefully to the presenter and follow the directions about where and how to sit in the dome. With a wry, half smile and a raise of one eyebrow, she adds pointedly that while the "younger kids" are "fairly good" at following those kinds of directions, "fifth graders often think the rules don't apply to them." As the presenter calls for the next class, Ms. Hudson ushers her students inside, reminding them quickly as she does so to save any questions for the end, because "each class only has a limited amount of time."

As demonstrated by this example, there were times when teachers discouraged students from asking questions as part of a lesson about respect, responsibility, and hard work.

In other cases, teachers' preferences for strategies of deference seemed to be a response to momentary frustrations. Those frustrations most often involved students who failed to demonstrate sufficient respect, work ethic, or personal responsibility. Mr. Potter, for example, had more than 10 years of experience and was generally patient and good-natured with his fifth graders. One afternoon, however, when Mr. Potter's advanced math class (the students were ability-grouped for math) was working on word problems, that patience was tested. After posting the assignment on the Smart Board, Mr. Potter circled around, glancing over students' shoulders as they worked. Almost immediately, Julie, Riley, Jamie, Aidan, Christian (all middle-class, white), and Steve (middle-class, Asian American) raised their hands or called out for help, making statements such as "I don't get number eight," "What does this one mean?" and "Is this right?" Mr. Potter patiently answered those initial questions, giving the students hints, reminding them of strategies that they had learned for solving word problems, and sometimes providing concrete examples to help students better conceptualize the problems. As Mr. Potter answered those initial questions, other students also began to call out and raise their hands, and some even got up to follow behind Mr. Potter, waiting at his side with their math notebooks in hand and then interjecting as soon as he was free. The questions persisted like that for more than 10 minutes. As time went on, Mr. Potter appeared increasingly agitated. His tone grew sharper. His answers grew shorter and more critical. His shoulders appeared tense, and his brow was deeply furrowed. Despite Mr. Potter's apparent frustration, however, the requests continued, with many of the students getting up repeatedly to trot over to Mr. Potter and ask, "Is this right?" Eventually, after enduring 20 minutes of near-constant questions, Mr. Potter finally hit his breaking point:

> Mr. Potter stops suddenly and growls: "Fifth grade!" As the students look up, startled, Mr. Potter gestures wildly in the air: "Every time we do word problems, you guys say you can't do it! You guys who are so used to getting it immediately, you say 'I don't get it' and you give up!" Mr. Potter continued his diatribe for more than a minute. At first, he seemed incredulous, saying shrilly: "Roger [a middle-class, Asian American student and a recent immigrant to the United States] had this done in two minutes. And English isn't even his first language!" Mr. Potter picked up Roger's paper and waved it in the air, shouting: "All you have to do is focus. I wanna see work. I wanna see attempts. If you guys actually tried, you could do anything!"

By that point, the students were squirming in their seats, but Mr. Potter continued:

> Shaking his head, Mr. Potter laments: "This class is by far the worst at actually giving it full effort and working at problems you find difficult." He went on, adding: "You're so used to getting things easily that as soon as you get stuck, you whine about it and you don't do it!" Mr. Potter pauses, picks up a piece of chalk, and asks mockingly: "Should I write on the board that my math class is a bunch of crybabies?" A few students shift nervously in their seats, but no one says a word for the next three minutes, when Mr. Potter finally dismisses the students for lunch.

Such vitriolic outbursts were extremely rare for the teachers at Maplewood. The frustration that sparked the tirade, however, was a common one. Teachers would often pull me aside in the hallway, or during lunch, or even at the back of the classroom to "vent" about students and parents who made "constant" or "ridiculous" requests. They complained about students trying to "get around" junk-food bans, about parents writing e-mails to excuse kids from homework, and about students who "lacked problem-solving skills."[5] In those moments of frustration, teachers were essentially expressing a preference for more deference-based approaches to problem-solving.

Those preferences were sometimes explicit. In some situations, teachers told students that they wanted them to work through difficult problems on their own. One Thursday in math class, for example, Ms. Dunham gave her fifth graders a geometry test. Ms. Dunham took the papers home that night to grade, but in reviewing them, she realized that the students had not done very well—many students made "careless" mistakes and others did not have time to finish, leaving blank problems at the end of the test. Rather than just give the students the grades they earned initially, Ms. Dunham decided to give the students a chance to correct their work. Before doing that, however, Ms. Dunham went through all of the tests and marked each correct answer with a large, blue "C." On Friday morning, Ms. Dunham gave the tests back to the students. She announced that they would have 15 extra minutes to work on the tests and that she would not be answering any questions about the test during that time:

> Sitting perched atop the file cabinet, Ms. Dunham mimics the whining voice that students often use when asking for help: "I don't want you to come up to me and say 'I don't know what the answer is!' I'm gonna send you away!" Ms. Dunham continues, her voice firm and punctuated with emphasis: "I want you to go back and *find your mistakes.*" Without missing a beat, Hunter (middle-class, white) retorts indignantly: "That's mean!" Ms. Dunham sighs, glances at the clock, and says: "How about this. Let's do

one problem together so you'll know what to look for." Hunter and a few of the other students cheer.

Ms. Dunham wanted her students to do well on the test. She gave them extra time to fix their mistakes and even went through a sample problem with them. At the same time, Ms. Dunham did not want students asking for help in finding or fixing their mistakes. She wanted students to take responsibility for carefully checking their own work instead, and she made that expectation very clear and firm.

More often, however, when teachers expected deference, those expectations became apparent only when teachers responded negatively to students who sought support.[6] Mr. Fischer's fifth-grade class, for example, was having a paper airplane competition to celebrate the end of their unit on early 20th-century innovation. Reviewing the rules, Mr. Fischer explained that the students would take their planes out into the hallway. They would each have one chance to toss their plane. The student whose plane went the farthest would be declared the winner. Mr. Fischer then told the students that they would watch a brief video about the Wright Brothers before the competition. As Mr. Fischer went to set up the video, Zara (middle-class, Asian American) and Lindsey (middle-class, white) got up from their seats. They hovered around Mr. Fischer, asking about the "record" for the farthest flight in previous years' classes, how long the record had held, and whether Mr. Fischer thought it would be broken this year. Lindsey then began peppering Mr. Fischer with questions about the rules for the competition:

> Pantomiming her throwing technique, Lindsey asks: "So . . . can we, like . . . take a step to throw, so like, if our front foot is on the line but the back one goes over?" Mr. Fischer lets out a breathy laugh and shakes his head. As soon as Mr. Fischer does this, however, Lindsey immediately hits him with another question, as if she already had it prepared in her head: "Well, then is it okay if our hand goes over the line when we throw it?" Instead of answering Lindsey's question, Mr. Fischer turns and asks dryly: "Do your parents go through this every night with you?" Lindsey blinks coyly, as if to ask: "What do you mean?" Mr. Fischer continues, deadpan: "Like, they say no, and then everything's a negotiation?" Lindsey smiles mischievously: "Of course!" Mr. Fischer sighs and rolls his eyes.

At first, Mr. Fischer jovially answered the girls' questions—he was all smiles and big hand gestures recalling stories of past years' competitions. As the requests continued, however, Mr. Fischer's patience seemed to wane—he stopped making eye contact; his shoulders got tense; his tone got gruffer. Mr. Fischer could have just said "no more questions," but he took a more indirect approach—teasing Lindsey about making everything a "negotiation"—instead. Such subtlety in conveying expectations was common among the teachers at Maplewood. Rather than reject students' requests outright, they would usually try to dissuade students from continuing through their tone of voice, their body language, and even occasionally through joking reprimands.

AMBIGUITY AND ITS AFTERMATH

Teachers' ambiguous and inconsistent expectations created an environment of uncertainty for students. With respect to problem-solving, for example, students could not easily predict whether asking a teacher for help would lead to rewards or reprimands. A similar request might generate a very different response, depending on the situation at hand. Mr. Fischer, for example, was generally very open to answering questions. During tests, there would often be a line of students stretched across the room, waiting to ask for clarification about directions or even to have Mr. Fischer check their work. During one social studies test, however, Mr. Fischer suddenly balked at the flood of requests. The last part of the test instructed students to "Write a diary entry about an event during the Revolutionary War from the perspective of a patriot." Upon reaching that part of the test, a number of students got up to ask for clarification. Mr. Fischer, however, seemed to believe that students should know what it meant to write a "diary entry," and he quickly became frustrated with their confusion:

> Nate (middle-class, white) gets up and moves quickly to Mr. Fischer's desk, gripping his test paper in both hands. As he approaches, Nate calls out hopefully: "Mr. Fischer?" Mr. Fischer hears this and looks up from his computer, asking lightly: "What's up?" Nate launches into a long question about the diary essay, asking "Are we supposed to pick a specific patriot like George Washington?" and "Does it have to be someone who was at that event?" and "Are we supposed to say what they did?" As Nate continues his meandering question, Mr. Fischer interrupts. He responds gruffly, in a loud, insistent whisper: "No! Diary entry! You. You're that person." Nate looks up at Mr. Fischer with a blank, puzzled stare. Mr. Fischer shakes his head in frustration.

By this point, Lindsey, Colin, and Kal, all middle-class students, were lined up behind Nate to ask the same question, and they all started calling out clarifying questions:

> Kal (middle-class, Asian American) asks if he should pick a specific person and use quotes that they said and Lindsey and Colin (both middle-class, white) chime in,

talking over each other as they ask questions about the question. Mr. Fischer hears this and holds up his hands, palms out, as if to say "Stop!" Frowning, Mr. Fischer interjects sharply: "Guys!" Nate, Kal, Lindsey, and Colin all stop suddenly. Mr. Fischer lets out a long sigh and then continues, explaining in a low growl: "Diary entry. You become the patriot. You were there." Nate, Kal, Lindsey, and Colin squirm uncomfortably. After a moment, Nate sputters: "But do you mean . . ." Mr. Fischer lets out a frustrated sigh, folds his arms, and launches into a longer explanation.

Eventually, Nate, Kal, Lindsey, and Colin seemed to understand that they were supposed to pretend that they (as themselves) were present at one of the events of the Revolutionary War and that they were supposed to write a diary entry describing what they saw. After that first group of students went back to their seats, however, Joanna, Melanie, Anna, Ashley, and Kelly (all middle-class, white students) got up to ask Mr. Fischer the same question:

Mr. Fischer responds in a gravelly voice. He tells the girls that they need to be better "problem solvers," instructing them to think about what a "diary entry" is, and about what a patriot would write in a diary about the Revolutionary War. When Anna tries to ask a follow-up question, Mr. Fischer interrupts, telling the girls to "go back and read it [the question] again" if they are still not clear. Melanie tries to protest, but Mr. Fischer holds up his hands and refuses to say another word.

Like Mr. Fischer, the teachers at Maplewood had great power to determine whether students' problem-solving strategies resulted in success or failure. Unfortunately, they did not always wield that power in consistent ways. As demonstrated in this example, both groups of (middle-class) students approached Mr. Fischer to ask the exact same question. Despite that similarity, however, the first group got the help they needed to proceed (albeit with some pushback), whereas the second group got only a gruff reprimand.

That uncertainty put the burden on students to decide how best to proceed when managing problems at school. As a result, students responded to teachers' inconsistent and ambiguous expectations by relying more heavily on the class-based coaching they received at home. When expectations were clear and direct, students responded in more similar ways. When expectations were not clear or direct, middle-class and working-class students anticipated different outcomes and thus opted for very different strategies.

Middle-Class Students: Expecting Rewards

In ambiguous moments, middle-class students seemed to operate under the assumption that support-seeking would ultimately lead to rewards.

They focused on the potential benefits that teachers could provide, and they rarely considered the potential drawbacks. In an interview during the summer after fifth grade, I asked Ethan (middle-class, white) what he would usually do if he was confused or stuck on something in class:

> JMC: What do you usually do if you get stuck on something, or if you don't know what to do?
>
> ETHAN: [matter-of-factly] Uh, go ask Mr. Fischer.
>
> JMC: And what happens when you ask him?
>
> ETHAN: He normally tells us, like: "Well, you're not reading the problem correctly." So I go read it again. Then I ask him again, and then he'll normally tell me after a couple of times of telling me the same thing. Like: "Well, it's like this."
>
> JMC: Oh, okay. So if you ask him a couple times, then he'll eventually just help you figure it out?
>
> ETHAN: Yeah.

Even when teachers were reluctant to answer questions, they rarely denied students' requests outright. Instead, and like Mr. Fischer saying the "same thing" in response to repeated requests, teachers typically used more subtle tactics of evasion. Such indirect rebuffs, however, did not usually persuade middle-class students to concede. Instead, and because they viewed ambiguities as opportunities for reward, middle-class students like Ethan were very willing to ask "a couple of times"—until teachers granted or more firmly denied their requests.

Although some middle-class students were more socially aware than others, they often seemed either oblivious or indifferent to teachers' moods and temperaments. One morning in fourth grade, for example, Ms. Nelson was reviewing the instructions for the spelling homework. The students had to complete a series of activities (finding antonyms, finding synonyms, making "word triangles," making a word search, etc.) using their spelling words. For some activities, they had to use all of their spelling words; for others, they could choose 10 words to use:

> As Ms. Nelson reviews the directions, Drew (middle-class, white) begins complaining aloud that this assignment is "going to take forever." Ms. Nelson hears this and lets out a long breath through her nose. She catches my eye and shakes her head as if to say: "Can you believe these kids?" As I smile back, Natalie (middle-class, white) calls out: "Can we just do five words, instead?" Ms. Nelson raises her eyebrows skeptically. She pauses and then explains slowly, in a careful, measured tone, that they have to "look at the orange sheets," and that the orange sheets tell them how many words to do. She adds, sharply: "It will always be either ten words or all of the words, but not five." Ignoring Ms. Nelson, Drew calls out eagerly, asking: "If

we do ten for one, can we just do five for the next one?" Ms. Nelson crosses her arms firmly across her chest. She glares pointedly at Drew and says brusquely: "Just do what the orange sheet says." Drew tries to protest again, but Ms. Nelson ignores him and moves on.

Although Ms. Nelson never explicitly told the students "no" or to stop pressing, her tone and body language seemed to indicate that she was tired of all the questions and just wanted to move on with the activity. Drew and Natalie, however, seemed either oblivious or unconcerned, continuing to push back with more requests to simplify the assignment.

Given their assumption that requests would lead to reward, middle-class students would usually press forward in seeking support and accommodations, even in the face of possible reprimand. Ms. Nelson, for example, regularly gave her fourth graders "morning work" (a vocabulary and grammar exercise) to complete while she circled around checking homework. During that time, middle-class students would often get up and approach Ms. Nelson with questions and requests:

> The students are working at their desks while Ms. Nelson checks homework. Meanwhile, Gina (middle-class, white) gets up numerous times from her seat, scampering over to Ms. Nelson to ask questions about the morning work assignment (e.g., "Are we supposed to circle the nouns?"), and about the schedule for the day (e.g., "Are we having a quiz in science?").

Gina could have answered all those questions on her own—the answers were in the directions for the morning work or in the daily schedule on the whiteboard—and Ms. Nelson could have told her to do so. Instead, Ms. Nelson just grew gradually less patient and polite in her replies:

> With the first few questions, Ms. Nelson patiently reminds Gina of the directions on the worksheet, or reviews the schedule for the day. Over time, Ms. Nelson's answers get shorter and curter. By the fourth or fifth question, she no longer looks up, but just says a one word "yes" or "no." Despite these short replies, Gina repeatedly pops up with more questions.

Ms. Nelson never explicitly told Gina to stop asking questions, but her increasingly curt replies seemed to indicate her mounting frustration with Gina's requests. Like other middle-class students in similar situations, however, Gina seemed unfazed by the teacher's mounting frustration. She just focused on getting the assistance, accommodations, and attention she desired.

Working-Class Students: Expecting Reprimands

In ambiguous moments, working-class students seemed to operate under the assumption that seeking support would ultimately lead to reprimands or other negative outcomes. They worried about how teachers might perceive their actions, and they worried about getting in trouble if they misbehaved. In an interview during the summer after fifth grade, I asked Amelia (working-class, white) what she does if she gets confused or stuck on something in class. She answered hesitantly,

> I don't know . . . sometimes [Mr. Fischer] tells us to stay at our seat, but sometimes he tells us to go up to him. Sometimes it makes me nervous. Like, sometimes it's kind of like, you would ask the question, and they might say: "You should have been listening. I just said that." But I'm thinking in my head, "I was listening. I just didn't catch that." But I just think it in my head. Because I might get in trouble, like, even more trouble, if I say that. Because they're like, I don't know what they would say, but just be like: "Not now!"

As can be seen with Amelia, ambiguous expectations often left working-class students feeling "nervous." When the appropriate course of action was not clear, they worried that they might misstep, that teachers would mistakenly assume they were being disrespectful or off task, and that such assumptions would lead to reprimand.

Compared to their middle-class peers, working-class students seemed much more keenly attuned to teachers' moods and temperaments. As Jared (working-class, white) explained,

> Most of the time, [teachers] explain too much, and you can't follow it all. So, I get lost, and I would just ask the person next to me. But, half the time, like, the teachers don't want us talking. So it's hard. Like, I don't know if I should go up and talk [to the teacher], or if I should ask the person next to me. So, I mean, sometimes I go up to the teacher and say "I don't get this." But she might say: "Ask your partner," or "Ask your neighbor." So, I don't know if she'll get mad, or if she wants me to do that.

Because of their concerns about the possibility of reprimand, working-class students like Jared often spent class time trying to gauge teachers' attitudes and dispositions. In doing so, however, working-class students generally erred on the side of assuming anger and thus adopted a more cautious approach.[7]

In some circumstances, that cautious approach did help working-class students avoid reprimand. Amelia, for example, was present in Mr. Fischer's class for the social studies test described in a previous example. Like most of her classmates, Amelia was confused about the "diary entry" question—I watched her stare at the question, write, erase, and rewrite her answer for more than 5 minutes with a deep, puzzled frown on her face. Unlike her middle-class peers, however, Amelia never got up to ask for clarification. As a result, and unlike Nate, Lindsey, Colin, Kal, Joanna, Melanie, Anna, Ashley, and Kelly (all middle-class students), Amelia avoided Mr. Fischer's admonishment. Ultimately, Amelia also got the clarification that she needed—she was sitting close enough to Mr. Fischer's desk that she heard his explanation to the middle-class students, prompting her to correct her own answer.

However, although working-class students' strategies of deference sometimes helped them avoid individual reprimand, those strategies did not help them avoid reprimands directed at the class as a whole. Both Jared and Amelia, for example, were in Mr. Potter's math class, and both were present during the incident discussed previously in which Mr. Potter got frustrated and ultimately called his class "a bunch of crybabies." Neither Jared nor Amelia asked any questions about the word problems. They both just worked through the problems on their own. Thus, Mr. Potter's vitriol was not technically directed at them. Ironically, however, and as I later learned through interviews with the students after fifth grade, it was the working-class students who most deeply internalized those kinds of whole-class reprimands. As Amelia explained, "Even if I didn't do anything wrong, I feel like they're yelling at me."

Although strategies of deference sometimes helped the working-class students avoid personal reprimand, the same strategies also prevented them from reaping rewards. During gym class, Ms. Winters informed the fifth graders that they would be running to determine which students would qualify to represent their grade in the annual Field Day race. Ms. Winters had laid out a course around the school grounds, marking the running route with orange cones. Fifth graders had to complete the course in 3 minutes or less to qualify. While the students ran, Ms. Winters set up for the next activity and chatted with two students who were unable to run because of asthma and a sprained ankle:

> At 3:15, Sammy (middle-class, white) crosses the finish line, red-faced and gasping. He immediately begins to complain to Ms. Winters about how his stomach cramped up and how he would have been able to run faster if he did not eat such a big breakfast. Sammy explains that he is one of the fastest runners on his soccer team, recounting how he "flew past" the defenders in a game last week. Ms. Winters nods understandingly, telling Sammy that he can try again during recess tomorrow.

Meanwhile, Cody (working-class, mixed-race) had been running the whole race with a broken shoelace. His shoe kept sliding off his foot. Each time, he stopped, quickly slid his foot back in, and continued on:

> At 4:10, Cody finally stumbles across the finish line. He immediately collapses on the wet grass, flopping heavily on his back in frustration. Cody glances over at Ms. Winters, but Ms. Winters is talking to Lizbeth (middle-class, white). Lizbeth is grinning, wide-eyed, as she explains triumphantly that she beat her time from last year. Ms. Winters congratulates her, asking her about how she "improved her technique." Finally, almost a minute later, Ms. Winters notices Cody lying on the ground. Rather than ask if he is okay, Ms. Winters instructs Cody to get up. "Cody!" she barks, "Get up and walk! Your muscles are going to tense up if you just lie there." Cody sits up quickly. His mouth is hanging open and his eyes are wide with surprise. He starts to mouth something, but ultimately stops. Instead, he lets out a heavy sigh and gets up to join the rest of the class.

Because she was busy talking with other students, Ms. Winters never noticed Cody's broken shoelace. As a result, and in light of the frequent reminders she gave students about the importance of "cool downs," Ms. Winters seemed to assume that Cody was lying down out of laziness and not out of frustration, and she criticized him for doing so. Cody, meanwhile, could have tried to protest or explain. Had Cody done so, Ms. Winters might have allowed him to run the course again, as she did with middle-class student Sammy. Instead, and seemingly because of Ms. Winters' gruff admonishment, Cody opted to stay silent. In doing so, however, and like other working-class students, he was unable to reap the rewards that might have come from a more influence-based approach.

SUMMARY AND CONCLUSIONS

This chapter sets the stage for subsequent chapters by revealing teachers' expectations for student problem-solving and the extent to which those expectations aligned with the strategies that children learned at home. Teachers' expectations, I found, were often ambiguous and inconsistent. Teachers shifted their preferred approaches to problem-solving throughout the school day. There were situations in which teachers expected students to work independently or wait patiently with hands raised. There were other situations in which they expected students to seek support and even call out or approach them directly with questions. Those shifts, however, were rarely explicit, leaving students to decode for themselves which strategy would be best for a given situation.

This chapter also highlights the critical role that teachers played both in prompting students to activate class-based problem-solving strategies and in determining whether those strategies resulted in reprimands or rewards. When confronted with vague or varying expectations, children relied on their parents' coaching as a guide. In those ambiguous moments, middle-class children focused on the possibility of reward and thus opted to push ahead with strategies of influence. Working-class children, meanwhile, focused on the possibility of reprimand and thus opted to fall back on strategies of deference.

The findings in this chapter build on research on cultural capital, teacher authority, and the hidden curriculum of schooling. Consistent with prior research in those areas, this chapter demonstrated that teachers acted as gatekeepers on a poorly-lit path to success (Anyon 1980; Mehan 1980; Wren 1999). Teachers rarely made their expectations for student problem-solving explicit, but they still judged students on their ability to comply with those hidden demands. As a result, and as discussed in more detail in subsequent chapters, teachers played a critical role in determining whether students' problem-solving strategies resulted in reprimands or rewards.

At the same time, this chapter also challenges some common assumptions regarding the relationship between class-based cultures and larger patterns of inequality. According to cultural capital theory, teachers should have fixed expectations that always favor the middle class (Bourdieu 1996; Lareau and Weininger 2003). By contrast, the teachers at Maplewood allowed their expectations to shift from moment to moment throughout the day, and they had good reasons for doing so.[8] A consequence of those fluctuations, however, was that teachers' responses to particular problem-solving strategies were not fixed. There were times when teachers favored a more deference-based working-class approach to problem-solving (e.g., when they wanted students to raise their hands or work through difficult tasks on their own) and times when they instead favored a more influence-based middle-class approach (e.g., when they wanted students to acknowledge their struggles and speak up in seeking support). These findings question the presumption— common in research on social class and cultural matching (Lareau 2000; Lubienski 2000; Stephens et al. 2012)—of a one-to-one correlation between institutional standards and middle-class behavior. They also challenge the idea—central to research on cultural capital and even non-cognitive skills (Carneiro and Heckman 2003; Farkas 2003; Heckman and Rubinstein 2001; Jennings and DiPrete 2010; Tach and Farkas 2006)—that certain strategies are consistently beneficial or detrimental for students. Instead, this chapter revealed that the profits of a given strategy could vary across situations in school.

That does not mean, however, that schools are neutral institutions. Rather, as demonstrated in Chapters 3–5, middle-class students received the bulk of teachers' assistance, accommodations, and attention. In some cases, those rewards reflected middle-class students' compliance with teachers' expectations. In other cases, however, and in contrast to what cultural capital theory and research on the hidden curriculum might predict, teachers granted middle-class students' requests for assistance, accommodations, and attention even when those students made the requests in ways that clashed with teachers' expectations.[9] Thus, as I argue in the following chapters, teachers' favoring of the middle-class resulted not (or at least not just) from middle-class compliance with teachers' demands but, rather, from the middle-class's willingness and ability to request support in excess of what was fair or required and to pressure teachers to grant those requests, even when teachers might have preferred to say "no."

CHAPTER 3

Seeking Assistance

One warm afternoon in early April, the students in Mr. Potter's fifth-grade class were all sitting at their desks. They had just returned from recess—there was a faint smell of sweat in the air and a buzz of happy chatter. Mr. Potter, a willowy man in neatly pressed slacks and a button-down shirt, was leaning casually against a file cabinet. Calling for the students' attention, Mr. Potter enthusiastically announced that they would be doing a "fun" creative writing activity. Mr. Potter directed the students' attention to the writing prompt posted at the front of the room. It read, "Goats, sheep, and chickens belong on a farm, not in the middle of . . ." Below the prompt were the following instructions:

1. Copy the prompt into your writing journal.
2. Finish the sentence.
3. Add one more sentence.
4. Pass your journal three times to your left.
5. Read your new story.
6. Add one more sentence.
7. Repeat 4–6.

Mr. Potter gave his fifth graders 2 minutes to complete the first three steps. As the students worked, Mr. Potter circled around, checking their progress. After 2 minutes, Mr. Potter had the students stop writing and pass their journals to the left. Glancing at the clock, Mr. Potter told the students they now had 2 more minutes to read their new story and add a sentence. As the students set to work, Mr. Potter surveilled the room:

Jeremy, a working-class, white student with a thin face and a poof of wavy blonde hair, is squinting hard, and his brow is deeply furrowed. Jeremy appears to be struggling to decipher what the paper says, but he does not raise his hand or call out for help. Mr. Potter, standing in the middle of the room, watches Jeremy for a moment, and then starts to move toward him.

Meanwhile, Julie, a white middle-class girl wearing track pants and a soccer T-shirt, had been glaring at the journal in front of her. As Mr. Potter started to move toward Jeremy, Julie called out loudly, "Mr. Potter!"

> Mr. Potter hears his name and looks up at Julie, lifting his eyebrows questioningly. Julie contorts her face into a pained expression. She slumps forward over her desk and whines loudly: "I can't *read* this." Hearing Julie's complaint, Mr. Potter nods and quickly changes course. Instead of heading toward Jeremy, he makes his way directly to Julie, helping her decipher the handwriting in the journal.

Like Julie, Jeremy appeared to be having trouble reading what was written in the journal he received. Unlike Julie, however, Jeremy did not ask for help. Although Mr. Potter could have helped Jeremy before going over to Julie, it would have been awkward to do so because Jeremy had not actually voiced a need for assistance and Mr. Potter had not yet offered help, meaning that Jeremy had no official claim on Mr. Potter's attention when Julie asked. As a result, Julie got the help she needed and immediately continued the activity. Jeremy, meanwhile, did not have a chance to add his own sentence to the story before it was time to pass the journals again.

OVERVIEW

In the classrooms at Maplewood Elementary, social class was particularly salient in three types of student–teacher interactions: requests for assistance, requests for accommodations, and requests for attention. Those patterns were generally consistent across teachers, although they did become more pronounced over time as children gradually internalized the lessons and worked through the pushback described in Chapter 1. As a result, most of the classroom examples I present in this chapter and Chapters 4 and 5 are from fourth-grade and especially fifth-grade classrooms. Chapters 4 and 5 focus on differences in accommodation-seeking and attention-seeking.[1] This chapter focuses on assistance-seeking—students' decisions about whether and how to ask for help from teachers when they encountered confusion or consternation at school.

Those moments of frustration were common for students at Maplewood. Some of the problems they experienced were small—pencil sharpeners got jammed, books got misplaced, and computer passwords got forgotten. Other problems were larger—absences that resulted in missed material, confusion about directions on tests, not having the materials needed to complete a project, or even being teased by a classmate on the playground.

Regardless of the size of the problem, children generally responded in class-based ways. Like Julie in the previous example, and drawing on the strategies of influence they learned at home, middle-class students typically sought assistance from teachers and were proactive and persistent in making those requests. Like Jeremy, working-class students instead drew on strategies of deference and dealt with problems on their own. Furthermore, when working-class students did seek help from teachers, they waited for signs that such requests were welcome (e.g., when teachers approached them to offer assistance). They also fielded their requests politely (e.g., raising hands rather than calling out) and with deference to teachers' authority (e.g., not asking follow-up questions, even if they were still confused).

Those decisions about whether and how to seek assistance had real consequences in the classroom. As discussed in Chapter 2, middle-class students sometimes faced reprimand when teachers became frustrated with their frequent and persistent requests. More often, however, middle-class students succeeded in securing the assistance they desired, and they used that assistance to complete their work quickly and accurately. Working-class students, meanwhile, were sometimes able to avoid reprimand by working through problems on their own. Hard work alone, however, was not always sufficient to overcome classroom problems. In those situations, working-class students spent more time struggling and often went without the help they needed to succeed.

ASSISTANCE-SEEKING IN CONTEXT

Existing research offers potential explanations for the previously mentioned unequal outcomes. It is known, for example, that students who seek support from their teachers tend to do better in school. Although help-seeking was once regarded as an indicator of excessive dependence, scholars and educators now recognize it as an achievement-oriented behavior (Karabenick and Knapp 1991; Patrick et al. 2001). Quantitative studies even show that frequent help-seeking is associated with higher levels of subsequent achievement (Gall 1985; Newman 2000; Ryan, Hicks, and Midgley 1997).

Given those apparent academic benefits, it seems possible that teachers expect students to seek help and reward those who do so. If so, then help-seeking is essentially a form of cultural capital in the classroom—a skill or strategy that can be activated to generate advantages in a particular setting (Lareau and Weininger 2003). According to cultural capital theory, there is a "cultural match" between the behaviors that schools value and the behaviors that middle-class families value in their children at home (Bernstein 1990; Bourdieu 1996; Foley 1990; Lareau 2000; Lubienski 2000; Stephens et al. 2012).[2] That match facilitates middle-class students' compliance with teachers' expectations and thus allows them to reap more rewards (Calarco 2011; Florio and Shultz 1979; Heath 1983). Working-class students, meanwhile, remain at a disadvantage because schools do not teach the behaviors they reward; instead, those behaviors remain part of the "hidden curriculum" of schooling (Apple 1980; Contreras, Brint, and Matthews 2001; Halstead and Xiao 2010; Jackson 1990).

My findings are at least partially consistent with this cultural capital model of middle-class advantage. As discussed in Chapter 2, there were times when teachers wanted students to ask for help. In general, however, teachers did not make those expectations explicit. As a result, middle-class students—who learned help-seeking and other strategies of influence at home—were better able to comply with teachers' expectations and reap the rewards for doing so.

Simultaneously, however, my findings suggest that compliance alone is insufficient to account for the advantages middle-class students secured through their assistance-seeking efforts. As mentioned in Chapter 2, there were times when teachers expected students *not* to ask for help. In those moments, working-class students found it easier to comply, whereas middle-class students felt compelled to forge ahead with their requests, even at the risk of reprimand. Furthermore, as this chapter will show, that persistence paid off. Even when they frustrated teachers with their requests, and even when teachers wanted to say "no," middle-class students were often successful in securing the assistance they desired.

Such findings suggest that the middle-class advantage in school was, at least in part, a negotiated advantage. Middle-class students reaped rewards not just for complying with the expectations of the school but also by requesting support in excess of what was fair or required and by pressuring teachers to grant those requests, even when teachers might have preferred to say "no." Whereas prior research has shown that middle-class *parents* are often successful in lobbying schools to provide additional (and often unfair) advantages to their children (Baker and Stevenson 1986; Lewis and Diamond 2015; Lewis-McCoy 2014; Useem 1992), this chapter demonstrates how middle-class *children* activate similar behaviors and how schools respond to those behaviors in ways that create unequal advantages.

This chapter focuses on the advantages that middle-class students secured through their assistance-seeking efforts. Chapters 4 and 5 show how similar patterns extended to accommodation-seeking and attention-seeking as well.

DEALING WITH PROBLEMS IN THE CLASSROOM

When confronted with moments of frustration or confusion, the students at Maplewood often sought guidance from their parents' lessons about influence and deference. Middle-class students readily acknowledged their struggles and were proactive and persistent in making requests. Working-class students instead tried to deal with problems on their own, or if they did seek help, they did so patiently and politely.

Students' Willingness to Seek Assistance

These contrasting strategies could be seen, in part, through students' willingness to seek assistance from teachers. Most of the middle-class children seemed comfortable asking for help with any problem at any time. They openly acknowledged their struggles, often proclaiming (loud enough for the whole class to hear) "I don't get this!" and "I need help!" Middle-class students also asked for help with a wide variety of academic, personal, and social problems, including problems with people ("Phillip is calling me names") and objects ("Can you open this for me?"), problems with understanding directions ("Does this mean that I'm supposed to . . . ?"), and problems understanding the material ("I can't figure out how to do number 17").

Middle-class students even asked teachers to use class time to address their individual questions and concerns. During language arts, for example, Ms. Nelson announced that they would be starting a new story. As the students got out their reading anthologies, Ms. Nelson made a brief announcement about the homework, which had been posted on the board all day. Directing students' attention to the spelling homework, Ms. Nelson noted that students should "be sure to take some graph paper for the word triangles":

Hearing the announcement, Lindsey (middle-class, white) thrusts her hand high in the air and cocks her head to the side, puzzled. Before Ms. Nelson can acknowledge her raised hand, Lindsey calls out: "I wasn't here last week when we did the triangles, so I don't know how to do it." Hearing this, Ms. Nelson glances quickly at the clock, hesitates a moment, and then concedes: "I can show you real quick on the board." Lindsey nods encouragingly, and volunteers "minor"—a word from her spelling list—when Ms. Nelson asks for a word to use as an example. Stepping up to the Smart Board, Ms. Nelson then demonstrates how to make a "triangle" out of the word "minor," explaining over her shoulder as she writes:

M
M I
M I N
M I N O
M I N O R

Lindsey could have chosen a more convenient time (e.g., before school, after school, before lunch, or after lunch) to ask Ms. Nelson to review the spelling strategies she missed while she was absent. Instead, and like middle-class students in general, Lindsey expected teachers to use class time to help her with individual problems.

Unlike their middle-class peers, working-class students rarely acknowledged their struggles aloud. Instead, they typically tried to work through problems on their own. One cold, December morning, Mr. Potter's fifth graders were taking a social studies test. In one section of the test, students were presented with a Venn diagram and a list of numbered statements (e.g., "They wanted to protect their lands"). Students had to indicate whether each statement would be made by the Native Americans, the frontier settlers, or both groups. After handing out the tests, Mr. Potter spent 7 minutes explaining the directions. He then paused, asking, "Any questions?" A few of the kids looked nervous, but none of them raised their hands. Mr. Potter gave the students a playful shrug, saying, "All right, then you may begin!" For the next 12 minutes, the students worked silently at their desks, and Mr. Potter sat at the front table, grading papers. Eventually, however, and as the first students reached the Venn diagram, confusion set in. Brianna and Vanessa (both middle-class, white) got up and made their way over to Mr. Potter. As Brianna asked a clarifying question about the Venn diagram, Vanessa stood "in line" behind her. As Mr. Potter answered their questions, Julie, Lisa, and Owen (all middle-class, white) got up to join the line as well. Meanwhile, Shannon (working-class, white) was clearly struggling, but she did not ask for help:

> Shannon sits hunched over her desk, glowering as she reads and re-reads the statements under the Venn diagram. Shannon sits like this for almost ten minutes, occasionally writing something on the page, then erasing it again. Although there are other students asking for help, Shannon never gets up to join the line.

As Shannon continued to struggle with the Venn diagram, the rest of the students finished the remaining sections and started to turn in their tests:

> When the line of students waiting for help finally dissipates, Mr. Potter looks up and scans the room with his eyes. He stops his gaze on Shannon, noticing the sag of her shoulders and the pained expression on her face. Getting up from the table, Mr. Potter makes his way over to Shannon's desk, asking gently, "You okay? Not sure what to do?" Shannon looks up at Mr. Potter sheepishly and gives a slight shrug. Mr. Potter nods and squats down beside Shannon. He then begins to walk her through the Venn diagram section, pointing at each sentence, reading it aloud in a soft voice, and encouraging Shannon to think through whether the statement applied to the Native Americans, to the frontier settlers, or to both. Shannon is hesitant at first, tentatively identifying where each statement should go. Mr. Potter praises her warmly for each answer, and Shannon begins to smile as she writes down the correct answers.

Mr. Potter asked for questions after reviewing the directions, but it was common for students to realize they were confused only when they actually started to work through tests and assignments. Faced with such confusion, middle-class students readily sought help, but working-class students such as Shannon rarely did the same. Although Mr. Potter eventually noticed Shannon struggling and offered assistance, it took Shannon significantly longer than the rest of the class to finish the test.

Working-class students did occasionally request help from teachers, but they almost always waited to do so until it was clear that their requests would not result in reprimand. As with Shannon in the test example, that often meant waiting for teachers to offer unsolicited assistance. In other cases, that meant waiting for middle-class students to successfully make similar requests. During a science lesson on biomes in Ms. Nelson's fourth-grade class, for example, the students were using their textbooks to complete a fill-in-the-blank note-taking packet:

> Ms. Nelson calls the whole class back together to review the correct answers. As she does so, Kelly, Elliot (both middle-class, white), Alan, Zara, and Kal (all middle-class, Asian American) call out with clarifying questions like: "Can we also put arid for number five?" Ms. Nelson nods, explaining that "arid" is another good description of a "subtropical" ecosystem. Eventually, Sadie (working-class, white) raises her hand. Ms. Nelson calls on her, and Sadie asks quietly: "For climate, can we put warmer?" Ms. Nelson smiles, explaining that, yes, "warmer" would also be a fitting description of a "temperate" climate.

Like Sadie, working-class students avoided asking for help from teachers unless it was clear that requests for assistance were welcome. They waited for teachers to approach them or to see that other students had success-fully made similar requests. The reassurance provided in those situations seemed to make it easier for working-class students to acknowledge their concerns.

Students' Frequency of Help-Seeking

Social class differences in students' willingness to acknowledge their struggles could also be seen in the frequency of their requests for help. This study cannot assess the precise correlation between social class and help-seeking. However, my observations did consistently show a disproportionate proportion of requests coming from middle-class students.

In order to clarify and search for disconfirming evidence of those patterns, and as a supplement to the larger ethnographic study, I conducted 16 hour-long count sessions in which I strategically tallied students' direct (e.g., "Can you explain number 7?") and indirect ("I don't get this") requests for assistance, clarification, information, and checking of work. Those count sessions occurred during the last 6 months of fieldwork in the same classrooms in which I conducted the rest of my observations.

These counts provided further evidence of class-based patterns in the frequency and scope of students' help-seeking. As Table 3.1 shows, questions and requests were very common—fifth-grade teachers at Maplewood received at least 80 requests for help during a typical school day.[3] Those requests, however, were not evenly distributed. Rather, the average middle-class student made more than seven requests for help from teachers on a typical day, whereas the average working-class student made one. Middle-class students also made a wider variety of requests for help. They asked for assistance, clarification, information, and checking of work, whereas working-class students only made requests for assistance and clarification.[4] Even within the two shared categories (assistance and clarification), middle-class students asked for more help than did their working-class peers.

Styles of Help-Seeking

Count data provide useful evidence of the frequency of students' help-seeking, but field notes are better suited for describing the nature and consequences of class differences in students' problem-solving. They reveal that students differed not only in frequency of help-seeking but also in styles used when making requests.

Table 3.1 STUDENTS' REQUESTS FOR HELP FROM TEACHERS, BY SOCIAL CLASS AND 60-MINUTE SUBJECT PERIOD[a]

	Math (Test/Quiz)		Language Arts (Writing Activity)		Science (In-Class Project)		Flex Time (Various Activities)		Total	
	MC	WC	MC	WC	MC	WC	MC	WC	MC	WC
Students present	41	11	39	11	39	14	41	14		
Types of Requests										
Assistance[b]										
Requests per student (total requests)	0.88 (36)	0.27 (3)	0.36 (14)	0.18 (2)	0.36 (14)	0.00 (0)	0.27 (11)	0.14 (2)	1.88 (75)	0.56 (7)
Clarification[c]										
Requests per student (total requests)	1.02 (42)	0.18 (2)	0.87 (34)	0.18 (2)	0.82 (32)	0.21 (3)	0.73 (30)	0.07 (1)	3.45 (138)	0.64 (8)
Checking of work[d]										
Requests per student (total requests)	0.56 (23)	0.00 (0)	0.33 (13)	0.00 (0)	0.26 (10)	0.00 (0)	0.46 (19)	0.00 (0)	1.63 (65)	0.00 (0)
Information[e]										
Requests per student (total requests)	0.10 (4)	0.00 (0)	0.28 (11)	0.00 (0)	0.23 (9)	0.00 (0)	0.20 (8)	0.00 (0)	0.80 (32)	0.00 (0)
Total requests per student (total requests)	2.56 (105)	0.45 (5)	1.84 (72)	0.36 (4)	1.67 (65)	0.21 (3)	1.66 (68)	0.21 (3)	7.75 (310)	1.20 (15)

[a]Within each subject period, requests are aggregated across the four classrooms in fifth grade. Counts include only white students. Counts were conducted on days when all working-class students in a class were present. However, 3 of the 14 working-class, white students received learning support for math and language arts and thus are not included in the counts for those subjects.

[b]Assistance: Direct ("Can you help me?") and indirect ("I don't get this") requests for interactive support for problems students are having with projects, activities, assignments, and physical aspects of the classroom environment.

[c]Clarification: Direct ("What does this mean?") and indirect ("This doesn't make sense") questions about general classroom instructions; directions for specific activities; and questions on tests, worksheets, and assignments.

[d]Checking of work: Direct ("Can you check this?") and indirect ("Is this right?") requests for teachers to look over or judge the accuracy of students' actions during classroom activities and their completed work on assignments, projects, and tests/quizzes.

[e]Information: Requests for teachers to provide additional knowledge or instruction (e.g., "Did they find water on the moon?" and "How do you use a protractor to draw 420 degrees?").

MC, middle class; WC, working class.

Rather than sit and wait with raised hands, middle-class students generally took a proactive approach to help-seeking that involved calling out or approaching teachers with requests. One late October afternoon in fifth grade, Ms. Hudson told her fifth graders to copy a set of upcoming project deadlines into their assignment books while she set up for the next activity. One of the projects on the list was the November book report:

> After going over the project deadlines, Ms. Hudson sets the students to work. She then heads to the cabinets on the side of the room. She takes out three large bins, carries them to a table at the back of the room, and then sorts through the contents in preparation for the next activity.

Meanwhile, Drew (middle-class, white) was tapping his pencil lightly on his assignment book and frowning thoughtfully:

> Drew raises his hand high in the air, simultaneously twisting around in his seat to look for Ms. Hudson. Spotting her at the back of the room, Drew immediately puts his hand down and pops up out of his seat. He trots over toward the table where Ms. Hudson is working, calling out as he approaches: "Ms. Hudson, I just have a quick question." Ms. Hudson looks up, startled. Before she can say anything, Drew continues, explaining: "Let's just say we're gonna start reading our book report books for November." Hearing this, Ms. Hudson interjects encouragingly: "And you should! Because it has to be a chapter book, so it's gonna take you some time." Drew, however, has continued with his question, so they are talking over each other. He asks: "Can we, like, make notecards and start taking notes?" Ms. Hudson nods vigorously, enthusing: "Oh! You should!" Ms. Hudson then launches into a long explanation of how notecards will be very useful as a way to keep track of characters and main events in a chapter book. Drew beams, looking pleased. He thanks Ms. Hudson and heads back to his desk.

Although Ms. Hudson was busy, and although his request was far from urgent, Drew did not hesitate to seek clarification. Furthermore, when it became apparent that hand-raising would not elicit an immediate response, Drew switched strategies, approaching Ms. Hudson directly with his request. That kind of proactive and even strategic help-seeking was common among middle-class students, who were keen on getting their questions answered as quickly as possible.

Middle-class students were also doggedly persistent in their assistance-seeking efforts. Even when teachers tried to deny their requests, middle-class students rarely conceded. During flex time in Ms. Dunham's fifth-grade class, the students were at their desks, working on various projects. Ms. Dunham noticed that Jesse (white, working-class) was struggling to assemble part of his diorama (although he did not ask for help), and she went over to offer assistance. As Ms. Dunham moved over toward Jesse, Mandy (middle-class, white) jumped up from her seat and trotted after Ms. Dunham, barraging her with questions about a poster she was making for her monthly book report:

> Coming up behind Ms. Dunham, Mandy thrusts out her poster and asks hopefully: "Is this okay so far?" Ms. Dunham is holding Jesse's diorama so that the pieces stay together while he staples them. She glances over her shoulder at Mandy's poster, nods, and whispers encouragingly: "Looks good!"

Ms. Dunham gave Mandy a reassuring smile, but Mandy continued to push with more questions, firing them one after another:

> "Are we supposed to type the captions?" Mandy asks, gesturing at the computers at the back of the room. Ms. Dunham puts down Jesse's diorama and turns to face Mandy. While Jesse waits quietly, Ms. Dunham explains that the posters are too large to fit in the printer, so they do not have to print the captions. Mandy, however, still does not seem satisfied, asking: "But, could I, like print out the captions and glue them on instead?" Ms. Dunham nods, saying flatly: "Yes. That's fine." Mandy asks three or four more questions, and Ms. Dunham becomes increasingly short in her replies, answering just "Yes," "Nope," and "Mmhmm." Finally, Mandy thanks Ms. Dunham and heads back to the computer station, leaving Ms. Dunham to go back to helping Jesse.

Ms. Dunham appeared frustrated with Mandy's questions, most of which could have been answered by reading the instructions for the project or reflecting on standard classroom procedures. Given those frustrations, Ms. Dunham could have said "enough" and turned Mandy away. Instead, however, Ms. Dunham relented, conveying her frustrations only obliquely—she seemed to feel pressured to continue answering questions until Mandy was satisfied with the response. Mandy, meanwhile, either missed or ignored Ms. Dunham's signals of mounting frustration. Like other middle-class students, she persisted with question after question until she had all the information she needed to proceed.

Working-class students typically took a more patient approach to help-seeking. They raised their hands and waited quietly—sometimes for a long time—even when it was clear that calling out or getting up would elicit a faster response. During a Spanish lesson, Mr. Pratt gave the fourth graders an assignment that involved using vocabulary words to write simple stories. Each student had to choose an insect and then write a whole paragraph describing, in Spanish, what that insect looked like and how it moved. As the students worked, Mr. Pratt fielded question after question.

In most cases, students wanted Mr. Pratt to translate a word they had not yet learned, although some students wanted Mr. Pratt to "check and make sure" their paragraphs were correct. Although most of the questions came from middle-class students, two working-class, white students—Ashleigh and Jared—asked for help as well. Unlike their middle-class peers, however, Jared and Ashleigh did so only after trying to solve the problem on their own and only by raising their hands:

> Ashleigh pulls the dictionary out from under her seat. She flips it open and begins thumbing through the pages. Eventually, Ashleigh stops and peers down at the page. She lets out a quiet sigh and taps the dictionary page with her pencil. Looking up, Ashleigh sees that Mr. Pratt is helping Lizbeth (middle-class, white) at his desk. Ashleigh raises her left hand over her head and uses her right hand to write as she waits. Ashleigh continues to wait as Mr. Pratt makes his way around the room, moving from student to student as they call out or approach him with requests for help. Meanwhile, Ashleigh has been sitting with her hand raised for more than three minutes. Eventually, Ashleigh stops writing, rests her left forearm on her head, and slumps low in her chair.

Finally, after Ashleigh had been waiting for more than 5 minutes, Mr. Pratt noticed her hand and moved to help:

> As Mr. Pratt approaches, he asks: "What's up?" Ashleigh explains quietly that she wants to write (in Spanish): "A spider makes a web." She explains that she looked up the word for "make" in the Spanish–English dictionary, but that there were multiple answers. Mr. Pratt explains that Ashleigh should just write "A spider has a web," instead, as they have already learned the Spanish word for "has" (*tiene*). Ashleigh looks somewhat disappointed, but she just nods, giving Mr. Pratt a quick smile and saying warmly: "Thanks."

Unlike her middle-class peers, Ashleigh checked the dictionary before asking Mr. Pratt to translate for her. Only when she was unable to find the answer on her own did Ashleigh eventually decide to ask the teacher. Even then, however, Ashleigh opted to wait with her hand raised, and she continued to wait as Mr. Pratt answered the questions of students who called out and approached him directly for help.

Compared to their middle-class peers, working-class students were also very polite in seeking assistance. They almost never pushed back if teachers denied their requests, and they rarely followed up with additional questions, even if they were still confused. During their weekly library lessons, the fifth graders were learning how to find and utilize online databases for "nonfiction research." The final project for the unit involved an online "scavenger hunt" that students completed over two class periods. The students had to think of three questions related to topics they were studying in science. Using the library's laptop computers and the online databases accessible from the library website, they then had to find answers to those questions. Finally, they had to type up and print their questions, their answers, and the links to the source material for each answer. On the second "scavenger hunt" day for Mr. Fischer's class, the librarian called the students to the rug to briefly review the directions. She then answered a number of clarifying questions, all asked by middle-class students. Kelly, for example, asked, "Do we print out our *answers*, too?" (yes). Then Ethan asked, "We have to go on *that* computer to print, right?" (yes again). After answering a few more questions, the librarian set the students to work finishing their projects. Meanwhile, Zach (working-class, white) had been sitting slumped forward, chin resting on his fist, with a completely befuddled look on his face. Zach was absent[5] 1 week earlier, on the first day of the scavenger hunt—a fact that the librarian, who taught all the students in the school, did not immediately recall:

> All the other kids are buzzing around, picking up laptops, finding their seats, and setting to work on their projects. Zach, meanwhile, trudges back to his library table. He stops to get a laptop along the way. He then sits down heavily, turns on the laptop, and stares blankly at the screen.

As the students worked, the librarian circled around, and some of the middle-class students stopped her to ask questions, which she answered warmly. Zach occasionally glanced up at the librarian as she worked with other students, but he said nothing:

> Zach glares at his computer, occasionally reaching out with one hand to click hard, almost angrily, on the touchpad. He eventually opens the library web page and starts clicking on random links. As he does this, Zach periodically glances up at the librarian, as though waiting for her to get to his table so that he can ask for help.

Zach continued like that for the next 9 minutes. Occasionally, Zach looked up at the other students at his table, as if waiting for an opening to ask them for help. However, they were all busy working and did not seem to notice Zach struggling. Meanwhile, the librarian continued circling around and answering questions such as "Is this the right way to write the source?" and "Can I print mine now if I'm done?" Eventually, the librarian made it to Zach's table:

> Approaching Zach's table, the librarian asks cheerfully: "Anybody need help? Everybody doing okay?" At this, Zach finally admits, his voice breaking with desperation: "I don't know what I'm supposed to be doing, cuz I wasn't here last class." The librarian looks puzzled, as though she is confused about why Zach did not speak up sooner. She briefly explains that Zach needs to think of a topic, write three questions about that topic,

and then go online and find the answers using "reputable" sources. She does not mention that they need to include a link to the source in their printout. Zach still appears puzzled—he is frowning and blinking as though trying not to cry—but he just nods and says nothing. At that moment, Brian (middle-class, mixed-race) calls out for help from another table. The librarian turns and heads over toward Brian.

Zach still seemed confused about the project, but he did not follow up with more questions. Ten minutes later, almost all of the students were finished and lining up to leave. Zach, meanwhile, was frantically finishing his answers and sending his document to the printer:

> After returning his laptop to the storage cart, Zach picks up his paper from the printer and dashes over to the librarian. As he approaches, Zach announces breathlessly and triumphantly: "I'm done!" Glancing quickly at the paper, the librarian remarks: "You didn't include the URLs for where you found your answers." Zach stammers: "I, uh . . . I guess I didn't . . . uh . . . okay." The librarian sighs and shakes her head, saying: "You don't have time to change it. You'll just have to turn it in like this." Zach opens his mouth as though he is about to say something but then stops. He just nods. His head hangs low as he trudges over to drop his paper in the basket and join the line of students at the door.

If Zach had initially followed up with more questions about the assignment, he might have learned that he needed to include the web addresses for the sites he used. Instead, Zach took a more polite approach—accepting the assistance he was offered without pushback. As a result, Zach completed the assignment incorrectly and only received partial credit.

GENERATING STRATIFIED PROFITS

As examples like that of Zach suggest, students' problem-solving strategies had real—and often contrasting—consequences. Compared to their working-class peers, middle-class students received fuller and more immediate assistance from teachers, and that extra support had numerous benefits.[6] They got help with peer conflicts, broken backpacks, and lost lunch money; in some cases, they even got an immediate leg up on assignments and exams.

Middle-Class Students Reaping Rewards

Over the course of my observations, I watched middle-class students make hundreds of requests for help. In some cases, teachers said "no." More often, however, middle-class students were successful in using their requests to secure the support they desired. That support also had real, academic benefits.

Because of the support they received from teachers, middle-class students were often able to complete their work more quickly than they could have completed it on their own. During a social studies lesson on the Revolutionary War, Ms. Hudson divided her fifth graders into groups. Ms. Hudson assigned each group a different section of the chapter to read, and she assigned each group member a different job (reader, scribe, timekeeper, or taskmaster). There was much commotion as students got up to find their groups, and many of the students seemed confused about the directions. In one group, Gina (middle-class, white), Drew (middle-class, white), Sidney (working-class, white), and Logan (middle-class, white) began debating about who was supposed to do what:

> After about thirty seconds of argument, Gina breaks off from her group and makes a bee-line for Ms. Hudson, who is standing near her desk at the front of the room. Approaching Ms. Hudson, Gina looks up pointedly, her chest jutted out and her shoulders held back confidently. She asks gruffly, as though trying to settle a debate: "Do we *all* have to write notes? Or just the scribe?" Ms. Hudson nods and explains, carefully enunciating each word so that Gina can hear her above the commotion: "You *all* write notes, but the scribe leads you in the discussion of what to write." Gina nods smugly and then scurries back to her group to report back on what she learned.

Like other middle-class students, Gina regularly asked clarifying questions about assignments and activities. In doing so, Gina prevented a long, drawn-out argument and gave her group more time to work on completing the assignment correctly.

Extra assistance from teachers also ensured that middle-class students' work was complete and correct. During a math test, Mr. Potter instructed the students to finish their tests and then put them on his desk. All of the working-class students followed those directions. Most of the middle-class students, meanwhile, opted to ask Mr. Potter to "check" their tests before submitting them for a grade. As they approached Mr. Potter, who was grading science projects at the back of the room, the middle-class students would make statements such as "I'm not sure if I get what the directions mean, here. Can you check to see if I'm doing it right?" In each instance, Mr. Potter took the test and reviewed it. In many cases, he looked not only at the problem in question but also at the test as a whole, flipping through the pages and offering suggestions such as "You need to show more work here" and "Watch your decimal points on this one." As a result, the middle-class students who asked for "checking" help were able to preemptively correct mistakes and avoid grade penalties for errors.

Working-Class Students Suffering Consequences

Working-class students occasionally reaped rewards from their more deference-based approach to problem-solving. More often, however, working-class students suffered real consequences when they opted not to ask for help. Compared to their middle-class peers, struggling working-class students received less immediate attention and less complete information from teachers. As a result, they also faced greater challenges in completing their work accurately and on time.

Working-class students were sometimes successful in overcoming problems on their own, and that success had meaningful benefits, including a sense of accomplishment and even praise from teachers. One morning during social studies, Ms. Nelson's fourth graders were getting ready to play a bingo-style review game for an upcoming test. As Ms. Nelson passed out the materials and explained the instructions, a few students got up to sharpen their pencils:

> Carter (working-class, white) is last in line at the electric sharpener. When it is his turn, Carter steps up and tries to insert his pencil into the slot. The pencil stops short, however, and nothing happens. Carter frowns deeply. Pulling his pencil back out, Carter leans down and peers into the hole at the front of the sharpener. Sitting a few feet away, I hear Carter grumble quietly to himself: "There's something stuck in there." Carter then pushes his pencil back into the slot, jamming it around and trying to dislodge whatever is stuck inside.

Carter continued working on the sharpener for more than 2 minutes, but he did not ask for help.[7] While passing out the bingo chips, Ms. Nelson noticed Carter struggling but did not intervene. Three minutes later, Carter was still tinkering with the sharpener:

> Ms. Nelson deposits a pile of bingo chips on the last desk. She then immediately heads toward Carter, who is still digging around in the pencil sharpener. She calls out: "You need help?" Just as she says this, Carter finally manages to dislodge the bit of pencil that was stuck. The pencil sharpener begins to whir loudly and Carter glances over his shoulder. He smiles triumphantly and calls back: "No, I'm okay!" Ms. Nelson nods and thanks Carter for his help fixing the sharpener, saying brightly: "Nice work!" Carter beams, proudly inspecting the neatly sharpened tip of his pencil as he trots back to his seat.

In some cases, working-class students were able to successfully overcome problems on their own, and those triumphs had significant benefits. Carter, for example, seemed proud that he had been able to fix the pencil sharpener on his own, and he seemed especially proud that Ms. Nelson praised him for his efforts.

Although there were some benefits to a more deference-based approach to problem-solving, not seeking help also had drawbacks. By trying to work through problems on their own, working-class students spent more time struggling. As a result, it often took them longer to complete their assignments, if they did so at all. During math class, for example, Ms. Nelson had her fourth graders work in randomly drawn pairs to identify patterns on a multiplication worksheet. Sadie and Carter (both working-class, white) were working together, sitting on the floor by the cubbies at the back of the room:

> Sadie and Carter are both bent over their worksheets, frowning. Carter grumbles quietly that he can't find any patterns. They begin to argue in hushed voices about what kind of patterns they are supposed to find.

During the activity, a number of middle-class students (Danny and Anna, Aidan and Adam, and Gina[8]) went to Ms. Nelson and asked her to clarify the directions. Each time, she provided a clearer explanations than the one on the worksheet. Sadie and Carter were clearly struggling with the worksheet—they were not sure what they were supposed to do. Unlike their middle-class peers, however, Sadie and Carter did not ask for help. Fifteen minutes after starting the activity, all of the other groups had finished, but Sadie and Carter were still working:

> Ms. Nelson says gruffly to Sadie and Carter: "You guys! Time's up. You were the only group that didn't finish. You guys need to work better together." Sadie and Carter appear to be upset, but they do not say anything. Hanging their heads, they get up silently and go back to their seats.

If Sadie and Carter had asked for help, they might have finished the activity on time. Instead, and because they opted to deal with the situation on their own, they failed to complete the worksheet and were (mistakenly) accused by the teacher of not working hard enough.

There were also drawbacks to working-class students' more polite and deferential approach to help-seeking. As demonstrated by the example of Zach in the library, working-class students rarely asked follow-up questions, even if they were still confused, and that confusion sometimes led them to complete their work incorrectly or not at all. Similarly, and as illustrated by the following example, teachers did not always notice working-class students raising their hands. As a result, working-class students often waited much longer for help and sometimes gave up before getting the support they needed to complete their work. As her fourth graders worked on a language arts quiz, Ms. Nelson sat at her desk, typing rapidly on her computer. The room was quiet except for the whir of the air vents and the rustling of papers. During the quiz, Phillip, Christian, Anna, and Maureen (all middle-class, white) and Zara, Kal, Alan, and Mason (all middle-class, Asian American) got up, sometimes repeatedly, with questions. They asked Ms. Nelson to clarify the directions, to check their work, or to tell them what to do when they were done. Meanwhile, Haley (working-class, white) was also struggling with the quiz:

> Haley is glaring at her quiz, eyes narrowed, lips pressed together. In the past three minutes, she has not written anything on her paper. Haley watches Anna trot back to her seat after asking Ms. Nelson a question. Haley then raises her hand slowly. Haley is sitting near the back left corner of the room, out of Ms. Nelson's eye line. Haley continues to wait with her hand raised, but Ms. Nelson does not appear to notice—she is busy answering Maureen's question about whether or not to include page number references in the essay portion of the quiz. Haley lets her raised hand flop down so that her arm is resting on her head. After another minute, Haley puts her hand down. Haley sighs quietly and then moves on, skipping over the question she was working on and never getting help from Ms. Nelson. Five minutes later, when all of the other students have finished and turned in their quizzes, Haley is still frowning at the paper in front of her.

Like Haley, working-class students were willing to wait a long time for help. When their polite attempts failed, however, they rarely tried alternative strategies (e.g., getting up) to get the teacher's attention. Instead, they often accepted defeat—even if it meant a lower grade.

SUMMARY AND CONCLUSIONS

In the classroom, students confronted a variety of challenges. They misplaced their notebooks and their lunch bags. They broke pencils, staplers, and backpack straps. They had arguments with classmates and friends. They struggled to understand concepts and directions and questions on homework and exams. These problems—some mundane, some serious—were an everyday occurrence at Maplewood. However, as this chapter has shown, middle-class and working-class students responded to such challenges in contrasting ways.

When confronted with classroom challenges, students used the class-based strategies of influence and deference they learned at home. Middle-class students treated help from teachers as a first line of defense and were very proactive and persistent in making requests. Working-class students, by contrast, typically tried first to deal with problems on their own, or if they did seek help, they did so patiently and politely and only when it was clear that their requests were welcome.

Those patterns of assistance-seeking had real consequences. Middle-class students were generally successful in asking for help, and the support they received generated meaningful advantages. They overcame their problems quickly and easily (or even preemptively avoided them), and they were often able to complete their work more accurately and without unnecessary delays. Working-class students were sometimes successful in overcoming problems on their own, and they sometimes avoided reprimand for not seeking help. Compared to their middle-class peers, however, working-class students spent considerably more time struggling and confused. In some cases, not asking for help even led working-class students to submit work that was incorrect or incomplete.

These findings suggest that assistance-seeking benefitted students in two different ways. The first way was consistent with prior research on cultural capital and the hidden curriculum (Bernstein 1990; Bourdieu 1996; Halstead and Xiao 2010; Lareau and Weininger 2003). In those cases, help-seeking generated advantages through its alignment with teachers' expectations for appropriate classroom behavior (at least in that particular moment). Middle-class students learned strategies of influence at home and thus had an easier time voicing their needs, particularly when teachers' willingness to grant requests was not explicit. Working-class students did sometimes ask for help, but their lack of familiarity with strategies of influence made them less inclined to use those strategies and less confident in doing so. Thus, although requests from both middle-class and working-class students were generally successful, middle-class students still received the bulk of the benefits associated with assistance-seeking in school.

The second way that help-seeking generated benefits was less consistent with existing theories. In those situations, middle-class students secured advantages by requesting assistance in excess of what was fair or required (e.g., asking teachers to check their tests) and making requests in ways inconsistent with teachers' expectations (e.g., calling out; not backing down). Given those additional benefits that middle-class students were able to secure, we might conclude that the middle-class advantage is, at least in part, a negotiated advantage—one that results from efforts to pressure institutions to grant requests for support, even when that support exceeds what is fair or required.

This idea of negotiated advantage has important implications not only for classroom inequalities but also for research on children's agency and teachers' authority. With respect to children's agency, and building on the contributions of childhood scholars (Adler and Adler 1998; Corsaro 2005;

Eder 1995; Thorne 1993), these findings also show how children's actions and interactions can contribute to inequalities in school. Research tends to focus on parents and schools as the primary drivers of inequality. From that perspective, middle-class children do better in school because they have access to more material resources and higher-quality schools (Hedges and Rowley 1994; Lareau 2000, 2011; Lee and Burkam 2002) and because they are generally placed in higher tracks and ability groups, where they receive higher-quality instruction (Eder 1981; Gamoran 1992; Oakes 2005; Rist 1970). As demonstrated here, however, children were not merely the passive recipients of unequal opportunities. Rather, children's actions—in conjunction with those of parents and teachers—helped perpetuate inequalities in school. These findings indicate that children's agency is more nuanced and more consequential than sociologists of child-hood have previously suggested. Whereas research on young children has provided evidence of their agency in interactions with peers and parents (Chin and Phillips 2004; Corsaro 2005; Eder 1995; Pugh 2009; Thorne 1993; Valentine 1997; Zelizer 2002), evidence of agency in interactions with teachers and other institutional authorities has typically stemmed from work on adolescents (Diehl and McFarland 2012; Hemmings 2003; McFarland 2001; Metz 1978; Pace 2003). As shown at Maplewood, how-ever, even young children could shape their own opportunities and experi-ences in school.

It is important to note that children's requests for assistance did not pro-duce advantages on their own. Rather, the benefits of help-seeking hinged on teachers' willingness to grant students' requests. Such findings are important both in highlighting the limits of children's agency and in their implications for research on noncognitive skills. Although there is consid-erable debate about which behaviors and traits "count" as noncognitive skills (Farkas 2003), scholars of noncognitive skills agree that success in school is not just a function of cognitive ability. Rather, behavioral traits and competencies—such as effort, motivation, help-seeking, and organiza-tional skills—are closely correlated with student outcomes (Carneiro and Heckman 2003; Farkas 2003; Heckman and Rubinstein 2001) and have long-lasting effects (Heckman, Stixrud, and Urzua 2006).[9] Given those findings, scholars typically treat noncognitive skills as inherently benefi-cial for learning. In light of the findings in this chapter, however, it seems that those benefits may be less inherent than scholars imply (Farkas 2003; Heckman and Rubinstein 2001; Tough 2012). Instead, those benefits were determined by teachers, who had the authority to grant or deny students' requests.

Simultaneously, however, these findings also show that student resistance can challenge teacher authority (Diehl and McFarland 2012; Hemmings

2003; Metz 1978; Pace 2003) and that such resistance is not reserved for the working class (McFarland 2001). Compliance and resistance are often viewed as competing behaviors with very different consequences for student outcomes (Bettie 2014; Fordham and Ogbu 1986; MacLeod 1995; Willis 1977). From that perspective, middle-class students comply with teachers' expectations and reap academic benefits for doing so. Working-class students, on the other hand, are thought to resist teachers' authority (and teachers' definitions of success) as a way to affirm their own social worth in the face of possible academic failure, but they ultimately undermine their academic success in doing so. At Maplewood, however, it was not—or at least not just—the working-class students who resisted teachers' authority. As noted in Chapter 1, working-class students did adopt alternative (character-based) definitions of success,[10] but they also worked hard to comply with what they thought teachers wanted. They tried to do well in school; avoid reprimand; and be viewed by their teachers as respectful, responsible, and hard-working. Those patterns may have changed by the time students got to high school (a point to which I return in Chapter 7), but they complicate the assumption that overt resistance to authority is synonymous with working-class culture. Those assumptions are also further complicated by the fact that resistance extended to the middle class as well. Certainly, and discussed in Chapter 1, the middle-class students accepted teachers' academic definitions of success. As demonstrated in this chapter, however, middle-class students were also willing to challenge teachers' authority to achieve those goals. Specifically, middle-class students secured assistance not just by complying with teachers' expectations for help-seeking but also by going outside of those expectations (i.e., by calling out, interrupting, or asking repeated follow-up questions) to get the support they desired. Those efforts often involved a subtle resistance to the teacher's authority—a willingness to push for "yes" even when teachers were clearly frustrated and wanted to say "no."

The purpose of this chapter is not to explain why middle-class students sought assistance from teachers when working-class students did not. However, the findings do raise questions about one standard explanation for differences in help-seeking. Specifically, they reveal that help-seeking cannot just be a function of students' goal orientations, as some scholars have suggested (Butler 1998; Karabenick 1998; Newman 2000; Newman and Goldin 1990). Dweck (1986) argues that help-seeking should come more naturally to mastery-focused students, who care more about learning than about looking smart. That mastery focus, however, is inconsistent with the emphasis on grades and competition that Nelson (2010) finds to be common among middle-class students. Thus, although differences in students' goal orientations might explain variations in help-seeking within social class groups, they seem largely incapable of explaining differences between middle-class and working-class students. Instead, it seems that class differences in student help-seeking reflect the lessons children learned at home—the kinds of lessons discussed in Chapter 1.

Overall, this chapter used evidence of social class differences in assistance-seeking to argue that the middle-class advantage is, in part, a negotiated advantage. Middle-class students secured more assistance from teachers not just by complying with teachers' expectations but also by challenging teachers' authority and pressuring them to provide assistance in excess of what was fair or required. Chapter 4 further explores how resistance to teacher authority allowed middle-class students to secure negotiated advantages in school. Specifically, I examine social class differences in children's efforts to change or exempt themselves from classroom rules and consequences. I also show how teachers responded to students' accommodation-seeking strategies and how those responses stratified students' experiences in school.

CHAPTER 4

Seeking Accommodations

One mid-March afternoon, I was outside with the students at recess. The air was chilly, but the sun was warm, with temperatures in the high 50s. After 5 minutes of running and playing, many of the students were sweating, and they began stripping off their coats and leaving them in piles. There were coats by the swings, by the monkey bars, by the basketball courts, on the blacktop, and by the slide. Seeing this, the playground aides sprang into action, circling around and sternly instructing the students to put on their coats.

The problem was that students were no longer allowed to take off their coats at recess. The winter had been a fairly warm one, and at almost every recess, coats got left behind on the playground and ended up in the lost-and-found. When parents started to call and complain, Dr. Weiss, the principal, established a new playground rule: Students who brought coats to recess had to wear them until they went back inside.

Students, not surprisingly, did not like the new rule, and they would often complain to me and to their teachers about how it was "unfair." In some cases, they also opted to ignore the rule entirely. On that day in March, for example, Shannon, a tall working-class, white girl whose brown curls framed her round face, and Maria, a petite working-class Latina girl with a long ponytail, left their coats under the monkey bars where they were playing:

> Ms. Bennett, one of the playground aides, spots the coats and makes a beeline for the monkey bars. As she approaches, she calls out sternly: "Remember the rule! Coats have to stay on." Shannon and Maria both frown and exchange frustrated glances, but they say nothing. Instead, they just drop from the monkey bars, retrieve their coats, and put them back on.

Shannon and Maria seemed annoyed about having to wear their coats, but they did not push back. Rather, they opted for a cooler activity—sitting in the shade under the playground equipment—instead of going back to the monkey bars.

Shannon and Maria were not the only students who disregarded the new rule. On the other side of the playground, six middle-class girls were playing four-square. They had all removed their coats, leaving them in a pile on the blacktop:

> As Ms. Bennett approaches, she points at the pile of coats and shakes her head. She calls out brusquely: "Coats on, girls. You know the rule." Middle-class Joanna, who was busy pulling her thick blonde hair into a ponytail, groans loudly, saying: "But it's boiling out here!" Ms. Bennett gestures at the pile of coats: "Dr. Weiss doesn't want you doing this anymore. Too many coats are ending up in the lost-and-found." Joanna, however, does not budge. Instead, she continues to protest, asking: "But it's so hot today. Can't you just go and ask Dr. Weiss?" Ms. Bennett laughs and shakes her head, repeating: "Coats on." The girls comply, but they take their coats off again as soon as Ms. Bennett continues on.

When Ms. Bennett circled past again, she saw that the pile of coats had reappeared on the ground:

> Ms. Bennett calls out loudly: "Girls! What'd I say before?" Anna, a middle-class girl wearing nylon track pants and a basketball sweatshirt, immediately turns toward Ms. Bennett, red four-square ball in hand, and moans: "Please? There's only five minutes left." The other girls then chimed in as a chorus, saying: "Yeah!" and "Please?" Ms. Bennett glances at her watch. Then she sighs, gesturing at the pile of coats and conceding: "Fine, but I better not find these here after you go inside." The girls all nod their heads vigorously and promise not to forget their coats.

With their coats still in a pile on the blacktop, the girls turned back to their four-square game. When the whistle blew, they grabbed their coats and lined up to head back inside.

Like Joanna and Anna, Shannon and Maria could have pushed back. Had they done so, Shannon and Maria might also have succeeded in convincing Ms. Bennett to let them leave their coats on the ground. However, because they did not challenge the rule, Shannon and Maria had to wear their coats—despite being too hot—and they even had to switch activities to make wearing coats more manageable.

These contrasting responses to Ms. Bennett and the new playground rule were not coincidental. Rather, they were part of a larger pattern of

class differences in accommodation-seeking—students' efforts to negotiate changes to or exemptions from rules, expectations, and consequences.

OVERVIEW

As with the playground coat rule, the expectations at school often conflicted
with students' individual needs or desires. Rules limited their creativity—
for example, by requiring students to follow a standard template when
doing a project, even when they had a more creative idea. Rules also limited
comfort—for example, by requiring students to wear their coats at recess,
even when they were hot and sweaty from running. In some cases, rules
also limited learning and achievement—for example, by requiring students
to stay in their seats, even if they were unable to see the chalkboard.

In this chapter, I explore how students dealt with those kinds of limitations. I ask: Did they accept the rules and their consequences? Did they just
ignore them and do what they wanted? Or did they try to negotiate with
teachers instead? I also describe how those efforts varied along social class
lines and how they generated stratified profits.

Through my observations, I found that middle-class and working-class
children dealt with rules and expectations in contrasting ways. Drawing
on lessons about deference, working-class children such as Shannon and
Maria treated rules as fixed. They almost never tried to negotiate changes
to or exemptions from standard protocols. Rather, they accepted rules and
expectations as fixed and adjusted their behavior accordingly. Furthermore,
when working-class students were caught skirting rules, they rarely offered
excuses; instead, they accepted punishment without complaint. Drawing
on lessons about influence, middle-class children such as Joanna and Anna
instead treated rules as flexible. They tried to negotiate with teachers, asking
for changes to rules and procedures or personalized exemptions from them.
Although middle-class children sometimes broke the rules (often after having their initial requests denied), those who were caught typically offered
impassioned excuses for their actions.

As I show in this chapter, class-based differences in accommodation-
seeking had real consequences. Middle-class students were often successful in convincing teachers to grant them the accommodations they desired.
Those accommodations also produced a variety of benefits, including more
opportunities for creativity, more comfort and convenience, and the chance
to avoid punishment for misbehavior. Working-class students, on the other
hand, did not enjoy this same level of customization in their school experiences. They generally accepted rules and punishments set for them, even

when doing so limited their creativity or their comfort and even when it resulted in reprimand.

ACCOMMODATION-SEEKING IN CONTEXT

Research on accommodation-seeking has focused on students with disabilities and the accommodations legally guaranteed to them through their Individualized Education Plans (IEPs) (Barnard-Brak, Lechtenberger, and Yan 2010; Hart and Brehm 2013; Smith, English, and Vasek 2002). Studies have shown, for example, that when students with disabilities learn to advocate for themselves and actively request accommodations, they do better in school (Gilberts et al. 2001). Accommodation-seeking, however, can also be defined more broadly. Specifically, we might think of how all students, regardless of disability status, negotiate changes to or exemptions from rules, expectations, and consequences.

Using that broader conceptualization, we can draw on existing research to see how accommodation-seeking might differ along social class lines and how it might contribute to inequalities. It is known, for example, that middle-class parents are more involved in their children's schooling (Domina 2005; Lareau 2000; Lee and Bowen 2006; Robinson and Harris 2014). It is also known that middle-class involvement goes beyond just volunteering in classrooms and reading to children at home. Middle-class parents also intervene at school—even challenging educators and their judgments—to ensure their children's well-being (Brantlinger 2003; Horvat, Weininger, and Lareau 2003; Lareau 2000; Lareau and Horvat 1999; Nelson 2010; Reay 1998). Those interventions have real consequences. Middle-class parents, for example, are often successful in lobbying to have their children placed in gifted programs or advanced tracks, even when their children do not technically qualify (Baker and Stevenson 1986; Lewis and Diamond 2015; Useem 1992).

Such interventions have been widely documented, and they provide important evidence of social class differences in the relationship between families and schools. However, existing research on social class and accommodation-seeking is also limited in important ways.

The focus on parental interventions, for example, has limited attention to children's own accommodation-seeking efforts. Numerous scholars have described parents' (especially middle-class parents') efforts to advocate on their children's behalf, seeking recourse for improper treatment from teachers, testing for special programs, admission to college preparatory tracks, and even interviews for jobs (Brantlinger 2003; Hardie 2015; Horvat et al.

2003; Lareau and Horvat 1999; Nelson 2010; Reay 1998; Useem 1992). Those studies, however, do not describe whether parents coach their children to be their own advocates, whether children activate what they have learned, or whether that activation generates advantages. As a result, relatively little is known about whether children try to change or exempt themselves from classroom rules and expectations. Nor is it known how those efforts vary along social class lines.

Accommodation-seeking, whether by parents or by children, has also been undertheorized. Teachers value and encourage "parental involvement" in schooling (Epstein 1986; Hoover-Dempsey and Sandler 1995; Lareau 2000; Robinson and Harris 2014). Given those findings, the benefits of parental involvement are generally treated as the result of a cultural matching process—one in which middle-class parents (and their children) are rewarded for complying with the expectations of the school (Lareau 2000; Lareau and Calarco 2012; Lareau and Weininger 2003; Reay 1998). Parental interventions are included under that larger umbrella of involvement (Baker and Stevenson 1986; Lareau 2000; Robinson and Harris 2014; Sui-Chu and Willms 1996; Useem 1992), but there is reason to suspect that they might operate differently from other parenting behaviors. Studies suggest, for example, that educators are often frustrated by parents' efforts to challenge them and their judgments. In those moments, teachers sometimes reject parents' requests (Lareau and Horvat 1999),[1] but there are also times when teachers give in (Lewis and Diamond 2015). Such findings indicate that compliance with expectations might not be the only way that middle-class families gain advantages in school. Despite those possibilities, however, there have been few efforts to interrogate whether such interventions operate as a form of cultural capital or whether they generate benefits in a different way.

Building on the arguments from previous chapters, I contend here that explaining the benefits of middle-class accommodation-seeking requires a more nuanced view of class and culture than research typically provides. The advantages of accommodation-seeking are not simply the result of compliance and cultural matching. Rather, those advantages are negotiated advantages—they derive from efforts to challenge teacher authority and to request resources and support in excess of what teachers expect (or even are willing) to provide. This means that following rules and meeting expectations may not be the only path to success in school. As this chapter demonstrates, students can also gain advantages by *not* following the rules or, more accurately, by negotiating changes to and exemptions from rules, expectations, and consequences. In summary, this chapter shows that middle-class strategies of influence generated advantages not only through their compliance with institutional expectations but also because they allowed students to negotiate those expectations to better meet *their* individual needs.

DEALING WITH RULE CONFLICTS

Problematic rules and procedures prompted different responses from students depending on their social class backgrounds. Drawing on the strategies of deference they learned at home, working-class students treated teachers' rules and expectations as fixed. Middle-class students drew instead on the strategies of influence and, in doing so, treated rules and expectations as flexible.

Rule Exemptions

Class-based approaches to accommodation-seeking could be seen, in part, in the extent to which students tried to exempt themselves from classroom rules. Those differences were particularly apparent one morning in Mr. Fischer's class. Like most teachers, Mr. Fischer expected his fifth graders to stay at their desks during teacher-led instruction. Mr. Fischer also regularly rearranged his classroom, trying out new desk configurations each month. On the first day of a new seating arrangement, Mr. Fischer announced that the class would be starting a new social studies project. While the students sat in their seats, Mr. Fischer used the digital Smart Board at the front of the room to project the instructions for the project:

> Almost immediately, Ted (middle-class, white) calls out loudly from the back of the room. As Mr. Fischer looks up, Ted explains: "My mom thinks I might need glasses. Can I move up to the rug so I can see?" Mr. Fischer nods and gives Ted a "come here" gesture, saying "Sure, that's fine." Ted grabs his social studies notebook and scampers up to the front of the room, settling on the rug a few feet from Mr. Fischer.

Meanwhile, Zach, a working-class student, was also struggling to see the instructions. Zach's desk was located at the very front of the room, perpendicular to the front wall (Figure 4.1). Zach had been having issues staying on task—frequently getting up to use the bathroom or sharpen his pencil or get a drink during class time (which students were permitted to do without asking)[2]—and Mr. Fischer wanted him up front so that he could "keep an

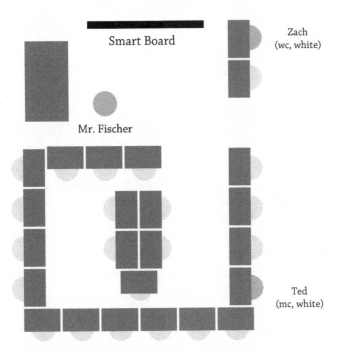

Figure 4.1 Mr. Fischer's classroom. mc, middle-class; wc, working-class.

eye" on him. Because of the placement of Zach's desk, however, he seemed to be having difficulty seeing the Smart Board:

> As Mr. Fischer talks with Ted, Zach leans to his left, craning his neck and trying to get a better view of the Smart Board. Zach then turns to watch Ted move toward the front of the room. As Ted finds a seat on the rug, Zach starts to get up from his own chair. Sensing this movement, Mr. Fischer turns abruptly toward Zach, saying gruffly: "Sit down. Now is not the time to use the bathroom or sharpen your pencil."

Given his gruff response to Zach's movement, Mr. Fischer did not appear to recognize that Zach was struggling to see the board. Instead, and likely in light of ongoing concerns about Zach's behavior, Mr. Fischer assumed that Zach was distracted or off task. Zach could have tried to correct that misperception, but he was reluctant to do so, possibly out of concern that such pushback would further frustrate Mr. Fischer:

> Zach sits back down silently, his eyes fixed on the desk in front of him. As Mr. Fischer continues reviewing the directions, Zach leans over to his left again. After leaning like this for about a minute, Zach gives up. He sits back in his seat, sliding down so that his shoulders are almost level with the top of his desk. In that position, it seems unlikely that Zach can see the Smart Board at all. Sitting low in his chair, Zach reaches both hands into

his desk and peers down to look inside. He finds a pink eraser and starts using his pencil to carve designs into the rubber.

As this example shows, a rule such as "stay in your seat" could be problematic if it meant that students could not see the board. In those situations, middle-class students regularly sought exemptions from rules, whereas working-class students rarely did the same. Like Ted, Zach could have asked to move or explained that he was having trouble seeing the board. However, because Zach tried to deal with the situation on his own, Mr. Fischer did not see that Zach was struggling and even reprimanded Zach for getting up.

Like Ted, middle-class students treated rules as flexible, and they often sought exemptions from them. In Ms. Hudson's class, for example, students who wanted to use the bathroom had to take a wooden pass from a hook by the door and place it on their desk (so that Ms. Hudson would know who was out). If one student was using the pass, no one else could use the bathroom until that student returned:

> Sidney (working-class, white) is supposed to be working on a practice test. Instead, she is using her pencil eraser to push the paper around her desk. Looking up distractedly, Sidney spots the bathroom pass—a long thin painted piece of balsa wood— hanging by the door. Sidney's eyes light up and she immediately darts across the room. She snatches up the pass, scampers back to drop it on her desk, and then dashes out the door.

Meanwhile, Gina (middle-class, white) was sitting on the rug near the blackboard. Ms. Hudson made her move up after repeatedly telling her to stop talking during the practice test. Gina agreed, but she asked Ms. Hudson for a clipboard so that she would not have to "write on the floor":

> After Sidney leaves, Gina stands up and moves toward the door. Getting closer, Gina sees that the pass is missing. Stopping in her tracks, Gina turns and looks for the pass, spotting it on Sidney's desk. Gina goes back to work on her practice test, but she keeps glancing up at the door, as if waiting anxiously for Sidney to return. About a minute later, Gina starts to bounce up and down, fixing her eyes on the door. After another minute, Gina looks up at the clock, lets out huffy breath, and drops her test and clipboard on the rug. Gina gets up and marches toward Ms. Hudson's desk. As Ms. Hudson looks up, Gina immediately begins to lament about how Sidney has been in the bathroom for "more than seven minutes" and how Gina "really" has to "go." Pausing, Gina asks hopefully: "So is it okay if I just go?" Ms. Hudson nods and waves her hand toward the door, saying: "Yeah, sure. Go ahead." Gina grins broadly and chirps: "Okay! Thanks!" She then whips around and makes a beeline for the classroom door.

Like Gina, middle-class students often searched for loopholes and wiggle room. With ease and confidence, they negotiated exemptions from bathroom policies, seating arrangements, snack rules, and assignment deadlines. Sometimes it seemed as though the requests were never-ending.

Working-class students, by contrast, treated rules as fixed. They almost never asked for extensions on assignments, more time on tests, or permission to call a parent if they left a project at home. They accepted when teachers told them to do a project in a certain way or bring in certain types of snacks. During flex time in Mr. Potter's class, for example, the fifth graders were working on their monthly book reports. Mr. Potter gave them an "options menu" with choices such as "make a diorama of a key event" and "make a mobile with pictures and descriptions of characters." Before getting started, the students had to "clear" their choice with Mr. Potter:

> Lucy (working-class, white) gets up from her seat, taking her bright pink options menu with her as she shuffles slowly to the front of the room. As Mr. Potter talks with another student, Lucy waits patiently, re-reading the options menu.

When Mr. Potter finished talking with the other student, he turned his attention to Lucy:

> Mr. Potter looks up at Lucy, asking pleasantly: "What's up?" Lucy takes a step forward, holds out her options menu, points, and asks hesitantly, as if expecting disappointment: "Can I do the 'paint a mural' one?" Lucy looks up at Mr. Potter and adds quickly: "If not, that's okay." Mr. Potter purses up his lips and pauses for what feels like a long moment. Then he looks Lucy in the eye, explaining firmly but apologetically that a mural generally requires "a really big space, like a whole wall." Saying this, he stretches out both arms wide to his sides, as if to indicate a very large area. Mr. Potter then points at another option on the sheet, explaining with forced cheer: "You could do a poster instead!" Lucy nods and shrugs: "Okay." Mr. Potter gives Lucy a reassuring smile and directs her to the poster paper in the supply cabinet.

Lucy could have protested that because "paint a mural" was included on the options menu, it was unfair of Mr. Potter to deny her request. Instead, Lucy simply accepted that a mural was not an option. Furthermore, although Lucy could have pushed back when Mr. Potter suggested the poster, she just accepted his choice instead. That deference, coupled with the fact that working-class students rarely asked for accommodations in the first place, helped ensure that working-class students did not receive the kinds of individualized accommodations that middle-class students were often able to negotiate for themselves.

Rule Changes

Social class differences in accommodation-seeking could also be seen in middle-class and working-class students' willingness to challenge teachers' rules and expectations. Middle-class students, for example, regularly lobbied for changes to classroom protocols, as can be seen in an example from Mr. Potter's class. Like most teachers, Mr. Potter expected his fifth graders to study for tests and memorize the relevant material. Using "cheat sheets" was not standard practice. One morning in math class, Mr. Potter told his students to clear their desks for a geometry test:

> As one student passes out the math tests, Mr. Potter starts to take down two posters hanging from the cabinets at the back of the room. The posters display formulas students will use on the geometry test (e.g., calculating the surface area of a cylinder). Seeing Mr. Potter remove the posters, Mandy (middle-class, white) calls out breathlessly: "Can you leave them up this time?" Jason and Joanna (middle-class, white) also call out, saying "Please! Please!" and "Leave them up!" As Mandy, Jason, Joanna, and other middle-class students continue their chorus of requests, Mr. Potter throws up his hands, saying: "Okay, I'll leave 'em up, but I better not see any careless mistakes."

Like Mandy, Jason, and Joanna, middle-class students requested changes to classroom rules and expectations, and even changes to standard testing procedures. Furthermore, as demonstrated here, middle-class students were often successful in securing the accommodations they desired.

Middle-class students' willingness to challenge teachers' rules and expectations could also be seen in the persistence they exhibited when teachers tried to deny their requests for accommodations. In fifth grade, the students were learning about the Progressive Era. While discussing the newsboy strikes of the 20th century, Diana (middle-class, Asian American) called out, "Can we watch *Newsies*?" (a Disney movie about the topic):

> Ms. Dunham shakes her head, saying "I wish we could." She then reminds the kids of the principal's policy banning the screening of "full-length movies" in class. Hearing this, Mandy (middle-class, white) sits up tall in her seat. She grins broadly, almost mischievously, and calls out playfully: "If you show everything but the last five minutes, it's not the full movie, so it's okay!" Ms. Dunham hears this and chuckles, smiling at Mandy as she replies: "You should be a lawyer." Mandy beams proudly. A few of the other middle-class students then start to call out that they could even watch everything but the last minute, or even the last five seconds of the movie, and that would be okay. Ms. Dunham smiles and holds up her hands, saying warmly: "Very clever. All right now, get to work."

Ms. Dunham ultimately denied the students' requests to watch *Newsies*. That rejection, however, left middle-class students undeterred. They almost seemed to enjoy the "game" of negotiations, taking pride in their ability to find new and "clever" ways to challenge the rules.

Working-class students, on the other hand, almost never tried to challenge teachers' rules and expectations. Furthermore, in the rare cases in which working-class students did ask for changes, they did not push back if teachers denied their requests. Mr. Potter passed out a math worksheet, which instructed the students to "use a protractor" to draw triangles with specific angles. After two middle-class students had called out with clarifying questions about the assignment, Jared, a high-achieving working-class student, raised his hand:

> Mr. Potter gives Jared a "go ahead" nod. Jared cocks his head to the side and asks hopefully: "Do we *have* to use a protractor to make the angles?" Mr. Potter smiles playfully and replies: "Well, angles have straight lines, and your 'straight' lines"—he makes air quotes with his fingers—"tend to look like this." He traces his finger in a wave-like pattern in the air. "So, use a protractor," Mr. Potter continues. Jared nods understandingly.

Requests for rule changes were extremely rare among working-class students. Jared, as explained in Chapter 1, was a high-achieving working-class student with upwardly mobile parents and many middle-class friends. Because of that liminal class position, Jared seemed more comfortable than other working-class students with making special requests from his teachers. However, even when Jared tried to change the rules (by asking to draw the angles by hand rather than using a protractor, as stated in the assignment), he quickly backed down when the teacher said "no."

Rule Consequences

Despite opportunities for negotiation, rule-breaking was not uncommon at Maplewood Elementary. Students forgot their homework. They talked when they were supposed to be quiet. They ran in the hallways. They got distracted and fell off task.

Those minor infractions were normal for both middle-class and working-class students. If anything, it seemed that middle-class students misbehaved more often and more overtly than did working-class students. Middle-class students, for example, would sometimes persist in off-limits behaviors even after hearing "no," whereas working-class students almost never did the same. Furthermore, although it was rare to see blatant disrespect for teachers or peers, when those incidents did occur, middle-class students were almost always the ringleaders. A number of the middle-class boys, for example, would often show off for each other by "messing with" their teachers (especially substitutes and playground aides) and classmates. During art class, the students were working on self-portraits:

> Ethan (middle-class, white) finishes his portrait and carries it up to the "inbox." Before dropping it in, Ethan looks down at Joanna's (middle-class, white) portrait atop the pile. Acting fast, Ethan snatches up Joanna's portrait, covers it with his own, and carries them both surreptitiously back to his seat. Ethan then reveals the smuggled portrait to his friends, Brian (middle-class, mixed-race) and Ted (middle-class, white), who watch, sti-fling giggles, as Ethan uses a red colored pencil to draw devil horns on Joanna's portrait. Meanwhile, Zach (working-class, white) looks on in horror, his mouth hanging open as he glances back and forth between the picture and the teacher across the room. Before Zach can say anything, Ethan slips Joanna's portrait back under his own, carries them back to in the inbox, and mixes them into the pile.

Although Zach initially looked like he might say something to the art teacher, he never turned Ethan in, and Ethan was never caught. Working-class students such as Zach were not immune from misbehavior—as noted previously, Zach regularly got "in trouble" for falling off task. However, they rarely exhibited the kind of meanness I sometimes saw among their middle-class peers.

Although the frequency of infractions seemed relatively similar across classes, there were stark differences in how students reacted when they got caught. In those situations, middle-class students often tried to negotiate their way out of punishment. Working-class students, on the other hand, generally suffered their punishment without complaint. After the bell one morning, Mr. Cherlin asked his fourth graders to take out their homework. He then circled around, using a clipboard to mark who had completed the homework:

> Lucy (working-class, white) does not have anything on her desk. Seeing this, Mr. Cherlin asks: "Lucy, do you have your homework?" Lucy shakes her head, not look-ing Mr. Cherlin in the eye. Mr. Cherlin sighs and explains matter-of-factly: "You'll be coming in for recess today since you forgot." Lucy says nothing, just looking down at her desk.

Mr. Cherlin then continued around the room, stopping next to Sarah (middle-class, white), who also did not have her homework out:

> Before Mr. Cherlin can say anything, Sarah looks up anxiously and immediately launches into an explanation, telling Mr. Cherlin that she couldn't do her home-work because she couldn't find her journal. Mr. Cherlin chides Sarah, saying that

she should have written her journal entry on a piece of paper instead and then put it in her journal when she found it. Sarah nods, then asks hopefully: "So do I have to stay in [for recess]?" Mr. Cherlin thinks about this for a moment and then shakes his head, saying that Sarah should just do the journal entry for homework tonight instead.

Both Sarah and Lucy came to school without their homework, but they dealt with the transgression in different ways. Like Lucy, Sarah could have accepted her punishment without complaint. Instead, and like other middle-class students in similar situations, Sarah offered an impassioned excuse. In doing so, Sarah avoided punishment for her actions. Unlike Sarah, Lucy did not offer an explanation for her forgotten homework. Like other working-class students, she seemed to accept that she had broken the rules and that she would have to deal with the consequences.

Even in the face of serious sanctions, working-class students rarely offered excuses to escape punishment. One afternoon, a substitute was watching Mr. Cherlin's class while he went to a meeting. The students were working on language arts packets, and the substitute was quickly getting frustrated with the noise level in the room:

Cody (working-class, mixed-race) leans across his desk, holds out his packet and whispers to Melanie (middle-class, white) who sits across from him. He points at the packet and asks Melanie for help clarifying one of the questions. Before Melanie can answer, the sub spots Cody talking. Wagging her finger at Cody, the sub asks challengingly: "Are you on task?" Cody looks up, startled. The sub shakes her head and huffs: "I'm gonna leave your teacher a note that you're not working." Cody gasps: "Wha…?" The sub turns on her heel and heads to Mr. Cherlin's desk, where she leans down to write a note in the plan book. Meanwhile, Cody looks like he might cry—he is slumped over his desk, head down, blinking back tears.

Despite the substitute's response, a number of middle-class students were still talking loudly. Glancing up from the plan book, the sub noticed two boys carrying on at the back of the room:

Will and Hunter (both middle-class, white) are talking and laughing loudly. Marching toward them, the sub bellows: "You should be working independently!" Will immediately protests: "But Mr. Cherlin said we could work with a partner!" The sub sputters, surprised, asking: "He did? Oh, uh, okay. Well, then, keep it quiet. No talking." Will and Hunter look at each other and roll their eyes. As the sub moves on, they continue talking again.

Mr. Cherlin initially told the students that they had to work "independently" on the packets—and that is what he wrote in the plans for the substitute. Right before the meeting, however, Joanna and Jamie (both middle-class, white) persuaded Mr. Cherlin to let them work with a partner instead. Will and Hunter, like other middle-class students, were quick to defend themselves by pointing out the change. Cody, meanwhile, did not try to use that change in rules as an excuse for his actions. He just accepted his punishment.

GENERATING STRATIFIED PROFITS

Class-based accommodation-seeking strategies had real consequences in the classroom. Middle-class students requested changes to and exemptions from rules, procedures, and expectations, and they persisted in those requests, rarely taking "no" for an answer. In doing so, middle-class students pressed teachers to grant them more opportunities for expressing creativity, more comfort and convenience, and a better chance at reprieve for misbehavior. By not seeking accommodations, or at least by backing down quickly when teachers said "no," working-class students were sometimes successful in avoiding reprimand. More often, however, working-class students' deference to teachers' rules and expectations left them with fewer opportunities for expressing creativity, less comfort and convenience, and more punishment for misbehavior.

Middle-Class Students Reaping Rewards

During my observations, it seemed that middle-class students were constantly asking for things—and they often received the accommodations they sought. They got extra time to study for their quizzes or complete their assignments. They got to choose topics for their projects that were not on the list of options provided. They got to use class time to work on their homework. They got to work with partners instead of by themselves. They got to sit on the floor or work outside instead of at their desks. They even got extra marshmallows for their hot chocolate. Although some of those accommodations might seem trivial, on the whole, the benefits were not.

One benefit was the creativity middle-class students were afforded in completing their assignments. In art class, Ms. Cantore announced that they would be making clay "pinch pots" and that they would each need to bring in a "Tupperware"-like container to use as a mold. Ms. Cantore spent almost 10 minutes explaining the directions for the project, and she was very explicit about the size and type of container the students would need.

Finally, Ms. Cantore paused, took a breath, and asked the students if they had any questions:

> Nate (middle-class, white) immediately thrusts his hand into the air, spinning sideways in his seat to look up at Ms. Cantore. She takes a step toward him and gives him a "go ahead" nod. Nate looks Ms. Cantore square in the eye, gives her a mischievous smirk, and asks: "What if we forget?" Ms. Cantore shrugs her shoulders and cautions him sharply: "Then you'll have to make it without one."

Ms. Cantore seemed to be trying to emphasize to the students the importance of bringing in a container. Her caution, however, prompted many of the middle-class students to begin thinking of alternative ways to complete the project:

> Hearing that it would be possible to make the pinch pot without a container, Brian (middle-class, mixed-race) calls out, smiling slyly: "What if we don't *wanna* use a container?" Ms. Cantore shakes her head and explains that if they don't use a container their pots will "look different" from everyone else's, because they won't be able to use the coil method that she showed them with the sample pot. Hearing that, Lindsey (middle-class, white) pipes up, saying: "But what if you want, like, a *different* shape. Like, something that they don't make a shape for in containers. Or something *different* different, like not a container or a pot or whatever?" Ms. Cantore sighs heavily. She stares at Lindsey for a long moment and then explains wearily: "The container *really* makes it easier. So you should bring one, just in case. I won't have extras to share." Lindsey just nods distractedly. She immediately turns and starts whispering to a friend about the "free-hand" pot she is planning to make.

Interestingly, whereas all of the working-class students brought in appropriate containers to use as molds, only half of the middle-class students did so—the others opted for free-hand instead. Like Lindsey, they wanted their projects to be unique, and they pressured teachers to grant them the creativity they desired.

The benefits of negotiating rules and consequences could also be seen in the comfort and convenience that middle-class students secured for themselves in school. During math class, Mr. Potter was reviewing a set of practice problems with his fifth graders:

> Finishing the last problem, Mr. Potter explains firmly: "If you're struggling with this at all, I want you to circle it and work on it during flex time and write out all of the work." Hearing this, Josh (middle-class, white) looks up anxiously and begins waving his hand in the air. Mr. Potter nods at Josh, and Josh asks hopefully: "I just made a small mistake. Do I still need to circle it?" Mr. Potter looks at Josh skeptically, raising one eyebrow. He

then explains slowly and dryly: "You need to practice these so you learn not to make the little mistakes." Josh lets his shoulders slump, pouting as he complains: "But I just copied the decimal point wrong!" Mr. Potter sighs and concedes in a tired voice: "Fine. I'll leave it up to you."

Like Josh, middle-class students used requests for accommodation to avoid discomfort and inconvenience. Mr. Potter wanted Josh to use his flex time to redo the problem, even if it was just to learn not to make small mistakes. When Josh persisted, however, Mr. Potter gave up, letting Josh decide for himself. By choosing not to redo the problem, Josh avoided the unpleasant task of correcting his work. Without any work to correct, Josh went straight to the computer station, meaning that he got to spend more class time playing games, as well.

In some circumstances, middle-class students even reaped academic benefits from their accommodation-seeking efforts. One Wednesday morning, the students were packing up their math materials and getting ready for lunch while Mr. Fischer wrote the night's homework on the board. One item read: "Reminder: March Book Report Due Friday (3/26)." The students had known about the book report for weeks, and they had a similar project every month. However, school had been closed Monday and Tuesday because of snow, so Mr. Fischer did not get to remind them about the project until Wednesday—2 days before it was due. As Mr. Fischer wrote the homework on the board, Colin (middle-class, white), Ethan (middle-class, white), Brian (middle-class, mixed-race), and Kal (middle-class, Asian American) stood together, debating in hushed voices. Then they dashed up to Mr. Fischer together, clustering around him and peppering him with questions and complaints:

Ethan's face is contorted into a pained expression. Stepping up to Mr. Fischer, he complains that it "doesn't seem fair" that they have to turn the book report in on Friday, because "March doesn't end for another week." Colin and Kal hear this and chime in, too, and the three of them all start to call out over each other, making various arguments about why the book report should be due after Spring Break (which lasts from March 26th through April 4th), instead of before.

Mr. Fischer was initially undeterred by the boys' complaints:

Mr. Fischer lets out a breathy, somewhat disparaging laugh. He turns around, a skeptical look on his face, noting somewhat critically: "You guys *really* should have it done by Friday. It *shouldn't* be that hard. It's just a list of fifteen to twenty fantasy events."

Eventually, however, and under continued pressure, Mr. Fischer conceded:

> The boys continue to whine and complain, following Mr. Fischer around the classroom
> as he packs up and prepares the classroom for the afternoon's activities. Finally, after
> dismissing the class for lunch, Mr. Fischer gives the boys his full attention. Sighing, he
> throw up his hands, saying: "All right, fine. You can turn it in after break if you need to."
> At this, Colin, Kal, Brian, and Ethan cheer and pump their fists in the air triumphantly.

Accommodation-seeking had real academic advantages. As demonstrated here, Colin, Kal, Brian, and Ethan persuaded Mr. Fischer to grant them an extension on the assignment. Furthermore, by the time the boys convinced Mr. Fischer, the other students had already left for lunch. As a result, Colin, Kal, Ethan, and Brian were the only students who knew about the extra time.

Accommodation-seeking also allowed middle-class students to avoid punishment for rule-breaking. Mr. Potter's class provides a useful example. The fifth graders were working on biography research projects, and they were supposed to bring all their materials (including library books, notecards, and Internet printouts) to and from school each day. Despite constant reminders from Mr. Potter, Michelle (middle-class, white) left her books at home:

> Michelle goes up to Mr. Potter's desk, waiting while he finishes answering Liam's ques-
> tion. As Liam (middle-class, white) heads back to his desk, Michelle shuffles forward
> nervously, explaining rapid-fire: "I left my book at home but I'm pretty much finished
> with it anyway." Gesturing over her shoulder with an outstretched thumb, Michelle
> adds: "Maybe I could go on the computer and do online research since that's what
> I would have to do next anyway?"

Mr. Potter looked at Michelle for a long moment before responding:

> Mr. Potter lets out a long breath and then asks disappointedly: "You forgot your book?
> Did you check your cubby and your backpack?" Michelle nods. She explains reassur-
> ingly that she knows she left it at home but that "it's okay" because she is "almost done
> with the book anyway." Michelle then asks again if she can go on the computer, using
> class time to gather Internet sources instead of taking notes from her book. Mr. Potter
> sighs softly. He half-heartedly reminds Michelle that if she does not have her book, that
> means that she is not prepared for class. Michelle starts to protest, but Mr. Potter cuts
> her off, conceding that he will work with her on the computer today, showing her how to
> find Internet sources, so that she will not waste class time. Michelle smiles broadly, look-
> ing relieved, and then trots off toward the computers with Mr. Potter trailing behind her.

Despite being unprepared for class, Michelle was not punished. She even managed to secure extra one-on-one help with her project. By offering justifications for their misbehavior, middle-class students such as Michelle were often successful in exempting themselves from normal consequences.

Working-Class Students Suffering Consequences

Working-class students rarely sought special favors. They accepted that tests had to be finished in 60 minutes and that projects had to be turned in on time and completed according to directions. They expected that teachers would make the rules and punish those who broke them.

One consequence of such deference was that working-class students had more limited opportunities to express their creativity in school. One afternoon, Ms. Nelson's fourth graders were painting mini pumpkins for Halloween. Ms. Nelson provided pumpkins, paint, and brushes. In addition to those basic supplies, many of the middle-class students brought in extra decorations—googly eyes, pipe cleaners for arms, felt to make hats and feet, and so on. Most of those students also kept their supplies for themselves or shared them only with close friends. As a result, all of the working-class students had pumpkins that—although still beautiful—were decorated only with paint, whereas many of the middle-class students had pumpkins that stood out much more prominently on display. Because they tried to stay within the parameters set for them, working-class students often did not get to express themselves as fully or creatively with their assignments. They may also have been perceived as less creative by their teachers or their peers, even if that was not actually the case.

Another consequence of deference to authority was that working-class students experienced fewer opportunities for comfort and convenience at school. By fourth grade, for example, teachers expected students to police themselves on bathroom rules. Students were typically allowed to get up and take the hall pass without explicitly asking for permission. However, most of the teachers did have rules about when students should use the bathroom. That usually included times when their absence would be both least consequential and least disruptive to other students—for example, between activities, during snack, on the way to lunch, and so on. Despite those instructions, middle-class students who needed to use the bathroom at less opportune times generally did so anyway and were rarely reprimanded. Working-class students, meanwhile, almost always waited for approved times, even if they became uncomfortable in the process. One afternoon in Ms. Burn's fourth-grade class, for example, I watched Jeremy (working-class, white) become increasingly fidgety as he waited for the break between social studies and flex time. He was watching the clock, tapping his pencil, and squirming in his seat. Finally, when Ms. Burns told the students to pack up their social studies books, Jeremy bolted out of his chair, grabbed the hall pass, and dashed out the door. I even heard one of the aides shout at him not to run in the hallways as he passed. If Jeremy had gone to the bathroom earlier, he would have missed some of the lesson. In waiting for the "right" time to go, however, Jeremy likely became so distracted that he missed much of the content anyway, and he may even have become a distraction to his peers. Thus, by trying hard to follow the rules, working-class students often found themselves in situations in which their comfort and convenience were compromised, sometimes even to the point of undermining their ability to learn.

By deferring to authority and not seeking accommodations, working-class students were also less inclined to avoid punishment for misbehavior. During a geology lesson, for example, Ms. Dunham had her fifth graders sit on the rug at the front of the room. However, because the rug was not very big, students who had desks near the front of the room (including working-class, white student Jesse) had to stay at their seats. Once all of the students were settled, Ms. Dunham took out a large case of rock samples. She presented them one at a time, asking students questions about the rocks and having them jot down notes in their "lab notebooks":

> Ms. Dunham pulls out the third sample and someone shouts out "That looks like a brownie!" The called-out response prompted a roar of laughter from the class and shouts of "Can I eat it?" and "I'm hungry!" The kids seem very excited about the activity, and many of them try to reach out and touch the samples as Ms. Dunham pulls them out of the case.

At first, Jesse was deeply engaged in the activity. Although the position of his chair made it difficult to see (Figure 4.2), Jesse twisted around in his seat and craned his neck to get a view of the rock samples. Over time, however, and because it was difficult to see, Jesse eventually fell off task, surreptitiously flipping through a comic book instead. Jesse had the comic book flat on his desk, partially covered with his lab notebook. He occasionally lifted the lab notebook to turn the page of the comic book underneath, and eventually Ms. Dunham caught him:

> Ms. Dunham notices Jesse turning pages and tilts her head to get a better view. Spotting the comic book, she says sharply: "Jesse! Eyes on me!" Jesse gasps and turns quickly toward Ms. Dunham. Ms. Dunham looks Jesse hard in the eye, saying firmly: "Put it on my desk." Jesse nods sheepishly and gets up from his seat. As the other students stare, Jesse hangs his head and trudges up to Ms. Dunham's desk. He sets the comic book

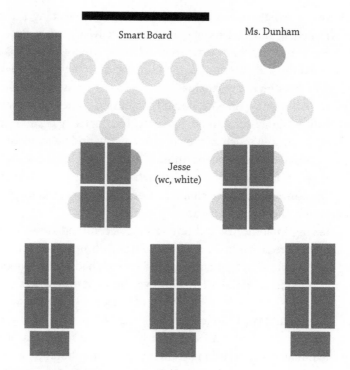

Smart Board

Ms. Dunham

Jesse
(wc, white)

Figure 4.2 Ms. Dunham's classroom. wc, working-class.

down lightly, then slinks back to his seat, where he sits down sideways so that he can see Ms. Dunham and the rock samples.

In similar situations, middle-class students were quick to let their teachers know if they were uncomfortable or unable to see clearly. Thus, when Ms. Dunham caught Jesse with the comic book, he could have explained that he was having trouble seeing the rocks. Instead, he just accepted his punishment, turning his comic book over to Ms. Dunham without complaint. By holding themselves accountable, and by accepting teachers' authority, working-class students such as Jesse faced more sanctions than did the middle-class students who talked their way out of punishment instead.

SUMMARY AND CONCLUSIONS

For the students at Maplewood, classroom rules, expectations, and procedures had a number of unintended consequences. Compliance with those standards often resulted in discomfort or disappointment and sometimes even stifled students' ability to succeed.

When confronted with problematic rules, expectations, and procedures, middle-class and working-class students used the strategies of influence and deference they learned at home. Middle-class students did not automatically comply with teachers' expectations. Instead, they treated expectations as flexible—challenging teachers' authority and requesting changes to or exemptions from classroom rules. Working-class students, by contrast, typically complied with teachers' expectations. They treated expectations as fixed—rarely challenging teachers' authority and rarely trying to change rules or seek exemptions from them.

Those patterns of accommodation-seeking had real consequences. Middle-class students were often (although not always) successful in challenging teachers' rules, expectations, and procedures, and those challenges generated a number of advantages. By requesting accommodations and by not taking "no" for an answer, middle-class students secured opportunities for creativity, comfort, and convenience. They also secured extra advantages on tests and assignments, and they avoided penalties for breaking the rules. Working-class students, on the other hand, were sometimes able to avoid reprimand by accepting the standards set for them and by not challenging teachers' authority. More often, however, working-class students' deference to teachers' rules, expectations, and procedures limited their opportunities for creativity, comfort, and convenience and also increased their chances of facing reprimand for misbehavior.

Building on the arguments developed in previous chapters, these findings suggest that class-based cultures contribute to inequalities in multiple ways. Using the framework of cultural capital, scholars often presume that advantages result when "individuals' strategic use of knowledge, skills, and competence" aligns with "institutional standards of evaluation" (Lareau and Weininger 2003: 569).[3] From that perspective, middle-class culture is consistent with institutional culture (Bourdieu 1996). That match facilitates compliance with institutional standards, and teachers reward students for their compliance, resulting in greater advantages for middle-class students (Stephens et al. 2012). As demonstrated in this chapter, however, students did not always profit by complying with teachers' expectations. Instead, as shown with the working-class students, compliance often limited students' opportunities for creativity, comfort, and convenience. Compliance also increased the chances that students would face reprimand for their actions, even when punishment was not really deserved (e.g., when the substitute yelled at Cody for talking, even though Mr. Cherlin had said that the students could work with partners on the activity).

These findings also support the idea that the middle-class advantage is, at least in part, a negotiated advantage. As shown in this chapter, middle-class children profited not only by complying with teachers' rules and expectations but also by challenging them. By persisting in their demands for accommodations, middle-class students pressured teachers to grant their requests, even when those accommodations were in excess of what was fair or required and even when teachers seemed inclined to say "no." Chapter 6 examines why teachers said "yes" to students' requests. Regardless of those reasons, however, these findings suggest that advantages can result not just from compliance with institutional standards but also from efforts to negotiate and challenge those standards for individual gain.

Given such findings, scholars might find it useful to broaden commonly used models of social class, culture, and inequality to incorporate the idea of negotiated advantage. Specifically, we might define cultural capital as individual knowledge, skills, and orientations that can be activated to elicit rewards from institutional authorities. The distinction is subtle, but it recognizes the importance of power in producing inequalities (Bourdieu and Passeron 1990). Power, as demonstrated here, is not exclusive to authorities who establish and enforce "institutional standards of evaluation." Rather, even children, when equipped with the right knowledge, skills, and orientations, can pressure institutions to accommodate their desires.

Moving beyond the central argument, the findings in this chapter are also useful for explaining persistent inequalities in school disciplinary practices. Research shows that less privileged students disproportionately experience harsh sanctions such as out-of-school suspensions, which have serious consequences for learning and achievement (Gregory, Skiba, and Noguera 2010; Perry and Morris 2014). Explanations for those patterns focus on educators' (implicit or explicit) bias against less privileged students (Skiba et al. 2002). As shown in this chapter, however, the reality may be more nuanced. Specifically, it seems that disciplinary inequalities might also result, at least in part, from social class differences in students' willingness to demand exemptions from rules and consequences.

As discussed in Chapter 6, those demands often pitted middle-class students against their teachers, and teachers were not always thrilled to comply. As Chapter 5 will show, however, relationships between students and teachers at Maplewood were generally very positive. The students, regardless of social class, craved attention from teachers, and teachers were quick to lavish students with praise. Where students differed, however, was in the strategies they used to capture teachers' attention and in the amount and type of recognition they received.

CHAPTER 5

Seeking Attention

As the first bell rang one Tuesday morning, Ms. Dunham was up at the front of the room, writing the morning work assignment on the whiteboard. A moment later, Danny, a small but bubbly middle-class, white student with a mop of brown, curly hair, burst into the room. Without stopping to take off his backpack, Danny rushed toward Ms. Dunham, calling out excitedly: "Guess what!"

> Ms. Dunham turns toward Danny, her whiteboard marker still in her hand. Before she can say anything, Danny holds up his right arm, which is wrapped in a cast. Proudly, Danny announces: "It's broken! Wanna see the X-ray?" Ms. Dunham blinks, surprised, and then sputters: "Uh, sure."

Danny immediately dropped his backpack, unzipped it, and began rifling through the heap of crumpled papers and books and other miscellaneous items at the bottom. Ms. Dunham waited patiently:

> Still digging through his backpack, Danny explains that it is "just a hairline fracture," but that doctors still put it in a cast so it would heal properly. Sighing dramatically, Danny then recounts how he and his dad waited at the hospital for "five hours." As he says this, Danny stops. Looking up apprehensively at Ms. Dunham, Danny adds quietly: "I didn't get my science homework done, though . . ." Ms. Dunham lets out a breathy laugh. Smiling sympathetically, she reassures him: "That's okay! You were at the hospital."

At that point, after more than a minute of searching, Danny finally extracted a CD case from his backpack:

> Danny holds up the CD, declaring: "X-rays!" Ms. Dunham raises an eyebrow skeptically, asking: "Really?" Danny nods, explaining assuredly: "That's how they do it now."

Pointing at the Smart Board, Danny asks if he can load the CD on Ms. Dunham's laptop "so everyone can see." Ms. Dunham pauses, then smiles: "Sure." She beckons Danny to follow her to her desk, where she helps him project the image on the screen.

Once the image was up, Danny and Ms. Dunham made their way over to the Smart Board, where Danny stood on his tiptoes to show Ms. Dunham where to find the hairline fracture.

By that point, a few other students had filtered into the room. Some of the students went to their cubbies to unpack while others gathered around Danny, listening as he recounted the story of his long trip to the emergency room. Meanwhile, Sadie, a tall, working-class, white student wearing purple leggings and a cat T-shirt, hummed softly as she unpacked her backpack. She occasionally looked up to watch the commotion at the front of the room. A few minutes later, when Ms. Dunham extracted herself from the crowd at the Smart Board and made her way to the paper cutter at the back of the room, Sadie turned around in her seat to watch:

> Ms. Dunham is slicing large pieces of tan construction paper into smaller chunks. Glancing up at Sadie, who is sitting about five feet away, Ms. Dunham asks: "Can you give me a hand for sec?" Sadie jumps up eagerly and scampers over to Ms. Dunham, saying: "Sure!" Ms. Dunham explains that she is making "notecards," and she could use Sadie's help passing out five to each student in the class. Pausing, she adds: "If you don't mind waiting a minute, I just need to make a few more."

As Sadie waited, she rolled up one leg of her cloth leggings and began inspecting a long, red scratch over her knee. A minute later, Ms. Dunham turned around to hand Sadie the stack of notecards:

> Cocking her head curiously, Ms. Dunham asks: "What's up?" Sadie lifts her knee for Ms. Dunham to see, noting matter-of-factly: "My cat scratched me." Sadie then explains that she was holding the cat in her lap so her mom could cut its nails, but it "got spooked" and jumped away. Sadie then pauses and asked: "Do you have any big bandages or anything?" Ms. Dunham shakes her head, explaining apologetically: "No, sorry. I don't have anything like that." Gesturing at Sadie's rolled up leggings, she adds gingerly: "You should probably keep it covered, though."

Sadie nodded, unrolled her pant leg, took the stack of notecards, and trotted off to go distribute them to the other students.

Danny and Sadie were both eager to tell Ms. Dunham about their injuries. However, they went about capturing Ms. Dunham's attention in different ways, and those efforts impacted the amount and type of recognition they received. Danny was very direct and dramatic in his bid for attention, going straight to Ms. Dunham, calling out with a tantalizing "Guess what!" and repeatedly engaging her for more attention. Ms. Dunham, in turn, showed a keen interest in Danny's injury, waiting for him to find the CD, talking with him about the trip to the emergency room, and letting him use her computer to show the X-rays to the class. Sadie, on the other hand, sought Ms. Dunham's recognition in a much more oblique way. Sadie never approached Ms. Dunham directly to tell her story—she waited for Ms. Dunham to ask about the scratch. She also did not push back or ask to go to the nurse when Ms. Dunham told her that she did not have a bandage to share. Ms. Dunham showed sympathy for Sadie, but she spent less than a minute talking about her injury and did not give her a chance to share her story with the rest of the class.

OVERVIEW

Regardless of social class, the students at Maplewood Elementary all seemed to want—even crave—individual attention from teachers. They searched for opportunities to talk about their interests, their experiences, their knowledge, and their lives outside of school. They relished praise and recognition for a job well done.

Teachers, however, had limited time to spend chatting one-on-one with students and recognizing them for their efforts. They had curriculum to cover, parent e-mails to answer, and meetings to attend. They rarely had time to make it through the lesson plan, let alone connect with 25 students one-on-one (Hallett 2010; Valli and Buese 2007).

In this chapter, I explore how students dealt with teachers' limited attention. I describe the strategies and styles that students used to elicit attention from teachers. I also discuss how those strategies and styles varied along social class lines and how those differences generated stratified profits.

Through my observations, I found that middle-class and working-class students took different approaches to attention-seeking. They sought attention for different types of behaviors and used different strategies to catch the teacher's eye. Specifically, middle-class students pursued recognition for their unique talents, skills, and experiences, and they did so overtly and throughout the school day. Working-class students, on the other hand, focused on getting attention for the connections they could make (with other people and with the material) and for the assistance they could provide. They also did so obliquely (rather than overtly) and only when it was clear that teachers had time to connect one-on-one.

As I show, those strategies had unequal consequences for students. Both strategies were useful for initiating positive interactions with teachers. Those positive interactions, however, disproportionately included middle-class students. Although teachers at Maplewood tried hard to engage with all of their students, they had limited time for individual stories, reflections, and contributions. As a result, teachers privileged first-movers—those who sought attention more quickly and more directly—and those with more unique or exciting stories to share. Those patterns ensured that middle-class students got the bulk of teachers' positive attention. Those patterns also amplified over time as students moved into the higher grades. By fifth grade, teachers had more curriculum to cover, leaving less time to connect with students one-on-one.

ATTENTION-SEEKING IN CONTEXT

Sociological research on children's attention-seeking has focused largely on their efforts to fit in with and secure recognition from peers (Fine 1987; Hatch 1987; Milner 2004). It is known, for example, that children derive their sense of dignity from their ability to take part in conversations with their peers (Pugh 2009). It is also known that having friends and getting support from friends are important for children's well-being (Ladd 1990; Wentzel and Caldwell 1997).

Although peer support is clearly beneficial, supportive relationships with adults are also crucial for children (Amato 1994; Harris, Furstenberg, and Marmer 1998; Pianta, Nimetz, and Bennett 1997). Teachers, for example, are a key source of support for children. Students who experience more positive interactions with teachers tend to do better in school (controlling for prior achievement) and have fewer behavior problems (Brophy and Good 1974; Cornelius-White 2007; Elias and Haynes 2008; Rosenfeld, Richman, and Bowen 2000). Teacher support is also particularly beneficial for children from less privileged backgrounds, who may have more limited access to adult support at home and in their communities (Baker 2006; Hamre and Pianta 2001; Harris and Marmer 1996; Stanton-Salazar 2001).

Despite those findings, research typically takes a negative view of children's efforts to seek attention from adults. Attention-seeking in child–adult interactions has even been described as delinquent or even disordered behavior (Campbell 1995; Spencer, Biederman, and Mick 2007). That negative view is problematic, however, in that it ignores the more positive side of attention-seeking, including children's efforts to make personal connections with their teachers and receive validation for their efforts. As a result, we know relatively little about the strategies children use to secure teachers' attention, how teachers respond to those efforts, or how those responses contribute to inequalities in school.

There is, however, some evidence that less privileged students—the very students who benefit most from close connections with teachers—may struggle more to secure one-on-one support. Ethnographic research in preschool settings, for example, finds that teachers give more positive attention to middle-class children than to those from poor and working-class backgrounds (Nelson and Schutz 2007; Streib 2011). Those studies, however, say little about the strategies children use to solicit teachers' engagement, how those strategies vary along social class lines, or how those variations prompt teachers to divide their attention in unequal ways.

This chapter answers those lingering questions. It also provides further evidence for the idea that the middle-class advantage in school is, at least in part, a negotiated advantage. Specifically, I show that middle-class students pressured teachers to provide them with attention and recognition far in excess of what was fair or required. Like Danny, middle-class students secured that extra support not by complying with teachers' expectations (i.e., following instructions and waiting for teachers to provide praise for doing so). Instead, middle-class students secured those advantages by creating opportunities for attention and by persisting in their requests until teachers relented.

SOURCES OF ATTENTION

Although middle-class and working-class students exhibited a similar interest in attention from teachers, they differed in the types of things for which they sought praise. In interviews, both middle-class and working-class students described how much they appreciated the chance to connect with their teachers one-on-one. They all fondly recalled times when a teacher had praised their hard work or laughed at one of their jokes. Despite that shared interest in attention, however, middle-class and working-class students often sought praise for different reasons. Middle-class children tried to gain recognition for their unique talents, skills, and experiences and for their creativity and cleverness (including their ability to make jokes at the teachers' expense). Working-class children instead sought recognition primarily for their commonalities with others, for the connections they made with course concepts, and for the assistance they provided to others.

Middle-Class Sources of Attention

Middle-class students regularly sought attention for their unique talents and skills. They rushed to tell their teachers about the goals they scored in soccer games, the pictures they drew in art class, the solos they played in the orchestra, their knowledge of complicated math formulas, and even their ability to spell ridiculously long words such as pneumononoultrami-croscopicsilicovolcanoconiosis. One morning, Ms. Filipelli was teaching about "squares" (i.e., a number multiplied by itself). Gathering her third graders on the front rug, Ms. Filipelli read aloud from a book titled *Sea Squares.* The first page had one whale with one tail; the second page had two gulls, each with two eyes; and so on:

> After reading each page, Ms. Filipelli asks the class how many features there are in total (one tail, four eyes, etc.). Each time Ms. Filipelli calls for answers, Mason (middle-class, Asian American) waves his hand eagerly, letting out little "Oo oo" noises. Rather than call on Mason, Ms. Filipelli tries to give other students a chance to answer, even cold-calling those who do not have their hands raised.

As the problems became more difficult, the other students struggled to answer when they were cold-called, but Mason continued to volunteer, eagerly waving his hand and calling Ms. Filipelli's name:

> When they get to eight octopuses with eight tentacles, it takes five tries for Ms. Filipelli to find someone who can get the answer right, but eventually Max (middle-class, white) answers correctly—sixty-four tentacles in total. As Ms. Filipelli praises Max for his correct answer, Mason blurts out: "I know a trick for eight times eight! I ate and I ate until I got sick on the floor." Mason was talking so quickly and breathlessly that Ms. Filipelli did not understand him the first time. She asks Mason to repeat himself, and Mason restates his "trick," more slowly and clearly this time. Ms. Filipelli smiles encouragingly, saying "That's a great one!" Mason beams, sitting tall in his spot and nodding approvingly as Ms. Filipelli explains the "trick" to the other students.

Mason could have raised his hand and waited quietly for Ms. Filipelli to call on him to share. Instead, however, and like the middle-class students more generally, Mason was so eager to share his unique knowledge and skills that he simply could not wait. He blurted out his "trick," and he seemed to relish the recognition he got from his teacher for doing so.

Seeking attention for unique knowledge and skills was relatively easy for high-achieving middle-class students such as Mason. However, even lower-achieving middle-class students found similar ways to elicit praise. In some cases, they did so by focusing on non-academic skills ("I scored three goals in my soccer game last night!"). In other cases, middle-class students tried to stand out by claiming that they were exceptionally bad at something ("I'm terrible at long division" or "I'm the *worst* at drawing!"). In those cases, middle-class children seemed to be using self-deprecation to elicit reassurance and praise from the teacher ("You're doing fine!").

Middle-class students also sought attention by sharing stories about unique experiences. They talked about taking vacations to ski lodges and Caribbean islands, earning badges on scouting trips, receiving expensive electronics as gifts, attending professional sporting events, and trying new foods at restaurants. During morning work in Mr. Potter's class, the fifth graders were supposed to unpack their bags and then complete an analogy worksheet. Mr. Potter, meanwhile, was setting up for the day's activities. As he did so, a number of middle-class students got up and approached him with questions and requests. Lisa (middle-class, white) got up three times with separate stories to share—all in the span of 10 minutes. The first time, she announced to Mr. Potter that she had memorized 53 digits of Pi. Mr. Potter urged Lisa to recite them on the spot and then praised her for knowing more than any other student he had ever taught. The second time, Lisa approached Mr. Potter to show him her math homework, asking him to check the answers (even though it was not time for math). He happily obliged, saying how impressed he was that she got them all correct. The third time, Lisa went up to tell a story about an argument between her mother and her middle-school-aged brother the night before:

> Lisa is standing at Mr. Potter's desk again, hip cocked to the side, one arm waving dramatically as she explains that her mom and her brother got into a "huge fight" and that her mom was "soooo mad." Mr. Potter listens interestedly, leaning in toward Lisa to hear over the din of chatter. Lisa is drawing out the story, repeatedly refusing to say what caused the argument. Eventually, Mr. Potter throws up his hands in frustration, pleading "Oh come on! What'd he do?" Lisa shakes her head playfully but then relents. Grinning, she reveals that her brother dropped his brand new iPhone into a "very full" toilet. Mr. Potter laughs heartily, saying: "What a story!"

In telling these stories, and like other middle-class students, Lisa seemed to be trying to captivate the teacher with her remarkable experiences.

As with Lisa's efforts to make the toilet story more interesting by withholding key details, middle-class students also tried to get attention through (and garner praise for) their displays of creativity and cleverness. One way they did so was by pointing out their innovative answers to questions in class. During "Daily Edit" one morning, Ms. Burns posted a set of grammatically incorrect sentences on the Smart Board. The fourth graders had to correct the sentences in their Daily Edit journals. The first sentence read

carol work on a farm take care of too dog for horse three cow

When it was time to review the answers, Ms. Burns pointed to the first sentence and asked for volunteers to share one mistake and correction. A number of the students offered corrections such as capitalizing "Carol," changing "work" to "works," and revising the spelling of "too" and "for":

> Ms. Burns then calls on Steve (middle-class, Asian American). He explains that he added "and" between "farm" and "take" and changed "take" to "takes." Ms. Burns praises Steve for "catching that one," explaining to the class the idea of a sentence with two parts.

Meanwhile, Mandy (middle-class, white) was waving insistently at Ms. Burns. As soon as Ms. Burns finished reviewing Steve's correction, she called on Mandy:

> Mandy gushes: "I found another way to fix that one." She then launches into an explanation of an alternative edit, saying excitedly that she "made it two sentences," instead: "Carol works on a farm." and "She takes care of two dogs, four horses, and three cows." Ms. Burns nods vigorously, explaining to the class that sometimes it is best to "break up complicated sentences" to make them easier to understand.

Mandy was very eager to share her alternative answer to the problem. Like other middle-class students, she seemed intent on demonstrating her creativity and cleverness, and she received warm praise for her efforts.

Middle-class students also sought attention for their cleverness by making "cheeky" or humorous remarks. During a math lesson on angles, Ms. Dunham had her fifth graders sit on the rug while she used an overhead projector to demonstrate using a protractor:

> Ms. Dunham explains that she will give the students their own protractors and a set of practice problems. She also notes that she and the classroom aide, Ms. Hughes, will be circling around to help them if they have questions. Pausing, Ms. Dunham looks around for the aide. Scrunching her eyebrows in a puzzled expression, Ms. Dunham asks: "Where's Ms. Hughes?" Without missing a beat, Greg (middle-class, white) retorts in a deep, Terminator-esque voice: "I *destroyed* her." Ms. Dunham laughs heartily, shaking her head.

The rest of the class was laughing too, and even I could not help but chuckle:

> Greg sits back and smiles contentedly at the response to his joke. Not to be outdone, Sammy (middle-class, white) chimes in: "She hates us, so she left and she's not coming back." Ms. Dunham laughs again: "We both *love* this class. You guys are hysterical!" Sammy beams proudly and a few of the other students smile and laugh approvingly.

Joke-telling as a form of attention-seeking was particularly common among middle-class boys. However, middle-class girls sometimes got in on the game, such as when Lindsey (middle-class, white) playfully corrected a substitute for mixing up the difference between "treat tickets" (given to individual students for good behavior) and "brownie points" (given to the class as a whole). Thus, while there were some differences (i.e., by gender or academic ability) in the specific skills, experiences, or attributes for which they sought attention, all of the middle-class students seemed particularly interested in receiving praise for being unique in some way.

Working-Class Sources of Attention

Working-class students, by contrast, seemed most interested in receiving recognition for the connections they could make (to others and to the material) and the help they could provide. During a Spanish lesson on fruit words, for example, Jesse (working-class, white) was thrilled to share that he had something in common with his teacher. Mr. Pratt explained that he wanted the students to use the phrases written on the board ("Me gusta/encanta" and "No me gusta/encanta") to explain whether they like/love or do not like/love particular fruits. Mr. Pratt gave the students a few examples aloud, saying (in Spanish) that he likes watermelon and that he loves strawberries (he did not mention disliking any of the fruits). Many of the kids then eagerly raised their hands to share, and Mr. Pratt called on them one by one:

> Diana (middle-class, Asian American) sits up tall in her seat, her hand waving rapidly in the air. When Mr. Pratt calls on her, she announces assuredly: "No me gusta las fresas" ("I don't like strawberries"). Mr. Pratt hears this and opens his eyes wide with disbelief. In a voice filled with mock horror, he asks in a mixture of Spanish and English: "What? No te gusta las fresas?" Diana scrunches up her face with disgust, shaking her head vigorously from side. Mr. Pratt gapes at Diana, his mouth hanging open incredulously. He then holds up one hand and pantomimes a pinching and sprinkling motion, asking "Even con azúcar?" ("Even with sugar?"). Diana shakes her head even more vigorously.

Seeing Diana's response, Jesse (working-class, white) thrust his hand high in the air, wriggling his fingers:

> When Mr. Pratt calls on him, Jesse explains breathlessly (in English): "I *love* strawberries with sugar!" Grinning, he adds: "Me gusta *all of them*." Mr. Pratt gives Jesse a broad smile. He nods encouragingly and responds slowly, enunciating each word: "Me gusta *todas las frutas*, también" ("I like all of the fruits, too"). Jesse grins.

In this exchange, Diana actively distinguished herself from her teacher—vehemently rejecting the fruit that Mr. Pratt professed to love. Jesse, on the other hand, and like other working-class students, seemed excited to connect with his teacher by acknowledging their common ground.

Working-class students also sought attention by connecting their personal experiences to things they learned in school. One morning in math class, Ms. Patterson explained to her third graders that it was a special day because they would be doing "Multiplication Mania":

> Ms. Patterson raises her voice excitedly as she announces this, and the students all echo her enthusiasm, shouting out "Yes!" and "Yay!" and "Oh yeah!" Ms. Patterson explains that the students will work in groups at different stations to complete different math games and activities, all of which will involve multiplication.

After explaining the directions for each station, Ms. Patterson passed out worksheets that the students would use to record the math facts they answered at each station. By that point, the students were all talking enthusiastically about the activities:

> Calling out above the din, Ms. Patterson adds: "Don't forget to bring the record sheets with you when you move to the next station!" As the other students get up from their seats to gather their materials and head to their first station, Carter (working-class, white) raises his hand. Ms. Patterson calls on Carter. Hearing his name, Carter grins and launches into a story about a time at Boy Scout camp when his brother had to keep a log of all of his activities. Carter explains that his brother accidentally left his log in his tent one morning and had to walk all the way across the camp to retrieve it. Ms. Patterson smiles, praising Carter and saying: "Nice connection, Carter!" Carter looks pleased, blushing red and giving Ms. Patterson an aw-shucks smile.

Carter's camp story reinforced Ms. Patterson's point about the importance of bringing the record sheet from station to station and not leaving it behind. Like other working-class students, Carter used personal stories not (at least primarily) to highlight his uniqueness but, rather, to forge connections with his teacher and with the topic at hand.

Working-class students also appreciated the attention they received for being "helpful" to others, and they often went out of their way to create opportunities for such help-related praise. Sadie (working-class, white), for example, frequently jumped to help her teachers with various classroom tasks. Whenever Ms. Dunham asked for someone to take the attendance folder to the office or clap the erasers outside or take down the chairs of students who were absent, Sadie's hand was almost always the first one in the air. By the end of fifth grade, Ms. Dunham would even allow Sadie to answer the classroom phone for her when it rang. In such helping situations, Ms. Dunham would also gush with praise, telling Sadie that she was so "helpful" and such a "good citizen." Sadie, meanwhile, appeared to crave that kind of positive attention, to the point that she actively avoided doing anything that might undermine Ms. Dunham's perception of her helpfulness and responsibility. During an interview after fifth grade, for example, Sadie asked me if I could return the dictionary that Ms. Dunham had leant her to use at home. Sadie recalled how horrible she felt when she realized she had forgotten to return the book, pressing both hands against her cheeks and opening her eyes and mouth wide to show me how she had looked upon first realizing her mistake. Shaking her head, Sadie lamented, her voice small and meek, "She used to tell me I was such a good citizen. She probably hates me now."

Working-class students also created opportunities for recognition by assisting their peers. Sadie, for example, served as a sort of self-appointed aide to the special education students in the grade. She would sit with them at lunch and help them unpack their backpacks, get materials in art class, and use equipment on the playground. Although other working-class students were not quite as committed as Sadie, they also would go out of their way to help classmates. That was apparent one day in Ms. Henderson's class. To help her third graders learn the scientific classification system, Ms. Henderson made "study books" by printing out fact sheets about different birds and stapling them together:

The students are sitting in a big circle on the rug at the front of the room, and they pass the books in a stack around the circle. Receiving his book, Shawn (working-class, white) grins, calling out: "Thank you, Ms. Henderson!" Other kids echo him, calling out: "Thanks!" and "You rule!" At this point, however, Christian (middle-class, white), who is last in the circle, realizes that there are not enough books to go around. He calls out: "I don't have one, Ms. Henderson!" Ms. Henderson frowns, grumbling to herself that she thought she made enough. She asks the students to "shake your books to see if anyone got two stuck together." There do not seem to be any more, and Ms. Henderson sighs heavily. She turns to the student next to Christian, asking: "Can you two share?" Before he can answer, Shawn, who is sitting across the circle, tosses his book to Christian, saying: "Here you go! You can have mine!" Ms. Henderson blinks, surprised, saying: "Thank you, Shawn! That was very nice of you!" Shawn grins and nods sheepishly.

Like Shawn, working-class students went out of their way to be helpful to others in the classroom. Working-class students also received accolades from their teachers for those efforts, and they seemed to deeply appreciate that praise and the positive relationships they formed with teachers in the process.

STRATEGIES FOR ATTENTION-SEEKING

Middle-class and working-class students differed not only in the types of things for which they sought recognition but also in the styles and strategies they used to catch teachers' eyes. Specifically, there were class-based variations in the timing of students' attention-seeking efforts and in the directness of their requests.

Middle-Class Attention-Seeking Strategies

Middle-class students sought attention more overtly. Rather than wait for teachers to notice them, middle-class students would call out or approach their teachers, exhorting them to "Listen to this story I wrote!" or "Guess what I did last night!" One morning, Ms. Nelson's fourth graders were completing a "multiplication patterns" worksheet—they had to identify "tricks" for memorizing multiplication facts. Calling the students together, Ms. Nelson asked for examples of patterns the students had found:

In response to Danny's (middle-class, white) comment, Ms. Nelson writes "even/odd alternating" on the easel next to "7 Patterns." Ms. Nelson then puts her marker down and starts to ask about the "8 patterns" students found. Before Ms. Nelson can finish, Kelly (middle-class, white) thrusts her hand high in the air, calling out: "Wait! I found another one for seven." Ms. Nelson looks surprised, asking: "Oh, really? Let's hear it!" Kelly explains that she found a pattern for the low sevens where the even tens digits repeat, up to 6, where the pattern stops (0, 0, 1, 2, 2, 3, 4, 4, 5, 6, 7). Ms. Nelson nods: "Very creative, Kelly. It's *almost* a repeating pattern." Kelly sits up tall with a satisfied smile. She turns to a friend nearby and points proudly at where she has written the pattern on her worksheet.

The class moved on to the 8 times tables. Again, the middle-class students called out with patterns to share and did not let Ms. Nelson move on until every avenue had been explored:

> Brian (middle-class, mixed-race) calls out to add that the ones digits are always even. Liam (middle-class, white) jumps in to describe how the ones digit repeats "every fifth time" (i.e., 8 × 1 = 08, 8 × 6 = 48, 8 × 11 = 88). Danny (middle-class, white) shows how the ones digit repeats in a pattern of 0, 8, 4, 2. When Anna (middle-class, white) tries to describe Danny's pattern in different words, she even gets into a brief debate with Ms. Nelson, insisting that she is describing a "different pattern" and "not the same thing."

Middle-class students were very direct in seeking recognition for their unique knowledge, skills, talents, and stories. Even when teachers tried to signal that they were ready to move on (as Ms. Nelson did by putting her marker down), middle-class students such as Kelly would often persist until they got the attention they desired.

That directness could also be seen in middle-class students' willingness to interrupt teachers and classmates with their bids for attention. Middle-class students called out with jokes and commentary, even when teachers were giving instructions. They waved their hands or interjected to share reflections, even when other students were talking or working. During Spanish class, for example, the fifth graders were writing short stories about animals. The students had to choose an animal (from the list of words they knew) and then describe how the animal looks, how it moves, and where it lives. Many of the middle-class students wrote fanciful rather than factual stories, and they wanted to show Mr. Pratt how clever they were in doing so. Rather than wait for the written feedback that Mr. Pratt had promised to provide, the middle-class students repeatedly called out or approached Mr. Pratt to tell him about their stories, even when he was working with other students and even, at one point, when he was talking with the principal, who had stopped by to chat:

> As Mr. Pratt talks with Ms. Weiss at the door, Colin (middle-class, white) calls out excitedly: "My giraffe eats pie!" Mr. Pratt laughs and smiles, asking him "Que tipo? What type?" Colin grins and calls back: "Cherry!" A minute or so later, Ashley (middle-class, white) calls out to Mr. Pratt, saying: "Listen to this!" She immediately begins reading her story about a "muy mediano mono" (very medium monkey) named Marvin. Mr. Pratt nods, praising her for using "Great alliteration!" Later, as the students pack up to leave, Zara (middle-class, Asian American) and Joanna (middle-class, white) run up to Mr. Pratt, who is writing the homework on the board. Joanna gestures at Zara excitedly and exclaims that despite working at separate tables, "We both did elephants that live at

the beach and hers is named Ella and mine is Ellie." Mr. Pratt nods, impressed, noting (in Spanish) that they must be "telepático" (telepathic) to have written stories so similar.

Before starting the activity, Mr. Pratt told the students that he would be collecting the stories and providing written feedback. The middle-class students, however, were not willing to wait. Like Colin, Ashley, Zara, and Joanna, they looked for opportunities to share their work and receive immediate recognition for their efforts, even if that meant interrupting or taking attention away from others in the process.

Working-Class Attention-Seeking Strategies

Working-class students sought attention more indirectly. Rather than call out—making statements such as "Hey! Listen to this song I know!" or "Look what I drew!"—they would wait for others to notice them. In Spanish class, the students were playing Simón Dice (Simon Says) to practice action verbs ("jump," "dance," "fly," "swim," etc.) they had learned:

> After a few rounds of Simón Dice, Mr. Pratt grins slyly, as though he is about to give the students a "tough one." Pausing for dramatic effect, he announces: "Simón dice nadar como un tiburón" (Simon says swim like a shark). Most of the students just look up at Mr. Pratt quizzically, not recognizing the last word (tiburón). A few students start to do a regular swimming motion, while others glance around to see what their peers are doing. Mr. Pratt sees this and calls out to clarify, explaining that "tiburón is like Jaws." Zach (working-class, white) glances around at his peers. Then, quietly, Zach begins to sing the theme from *Jaws* ("dunh-dunh, dunh-dunh-dunh-dunh-dunh-dunh"). As he does this, Zach puts his hands together over his head to form a "fin." He wiggles from side to side with a deep, war-like scowl on his face. Mr. Pratt laughs, points at Zach and exclaims: "Exactamente!" Zach smiles shyly, looking pleased as the other students copy his motion.

Working-class students were rarely overt in their attention-seeking efforts. Zach, for example, could have called out, saying, "Oh! I know! It's a shark!" or "Look at me!" Instead, he waited for Mr. Pratt to notice the connection he was making and to praise him for doing so.

Working-class students' more indirect approach to attention-seeking could also be seen in the timing of their requests. Whereas middle-class students interrupted with stories and requests for attention throughout the school day, working-class students generally reserved their attention-seeking efforts for moments when it was clear that teachers (or other adults) had time to provide one-on-one attention. One morning on the way to lunch, for example, I spotted Jesse (working-class, white) eyeing the sandwich I was carrying:

> "Ready for lunch?" I ask. Jesse nods vigorously and then explains that his mother over-slept, so he missed the bus and also missed breakfast. (Like some of the other working-class students, Jesse qualified for free lunch and also free breakfast at school.) "I'm so sorry." I sputter, "You must be hungry if you missed breakfast." Jesse looks at the floor and then shrugs, noting: "It's okay. I had a couple crackers in the car on the way here."

As noted in the Introduction, Jesse (working-class, white) would often sneak out of the cafeteria in the morning so that he could be the first one in the classroom and have an extra minute or two to talk with his teachers. During class, however, Jesse participated in activities and discussions, but he rarely tried to connect with his teachers one-on-one. Instead, like other working-class students, he waited for moments—such as before school or between activities—when teachers and other adults like me had more time to listen and share.

CONSEQUENCES OF ATTENTION-SEEKING

Although middle-class and working-class students were both successful in getting attention from teachers, the strategies they used were not equal in their consequences. Rather, middle-class students captured a disproportionate share of teachers' positive attention. They did so by engaging teachers more quickly, by offering more novel contributions, and by pressuring teachers to provide more one-on-one attention than they had initially planned. As a result, working-class students spent more time waiting for positive attention and also got less complete support. Those disparities seemed to increase from third grade to fifth grade (and also, as explained in Chapter 7, to seventh grade) because teachers in the older grades had less time for sharing and connecting one-on-one.

Middle-Class Students Reaping Rewards

Middle-class students captured a disproportionate share of teachers' positive attention, and they did so, in part, by engaging teachers more quickly and more directly than did their working-class peers. That was apparent one afternoon in Mr. Fischer's class. The fifth graders made paper airplanes as part of a lesson on the Wright brothers and "the age of invention." Each student then got to toss his or her plane down the hallway, and the furthest-flying plane was declared the winner. After the competition, there was much commotion in the hallway:

> Joanna (middle-class, white) dashes up to Mr. Fischer, calling out his name. At first, Mr. Fischer does not respond. It is very noisy, and he is trying to herd the students back into the classroom. Joanna, undeterred, moves around so she is directly in front of Mr. Fischer. She lets her whole body slump dramatically as she groans: "Mine hit the wall!" Mr. Fischer smiles sympathetically, saying: "It still went pretty far!" Still frustrated, Joanna thrusts out her plane and asks: "What do you think I did wrong?" Mr. Fischer leans down to inspect the plane. He points, explaining: "It's a little uneven here. One wing is bigger. That might've done it." Joanna sighs, lamenting tragically: "I should've used my other one." Mr. Fischer laughs and shakes his head.

Mr. Fischer again called out to the students to "head back inside." Meanwhile, Amelia (working-class, white) came up behind him, cupping her plane in her hands:

> Amelia says quietly, almost to herself: "Mine twirled." She is referring to how her plane flew straight up and then corkscrewed back down, landing just a few feet in front of the starting line. Amelia, however, is about a step behind Mr. Fischer when she says this, and with all of the commotion, Mr. Fischer does not seem to notice her. He just continues herding the students back into the room. Amelia does not say anything else. She just shuffles into the classroom.

Like Amelia, Joanna could have stopped after her first attempt to get Mr. Fischer's attention, accepting that he was simply too busy herding the students back inside. Instead, Joanna opted to try again, speaking louder and moving her body so that Mr. Fischer would be sure to see her. As a result, Joanna got the recognition she desired, while Amelia did not. Mr. Fischer sympathized with Joanna's frustration, praised her for a good flight, and offered her constructive feedback on her plane.

With respect to attention-seeking, middle-class students also benefitted from a sort of "first-mover advantage" (Kerin, Varadarajan, and Peterson 1992). With textbooks full of curriculum to cover, teachers rarely had time during class for individual stories and reflections. As a result, teachers privileged students who spoke first and students with more novel stories to share. In Ms. Patterson's third-grade class, for example, the students were learning about birds and their habitats. On Monday, Greta (middle-class, white) had gone up to Ms. Patterson to tell her about a birds' nest that she had found in her yard at home. She asked Ms. Patterson if she could show the class, and Ms. Patterson agreed, telling her to bring it in the next day. On Tuesday, Ms. Patterson had the students cluster on the rug as they took turns reading aloud from their science book. When they finished the chapter, Ms. Patterson looked over at Greta, saying "Okay, go ahead":

> Greta grins and pops up from her spot on the rug, dashing over to her cubby. Greta carefully extracts a shoe box and carries it slowly and gingerly back to the rug. Greta then opens the box and shows the rest of the class an empty birds' nest, describing how she did research online with her mother to determine that the nest probably belonged to a family of robins. The other students all crane their necks to try to see, chattering excitedly as they do so.

Ms. Patterson then told Greta that she could take questions from the class. Greta called on Carter and Rachel (both working-class, white):

> Carter asks where Greta found the nest, and Greta explains that she and her brother found it in the bushes by their back door. When Greta calls on Rachel, Rachel does not ask a question. Instead, she starts to tell a story about a time when she found a birds' nest at her own house. Before Rachel can go into detail, and as other students start to call out and raise their hands with their own wildlife stories, Ms. Patterson holds up her hands, saying apologetically: "Unfortunately, we don't have time for swapping stories. We have to move on."

Greta got to share her bird story (and take up class time doing so), at least in part, because she was the first to ask. Rachel, meanwhile, wanted to join in the conversation, but she asked second, and there was not enough time for "me too." Like other working-class students, Rachel sought attention by highlighting her similarities with others and not her unique experiences. Working-class students such as Rachel also used their middle-class peers' requests to gauge the appropriateness of attention-seeking in any particular moment. Because teachers tended to privilege the first movers, working-class students often ended up with fewer opportunities to share.

Middle-class students also captured extra positive attention by pressuring teachers to spend more time on individual stories, ideas, and questions than originally planned. On Election Day, Maplewood took part in "Kids Vote." Students got to use online ballot boxes to cast their votes for President of the United States. After lunch, at the beginning of social studies, Ms. Nelson gathered the students on the rug, asking them to turn to Chapter 12 in their textbooks:

> Despite Ms. Nelson's instruction, there is a lot of chatter—almost all of it about the election. Drew (middle-class, white) thrusts his hand high in the air, calling out loudly: "Ms. Nelson!" Ms. Nelson looks over at Drew, and he immediately exclaims: "Last week we got like *forty-nine* calls!" Ms. Nelson sputters, as though she thought Drew was going

to ask a question about the economics chapter. She explains haltingly: "Uh, okay. We're not gonna talk about that now." Undeterred, Drew fires back curiously: "But how come they called so many times?"

Hearing Drew's question, Elliot, Keri, and Gina (all middle-class, white) started calling out with their own questions and stories about campaign workers:

> Ms. Nelson sighs, glances disappointedly at the clock, and explains that people from both parties are just trying to remind everyone to vote and making sure they have rides to the polls if they need them. Ms. Nelson then describes how campaign workers try to convince anyone who still hasn't made up their mind. She notes that "This is it. This is their last chance to hit the public." As the questions and stories (all from middle-class students) continue, Ms. Nelson repeatedly tries to move on. Eventually, she throws up her hands, shouting: "Okay!" As the students finally quiet down, Ms. Nelson insists firmly: "We're *really* gonna move on, now."

Ms. Nelson was clearly frustrated with the stories and the questions. She had planned to read a whole chapter from the book and then have the students work in pairs to answer questions about what they had read. Instead, they only had time to read half of the chapter. The time Ms. Nelson had planned to spend on the lesson went directly to the middle-class students. They pressured Ms. Nelson to provide an extended sharing time during which they alone got to tell their stories and get answers to their questions about how elections work.

Working-Class Students Suffering Consequences

Although teachers gave the bulk of their positive attention to middle-class students, some of that attention did go to working-class students. Teachers praised working-class students for their hard work, for their helpfulness, and for the connections they made with teachers, classmates, and course material. However, working-class students' more deference-based approach to attention-seeking also had a number of drawbacks, at least in comparison to the more influence-based approach used by their middle-class peers.

One such drawback was that working-class students often spent more time waiting for teachers' recognition. During large group activities, middle-class students would keep their hands raised—or even wave them around excitedly—while others were talking. Working-class students, on the other hand, would put their hands down or lower them, often resting their forearms on top of their heads, while others were talking. They would then raise their hands again only when it was clear that the teacher was ready for additional volunteers. What that meant, however, was that when teachers looked for hands, the first ones they saw were usually those of middle-class students and not those of their working-class peers. Unfortunately, that split-second delay often meant the difference between having and not having an opportunity to share. Some teachers explicitly waited before calling on students to answer, giving others time to think and feel confident raising their hands. When pressed for time, however, even those teachers would often privilege students who appeared "ready" with answers.

Working-class students also found themselves at more of a disadvantage over time. As students got older, teachers had more curriculum to cover and less time available for individual stories and one-on-one attention. In third grade, teachers regularly included opportunities for student reflection in their lesson plans. While reading novels out loud, teachers would explicitly ask students to make connections between the story and their lives, and they would leave time for at least three or four students to share. Third- and fourth-grade teachers would also regularly encourage students to share their writing—especially personal narratives—aloud with the class. By the end of fourth grade and especially by fifth grade, however, teachers rarely saved class time for students to share personal connections with the material they were learning. During class discussions, for example, they privileged more analytical and fact-based contributions. They also spent less time on personal narrative writing (and more on persuasive and research-based writing) and gave students fewer chances to tell stories aloud. As the "built-in" opportunities for attention-getting grew fewer and farther between, middle-class students worked harder to assert themselves and garner attention, often by interrupting with the kinds of "clever" comments described previously. Working-class students, on the other hand, increasingly saved their attention-seeking efforts for the brief moments (e.g., before/after school and between activities) when teachers had more time for one-on-one conversations. Essentially, it seemed that working-class students were trying to find ways to connect with their teachers while maintaining deference to teachers' expectations and authority (i.e., not interrupting). Unfortunately, the growing intensity of the curriculum made it increasingly difficult for them to do so as they moved into the higher grades.

SUMMARY AND CONCLUSIONS

Attention-seeking was an important project for students at Maplewood. They relished praise from teachers and rare moments of undivided attention. As this chapter has shown, however, middle-class and working-class students sought recognition from teachers in contrasting ways. Middle-class students used frequent and overt attention-seeking efforts to highlight their unique talents and experiences, their creativity, and their cleverness. Working-class students instead used indirect and carefully timed bids to get teachers' attention. They also focused less on their unique talents and experiences and more on the connections they could make with others and the help they could provide to teachers and peers.

Those different attention-seeking strategies had real consequences for students. Both middle-class and working-class students were successful in securing praise and recognition from their teachers. However, teachers had limited opportunities for engaging students, and (as discussed in more detail in Chapter 6) the nature of the school environment made it difficult to allocate that time evenly. As a result, middle-class students received a disproportionate share of teachers' positive attention. Compared to their working-class peers, middle-class students got teachers to respond to their bids for attention more quickly and more completely. Middle-class students also pressured teachers to provide more individual attention than initially intended.

Building on the arguments in previous chapters, these findings provide further evidence for the idea of the middle-class advantage as a negotiated advantage. Given what is known from research on cultural capital, we might expect teachers to give students positive attention for meeting expectations in school.[1] Certainly, that did happen—teachers praised students for working hard, doing well on assignments, listening, and following directions. However, compliance with expectations was not the only reason teachers gave students positive attention. Rather, middle-class students were also able to secure recognition in excess of what was fair and in excess of what teachers initially intended to provide. They did so by calling out and interrupting with stories, comments, and jokes and by persisting in those bids for attention until teachers relented.

Beyond their implications for the idea of negotiated advantage, these findings are also useful in explaining how children try to seek attention from teachers and how those efforts can result in inequalities. Although it is known that support from adults is crucial for students and their well-being (Baker 2006; Hamre and Pianta 2001; Stanton-Salazar 2001), research on children's attention-seeking strategies has focused on efforts to be a part of a peer group (Fine 1987; Hatch 1987; Milner 2004; Pugh 2009). Building on that existing research, this chapter shows that students are not just concerned with winning the approval of peers. Rather, children actively try to gain recognition from their teachers, and they do so in ways that vary along social class lines (Streib 2011). Those variations mattered because middle-class students' attention-seeking strategies were generally more successful in capturing teachers' limited time and attention. Those inequalities are important, at least in part, because working-class students may have the most to gain from their connections with teachers (Harris and Marmer 1996; Stanton-Salazar 2001).

Chapters 3–5 have highlighted social class differences in the strategies children used when seeking assistance, accommodations, and attention at school. These chapters have also shown that those strategies, when activated, produced stratified profits in school. As noted in Chapter 2, however, those stratified profits hinged on teachers' responses to students' classroom strategies. Teachers had the power to deny students' requests for assistance, accommodations, and attention. In reality, however, and as previous chapters have shown, teachers generally said "yes" to middle-class students' requests, even when those requests generated support in excess of what was fair or required. Chapter 6 examines why teachers typically responded more positively to strategies of influence than to strategies of deference. It also shows how those responses helped ensure middle-class students' negotiated advantage.

CHAPTER 6

Responses and Ramifications

One morning, just before lunch, the students in Mr. Potter's fifth-grade advanced math class were all seated at their desks, getting ready for a math test. The room was bright from the sun streaming through the windows, but it was also frigidly cold—despite it being only March, the air vents were blowing a steady stream of cool air, and I kept having to pause my note-taking to warm my hands. Before passing out the tests, Mr. Potter reassured the students, telling them that their "past two quizzes were excellent," that they "know this material well," and that they "shouldn't have any problem doing well" on the test. During the test, however, a number of middle-class students went up to Mr. Potter with questions:

Steve, a middle-class, Asian American student wearing nylon track pants and a hooded sweatshirt, is working on the section of the test marked "complements and supplements." Each problem in that section shows a drawing of an angle with a specific measurement and then asks students to either "Find the supplement of this angle" or "Find the complement of this angle." With his lips pursed tight in concentration, Steve reads one problem, then starts drawing an angle, pausing to erase a few times as he tries to show the correct number of degrees. But then Steve narrows his eyes and reads the directions again, as if unsure whether he is doing the problem correctly. Letting out a loud breath, Steve rises from his seat, his jaw set with a look of determination. Steve strides confidently toward Mr. Potter, test in hand and head held high. Mr. Potter looks up from the stack of papers he is sorting at the front of the room. Steve explains, quietly but insistently, that he is not sure what to do with "the complement and supplement ones." Holding out his test, Steve asks: "Is this right?" Mr. Potter leans down to get a better view of Steve's paper. After a moment, he shakes his head, explaining in a low but pleasant voice: "You don't have to draw it. You just have to write the number of degrees you'd have to add to an angle to find its complement or its supplement." Steve's eyes widen, and he nods quickly, as though he suddenly understands.

After helping Steve, Mr. Potter stood up, crossed his arms, and turned his gaze slowly from one side of the room to the other. He then began to make his way toward Roger, a tall, soft-spoken, middle-class, Asian American student with thick glasses. Roger's family had recently emigrated from China, and he was still learning English:

> Squatting down next to Roger, Mr. Potter begins to whisper with him, asking him how he is doing with the test and whether he understands all of the questions. Roger nods, giving Mr. Potter a quick, reassuring smile. Mr. Potter peers at Roger's test for a moment, as though checking his work. Then he smiles, saying "You're right! Looks good!"

Standing up, Mr. Potter started to make his way back toward the front of the room. As he did so, however, he happened to glance at the test of another student, Jared, a short but athletically-built working-class, white student wearing track pants and a hoodie. Like Steve (one of Jared's close friends), Jared was trying to draw the angles rather than just write the number of degrees that would make a complementary or supplementary angle:

> Mr. Potter squats down next to Jared's desk. Jared looks up, surprised, and then back down at his test. "You okay?" Mr. Potter asks, giving Jared a warm smile. Hesitantly, and without making eye contact, Jared admits: "I don't think I get the complement and supplement ones." Mr. Potter nods, explaining quietly: "You don't have to draw it. You just have to write the amount of the complement or the supplement—whichever it asks for. Like, Number 9 says '57 degrees.' So what would you add to that to find its complement?" "Oh!" exclaims Jared, rocking back in his chair. He gives Mr. Potter a sheepish grin. Pointing to his paper, Jared explains meekly: "I was trying to draw it." Mr. Potter pats Jared on the shoulder as he stands up, and Jared shakes his head, letting out a breathy, self-deprecating laugh.

After helping Jared, Mr. Potter then called for the attention of the whole class. As the students looked up, Mr. Potter repeated aloud the clarification that he had just given to both Steve and Jared, explaining that the students did not need to draw the angles and that they only had to "write the amount of degrees you'd have to add to an angle to find its complement or its supplement." The announcement elicited a few exclamations of "Oh!" from students throughout the room, who nodded appreciatively before turning back to their tests.

This was a test. Mr. Potter did not have to help the students—if anything, he seemed to expect that the students understood the material and that they would be fine on their own. In light of Steve's question, however, Mr. Potter seemed to recognize that the directions were somewhat unclear, and he went out of his way to check in with students—Roger and Jared— who might be confused.

OVERVIEW

The teachers at Maplewood Elementary played a critical role in determining whether students' problem-solving strategies resulted in rewards or reprimands. As discussed in Chapters 3–5, strategies of influence generally elicited more support from teachers than did strategies of deference. Although strategies of deference did sometimes help working-class students avoid punishment, those strategies rarely led teachers to provide the kind of support that helped students get ahead. Strategies of influence, on the other hand, regularly prompted teachers to provide assistance and accommodations and attention in excess of what was fair or required, and to do so even when they wanted to say "no." But why?

One possibility is teacher bias. That could be bias against working-class students and/or bias toward middle-class behaviors. Research suggests, for example, that teachers are more likely to underestimate the effort and academic abilities of less privileged students (Kozlowski 2015; Ready and Wright 2011). Those underestimates also shape how teachers treat students, with teachers disproportionately assigning less privileged students to lower academic tracks and ability groups (Eder 1981; Oakes 2005; Rist 2000) and also judging less privileged students more harshly and subjecting them to more serious punishments (Duncan and Brooks-Gunn 1997; McLeod and Kaiser 2004; McLeod and Shanahan 1993).

This study is not designed to assess the prevalence of teacher bias or its impact on students' behaviors and outcomes. Thus, it is certainly possible that subconscious biases contributed to the inequalities I observed at Maplewood. However, although bias may have been a factor in that process, my observations suggested that there were other factors at play. As discussed in Chapter 2, teachers often got frustrated with middle-class students' incessant requests, suggesting that they did not view middle-class students or their behaviors in an unquestioningly positive light. Furthermore, as this chapter will demonstrate, the teachers at Maplewood cared deeply about all their students, and they tried to level the playing field. As shown in Chapter 3, teachers generally said "yes" to working-class students when those students requested support. Furthermore, like Mr. Potter in the previous example, they often went out of their way to offer unsolicited support to students who might be struggling.

So what else could explain the teachers' tendency to privilege influence over deference? Another possibility is that teachers felt pressured to grant students' requests for assistance, accommodation, and attention. Lewis and Diamond (2015), for example, found that parent pushback played a key role in maintaining racially segregated academic tracks in an affluent public high school. The teachers that Lewis and Diamond interviewed were aware of and frustrated by inequalities in the school (including inequalities they helped create by assigning students to different tracks). However, those teachers were also compelled to persist in those practices because of pushback (or "anticipated" pushback) from white parents (see also Cucchiara 2013).[1]

Teachers at Maplewood followed a similar pattern in responding to students' requests. Teachers who denied middle-class students' requests faced real pushback from middle-class students and from middle-class parents. In light of such pushback, it was often easier and less risky for teachers to say "yes" instead.

TRYING TO LEVEL THE PLAYING FIELD

The teachers at Maplewood wanted to create a level playing field for their students. They recognized that some students faced real barriers to success, and they worked hard to create an environment in which all of their students felt supported. On the second to last day of fifth grade, before the students arrived, I was chatting with Ms. Dunham in her classroom, helping her stack and put away textbooks. As we worked, Ms. Dunham gestured at a framed class photo on her desk. There was large white matte around the photo, and all of the students had signed their names and written little notes to Ms. Dunham:

> Ms. Dunham pointed at one of the messages, which read: "Ms. Dunham, thank you for giving us so much opportunity. Love, Jesse." Ms. Dunham smiles warmly, her eyes sparkling with tears. Ms. Dunham lets out a long breath and shakes her head sadly, saying "I really feel for Jesse, since things are so tough at home. He needs all the positive attention he can get." Wistfully, she adds: "Kids like that—Jesse, Sadie, Jeremy—this is all they have. They don't do anything all summer. They just hang out or watch TV. . . . It makes me think of my own kids, the opportunities, the things we take for granted." Ms. Dunham continues, saying: "It's hard, hard to see those kids who don't get that." Gesturing at the posters on the walls and the artwork still proudly displayed around

the room, Ms. Dunham adds, more firmly this time: "That's why, like I was telling you yesterday, I don't like to pack things up until the very end." I smile, echoing what Ms. Dunham told me the day before: "Yeah, you want them to feel wanted, like you're not pushing them out the door." Ms. Dunham nods vigorously in agreement, adding: "They need that stability, that consistency, and they don't get it at home."

At that moment, the bell rang. Ms. Dunham whispered cautiously that she "probably shouldn't say more" because Jesse was always the first one down the hall in the morning:

> Sure enough, as I turn to look, Jesse barrels through the door, bent forward from the weight of his backpack. Ms. Dunham gives me a knowing smile, and then turns to greet Jesse with a hearty "Good morning!" Jesse stops and stands up tall, giving us both a big grin.

Like Ms. Dunham, the teachers at Maplewood cared deeply about their students and especially those with "tough" home lives. They tried to provide as much "positive attention" as time allowed.

In light of that concern, teachers often went out of their way to offer unsolicited assistance to working-class students and other students who appeared to be struggling. During a Halloween activity in fourth grade, for example, students were using squeezable puff-paint bottles to decorate mini pumpkins. The bottles had not been used recently, and many were clogged. When they encountered a clogged bottle, Riley, Kyle, Lisa, Bradley (all middle-class, white), and Diana (middle-class, Asian American) immediately got up and went over to Ms. Phillips to ask for help. When Amelia (working-class, white) encountered a clogged paint bottle, she tried to deal with the problem on her own:

> Her face set in a grimace, Amelia turns the bottle over and squeezes hard, but nothing comes out. Then, frowning, with the bottle still upside-down, she gives it a good shake. All of a sudden, about a half-cup of red glittery paint explodes out of the bottle and onto Amelia's paper. Amelia's eyes open wide and fearful as she looks down at the paint.

Seeing the spilled paint, Ricky, a middle-class boy at the same table, started to tease Amelia for making a mess:

> As Ricky laughs, Amelia blushes a deep red and tears well in her eyes. She covers her face in her hands and puts her head down on her desk. Kyle, another middle-class boy at the table, gives Ricky a disgusted look. He then starts yelling at Ricky, telling him to stop being so mean.

Ms. Phillips, meanwhile, heard Kyle yelling and went over to investigate. Kyle immediately began to explain, recounting the spilled paint and Ricky's teasing:

> Ms. Phillips shakes her head. She gives Ricky a stern warning and then squats down beside Amelia. Putting a reassuring hand on Amelia's shoulder, she explains: "I understand—it was stuck." Amelia looks up slowly, her eyes still red from crying. Ms. Phillips smiles warmly and offers to help Amelia open the other paint bottles. Amelia nods timidly and gives Ms. Phillips a weak smile.

Like Ms. Phillips, the teachers at Maplewood looked for signs of struggle. They circled around while students were working. They gave students pretests to gauge their understanding. Sometimes they even had students close their eyes and raise their hands if they were confused about a concept during instructions. As Mr. Fischer explained, "I don't wanna embarrass kids. But I really need to know if they don't get it, and if their eyes are closed, they feel safer." Teachers then used that information to provide support, even when students did not actively ask for help.

That kind of unsolicited support seemed especially beneficial for working-class students. In an interview during the summer after fifth grade, I asked Zach (working-class, white) what teachers can do to help their students do well in school. He explained:

> ZACH: They can, um . . . they can talk with them more. Talk through tests with them and tell them what they did wrong.
>
> JMC: And were there ever times when teachers did that with you?
>
> ZACH: Yeah.
>
> JMC: Can you tell me about that?
>
> ZACH: It was, um . . . a pretty good experience, cuz it made me want to do better every test when they came to me and told me what I got wrong and how I could do better.
>
> JMC: And did you have to go to them to ask for that? Or did they call you up?
>
> ZACH: They, um . . . they called me up to talk to me about it.
>
> JMC: And how was that?
>
> ZACH: It made it easier to, like, talk to them about it.

As discussed in Chapter 2, working-class students worried that they might get in trouble for seeking support or doing so in the wrong way or at the wrong time. When teachers reached out with offers of unsolicited assistance, working-class students could be more confident that their requests would not result in reprimand.

THE LIMITS ON LEVELING THE PLAYING FIELD

The teachers at Maplewood wanted to create a level playing field for their students, but their actions often served to reinforce existing inequalities. As demonstrated in previous chapters, teachers provided more assistance, accommodations, and attention to middle-class students than to their working-class peers. Moreover, teachers said "yes" to middle-class students' requests, even when those requests were in excess of what was fair or required, and even when they might have preferred to say "no." As this chapter will show, teachers said "yes," at least in part, because of pushback (or even potential pushback) from middle-class students and middle-class parents.

Given the possibility of pushback from students, granting middle-class students' requests allowed teachers to avoid wasting class time. As shown in previous chapters, middle-class students were extremely persistent in their requests for assistance, accommodations, and attention. For teachers, that meant that saying "no" came with a real cost and that saying "yes" could avoid the hassle of prolonged negotiations. One morning in gym class, for example, the fifth graders were getting ready to play kickball. Hunter (middle-class, white) was wearing a plastic brace on his right ankle, which he had "twisted." School rules dictated that students who were injured had to sit on the sidelines during gym activities, but Hunter asked Ms. Winters, the gym teacher, if he could play anyway:

> As the other kids go to the closet to get kickballs and bases, Hunter heads toward Ms. Winters. Hunter has a plastic brace on his ankle, but moves fairly quickly despite his injury. Calling out to get Ms. Winters' attention, Hunter immediately begins to negotiate, asking if he can play kickball with the class despite his brace. Before Ms. Winters can say no, Hunter explains that he can "still play outfield." Ms. Winters thinks silently for a long moment, then concedes: "Well, lemme check with the nurse."

Hunter waited while Ms. Winters went into to her office to call the nurse. When Ms. Winters re-emerged a minute later, she explained in a cautionary tone: "Hunter, she says as long as you're not jumping or running, that's fine." Despite being allowed to play, however, Hunter continued to press for more:

> Hunter asks hopefully: "Well, can I kick if I kick with my left foot?" Ms. Winters frowns, furrowing her eyebrows. Crossing her arms across her chest, she responds skeptically: "But you can't run." Hunter pleads: "I know, but can I have someone run for me?" Ms. Winters lets out a tired sigh and concedes: "Sure." Hunter grins broadly and lets out

a little "Yes!" He then immediately turns and heads back over to his friends, talking with them and negotiating who will run for him when it is his turn to kick.

Whether they were asking for assistance, accommodations, or attention, middle-class children such as Hunter were rarely willing to take no for an answer. That doggedness often raked on the nerves of the teachers, but it was also a successful strategy for getting the support students desired. The distinct possibility of pushback, particularly when coupled with the kinds of time pressures described in Chapter 2, often prompted teachers to say "yes" to middle-class students so that they could move on and avoid wasting time.

Granting students' requests also allowed teachers to avoid pushback (or the possibility of pushback) from middle-class parents. In the spring of fifth grade, for example, all the classes were scheduled to go to a local theater to see a play. The day before the field trip, Mr. Fischer told his students that he expected them to "look nice" for the occasion. That meant slacks or skirts, a sweater or collared shirt, and "nice" shoes—not the nylon track pants and sneakers most students (boys and girls) typically wore to school. Ted (middle-class, white) and Brian (middle-class, mixed-race) immediately protested, insisting that they could wear "track pants" and sneakers and still "look nice." Mr. Fischer disagreed, explaining to Ted and Brian that athletic attire would not "show respect" for the theater. He also noted that students who failed to dress appropriately would face consequences. Ted and Brian tried to argue further, but Mr. Fischer ignored them and moved on. That night, however, Mr. Fischer received what he described as a "flurry of angry e-mails" from Ted and Brian's parents. The next day, after the field trip, Mr. Fischer pulled me aside to chat.

Before I can sit down, Mr. Fischer approaches with his arms folded tight and high across his chest. Mr. Fischer jerks his head toward where Brian and Ted (who are both wearing sneakers and black, athletic-style pants with a white stripe down the side) are sitting and eating their lunches. In a low but gruff voice, Mr. Fischer scoffs: "Apparently those two only wear sweatpants." Mr. Fischer's eyes are sharp, and his jaw is clenched tight—he seems both frustrated and incredulous as he explains that Brian and Ted's mothers both e-mailed him to complain about the "dress code" and inform Mr. Fischer that their sons would not be dressing up for the play. One of the mothers even tried to contend that "this is a public school" and that such demands constituted a "rights violation." Mr. Fischer describes how he e-mailed back, asking, "Doesn't he at least have a pair of khakis he could wear?" Mr. Fischer then shakes his head slowly, recalling disappointedly how the parents e-mailed him again, insisting that "that wasn't the point—it's that you're telling my kid what to wear" and threatening to "take it to the principal." I shake my head in sympathetic disbelief, adding a soft "Wow . . ." Mr. Fischer nods emphatically, then shrugs, letting out a frustrated "Pfft!" and asking dolefully, "What can you do?"

Mr. Fischer wanted his students to "look nice" out of respect for the theater and the opportunity they had been given to enjoy local arts. Ultimately, however, Mr. Fischer decided that it was not worth the fight—Ted and Brian got to wear what they preferred, and they did not face any consequences for doing so. Like Mr. Fischer, the teachers at Maplewood often responded to pushback from parents by granting requests that they might have otherwise denied.

Teachers' decisions to back down in those situations seemed to reflect, at least in part, a reluctance to jeopardize relations with parents. One working-class parent, Ms. Campitello, even went so far as to describe the teachers at Maplewood as being "afraid of the parents." Shaking her head, she sneered:

> I remember [when I was a kid] that if something happened at school, the teacher would call and tell our parents, and we would be scared to death and we wouldn't do it again. It doesn't seem like that anymore. It seems like the teachers here are afraid of the parents.

The teachers did not openly acknowledge such fear. During interviews, for example, most of the teachers at Maplewood were careful to avoid speaking ill of parents, especially by name. However, many teachers did speak, albeit in veiled terms, of concerns about contentious parents and of a desire to maintain good rapport. As fourth-grade teacher Ms. Burns noted in an interview,

> I think overall you'll meet the majority [of parents] that are grateful and supportive. But, you know, you have enough out there, and sometimes they become so contentious that it takes a strain on what you really want to be there for. You really just want to be there to teach the kids and make a difference in the kids' lives and the community. If we can make it so that it's not an "us and a them," that's a positive.

Like Ms. Burns, the teachers at Maplewood wanted to have a positive relationship with parents, and they often seemed wary of sparking the kind of contention that might jeopardize that relationship.

Teachers' desire to avoid conflict with parents seemed to reflect three key risks associated with such conflicts. First, teachers who challenged middle-class parents risked losing important resources. The teachers at Maplewood were deeply dependent on parents, especially middle-class parents, for the

time, money, and support they gave to the school. As third-grade teacher
Ms. Filipelli recalled,

> The parents here are unbelievable. They did this huge fundraiser night. It was a Mardi
> Gras-themed silent auction. And the school plays! The costumes and the props that are
> hand-made and purchased are the best I've ever seen. That was all the parents, the PTO.
> They're really supportive in all of their volunteer programs.

Through fundraisers such as the silent auction, the parent–teacher organization (PTO) at Maplewood regularly brought in more than $50,000 a
year for the school. That money paid for laptops and digital "Smart Boards,"
science equipment, books, art supplies, and countless other resources that
teachers relied on day-to-day. As volunteers, parents, especially middle-class
parents, spent countless hours going on field trips; hosting class parties; and
organizing school fairs, sports nights, and other after-school events. During
contentious teacher contract negotiations, middle-class parents were also
quick to defend the teachers and the local property taxes that paid their sal-
aries, regularly standing up at school board meetings and other community
events to speak about the quality of the education their children received
in Fair Hills schools. Given all that parents contributed, teachers may have
been reluctant to say "no" to parents' or students' requests.

Second, teachers who upset middle-class parents also risked challenges
to their professional authority. Like middle-class parents in other studies
(Horvat, Weininger, and Lareau 2003; Lareau 2000; Lareau and Horvat
1999; Nelson 2010), the middle-class parents at Maplewood were quick
to challenge teachers and bring complaints to higher authorities if they
believed that teachers were being insufficiently responsive to their children's needs. In an interview after fifth grade, for example, middle-class
mother Ms. Brauer was already anticipating problems with course placement in high school. She noted,

> The only two academically accelerated classes they offer [in ninth grade] are going to
> be language arts and math. I would expect Kyle to be able to be in the higher level for
> both. If he isn't, I know that I will address that with the teachers and probably with the
> principal, as well.

Those challenges to teachers' professional authority were particularly common with respect to children's academic placement. As I learned from informal conversations with teachers and from records in students' academic
files, at least five of the middle-class parents successfully lobbied the school
to move their children into the advanced math class or the gifted program.
In many of those cases, parents hired outside experts to test their children

when tests given by the school failed to yield a high enough score. In other cases, parents took their concerns to the principal or even talked of getting lawyers involved. By elevating their complaints in that way, middle-class parents effectively challenged educators' professional authority.[2]

Saying "yes" to middle-class parents and their children allowed teachers to avoid that risk. One middle-class parent, for example, sent an e-mail to her to son's third-grade teacher after receiving a letter with his standardized test scores. The e-mail was included in her son's academic file and read, in part,

> When you can, please contact me so we can discuss these test results. I have a few questions and I'd prefer we have a dialogue so I don't have to go in an unnecessary direction. He is testing only average for 3rd grade (which is fine with me), but I need to hear your opinion on his placement in advanced math. I've also been wondering on how I can help him with multiplication and division since these skills were not taught to him.

In writing that e-mail, the mother seemed concerned that her son's "average" test scores would prevent him from being included in the advanced math class in fourth and fifth grade. The mother also offered veiled threats of having to "go in an unnecessary direction" and even accused the teacher of not teaching multiplication and division skills, both of which were part of the standard curriculum. The teacher politely denied that accusation in a follow-up e-mail but also deferred to the mother's preference regarding placement, noting,

> I'm not sure about your question about multiplication and division. Did you get my letter in the beginning of the year? Have you seen his quiz that came home on multiplication and division and his homework? I spent the month of September teaching the concepts of multiplication and division. I do flash card and games each day for fact fluency. I teach them a times table each week and have them doing practice packets each day to reinforce the times table we are working on. So, as you can see I'm confused by your comment that multiplication and division hasn't been taught to him. It is an ongoing process and will take time for him to have them all memorized. . . . I'll give you a call next week so we can talk about it. Let me know if you prefer a meeting with the two of us [the teacher and the principal] instead of a phone call. We want you to feel comfortable with the placement for [your son].

Despite the harshness of the parent's message, the teacher was extremely polite and conciliatory in her response. It seemed that she wanted to avoid upsetting the parent further. Ultimately, the mother met with the teacher and the principal, who agreed to place the child in the advanced math class for fourth and fifth grade.

I experienced similar challenges first-hand when a middle-class parent complained about my study to the superintendent. When I tried to begin observations of the students in seventh grade at Fair Hills Middle School, a middle-class parent (of a student who was not part of the original cohort at Maplewood) sent me an angry e-mail (copying the principal and the superintendent) calling the study an invasion of privacy and insisting that it should not be allowed to move forward. In the end, and after more than 2 weeks of back-and-forth negotiations (and sleepless nights on my end), the parent agreed to drop the issue if I agreed not to observe in any classrooms in which his child was present. Ultimately, however, and because of that parent, district officials decided that I would not be allowed to complete any additional observations—beyond those planned for seventh grade—in Fair Hills schools.

A third risk that teachers faced in saying "no" to middle-class families was the risk of personal reprisal. The middle-class parents at Maplewood were quick to "blacklist" teachers who they viewed as unresponsive to their children's needs.[3] Mr. Fischer, for example, was one of the few teachers who tried to stand up to middle-class parents. He regularly got into what he called "e-mail battles" with middle-class parents about snack policies and homework and other classroom expectations. As a result, Mr. Fischer developed a reputation among parents as "harsh" and "unresponsive." That reputation also had real consequences for Mr. Fischer. In interviews (conducted after their children finished fifth grade), a number of middle-class parents reported asking the principal not to place their children in Mr. Fischer's class. Middle-class mother Ms. Shore even pulled her son Christian from Mr. Fischer's class after less than a week of school. She explained,

> My son Trevor did not have a good fifth-grade year with Mr. Fischer. It wasn't anything horrible. Trevor was part of the in-crowd, and they were always going for the laugh, and they would get in trouble. But Trevor isn't a behavioral problem. It was just a tough year for that group, and Trevor was a part of it. And I had been in there over and over trying to address the issue. So when it came time for Christian to be in fifth grade, I gambled, thinking Christian would never get Mr. Fischer. He did. And I know Christian could sense my frustration. Because it had been such a difficult year for Trevor—that negative experience had spilled over into our household. So, Christian became very anxious about the fact that he had Mr. Fischer. And after the first few days [of the school year], I just felt like it wasn't gonna go well. So I had a conversation with Dr. Weiss, and she was able to transfer Christian to Ms. Hudson's class.

Some of the middle-class parents who had "negative experiences" with Mr. Fischer also encouraged their friends to avoid his class as well. In interviews, the parents on the receiving end of such advice talked knowingly about how they tried to influence their children's placement by writing letters stating that "certain teachers" would not be a "good fit" for their child.

Mr. Fischer, meanwhile, seemed hurt by such actions. During the second week of fifth grade, after Ms. Shore had successfully lobbied to have her son Christian moved to another teacher's class, I was chatting with Mr. Fischer before school:

> Mr. Fischer notices the seating chart I'm drawing in my notes and lets out a nervous chuckle, "We're down to 24." he says sheepishly. Looking up, I see that Mr. Fischer has his arms crossed tightly across his chest. "What happened?" I ask. Mr. Fischer looks away. His usual playful gruffness is gone—his shoulders sag and he looks defeated, almost embarrassed. After a pause, Mr. Fischer continues, his voice breaking, as he explains that "One mom, I had her older son, too. She decided this wasn't going to be a good fit." At that point, students start to arrive, and Mr. Fischer stops abruptly. He gives me a wan smile and heads for the front of the room.

Like Mr. Fischer, the teachers at Maplewood seemed hurt by parents' criticisms and harsh words. In light of the possibility of pushback, then, and seemingly out of concerns about logistical, professional, and personal repercussions, teachers often found themselves granting requests—including requests from students—that they might have otherwise denied.

SUMMARY AND CONCLUSIONS

The teachers at Maplewood wanted to provide a level playing field. They cared deeply about their students, especially students with "tough" home lives. They also went out of their way to help students who might be struggling.

Ultimately, however, and as demonstrated in previous chapters, teachers' actions often served to reinforce existing inequalities. Teachers consistently said "yes" to middle-class students' requests for assistance, accommodations, and attention. They did so when those requests were in excess of what was fair or required, when granting those requests would privilege middle-class students over their working-class peers, and even when they wanted to say "no."

This chapter helps explain why, despite their good intentions, teachers translated students' class-based strategies into unequal opportunities in school. Specifically, I found that saying "yes" to requests for support allowed teachers to avoid real and potentially detrimental pushback. That included pushback from both middle-class students and middle-class parents. As discussed previously, middle-class students rarely took "no" for an answer. Instead, they treated "no" as teachers' opening gambit in a back-and-forth negotiation. As a result, saying "yes" meant that teachers could avoid wasting class time. Saying "yes" also helped teachers avoid getting parents involved. Middle-class parents were quick to challenge "unresponsive" teachers (i.e., complaining about them to the principal, the superintendent, and other parents and sometimes getting outside experts involved). Given middle-class parents' instrumental contributions, teachers who said "no" to middle-class parents risked losing important financial, logistical, and even political support for the school. Furthermore, and given middle-class parents' influence, those teachers also put their own personal and professional credibility in jeopardy. Faced with those possibilities, it seemed reasonable for teachers to say "yes" instead.

Teachers are an easy scapegoat for educational inequalities. For more than a decade, accountability has been central to education policy debates (Hallett 2010; Jennings 2010). Policymakers often assume that if we hold schools and teachers accountable—through high-stakes testing and more school choice—student performance will improve and inequalities will disappear. Scholars have also contributed to this air of teacher blame, although research has focused more on teachers' biases than on their lack of accountability. It is known, for example, that teachers typically underestimate the capabilities of less privileged students (Kozlowski 2015; Ready and Wright 2011), discipline them more harshly (Gregory, Skiba, and Noguera 2010; Kupchik 2009; Morris 2005), and provide them with fewer opportunities for high-quality learning (Eder 1981; Oakes 2005; Rist 2000).

Although my research was not designed to assess the prevalence of teacher bias or the impact of increased accountability, it does raise questions about the extent to which teachers deserve blame. As discussed in this chapter, the teachers at Maplewood wanted their students to succeed, and they often went out of their way to help students who appeared to be struggling. That combination of good intentions and unequal outcomes closely mirrors what Lewis and Diamond (2015) found in their research on racial bias in high school track assignments. The teachers they studied were aware that black students were being disproportionately assigned to lower tracks, and they wanted to increase equality, but their actions upheld the status quo. Like Lewis and Diamond, I found that teachers did so, at least in part, because of fear of pushback. Denying privileges to those who sought them had real consequences for teachers. It led to protracted negotiations that took up class time. In some cases, denying privileges even resulted in personal and professional attacks (see also Horvat, Weininger, and Lareau 2003). Given those risks, teachers who wanted to say "no" may have felt pressured to just say "yes" instead.

Unfortunately, however, those actions had real implications for inequalities. By saying "yes" to middle-class students, teachers privileged strategies of influence over strategies of deference. Through those positive responses, teachers ensured that middle-class students received the assistance, accommodations, and attention they desired, even when that support was in excess of what was fair or required. In doing so, teachers gave middle-class students an advantage over the working-class students who tried to manage on their own.

CHAPTER 7

Alternative Explanations

The primary goal of this book is to show how social class matters in the classroom. Consistent with that goal, the preceding chapters have shown how children learn class-based strategies from their parents, how they activate those strategies in interactions with teachers, and how teachers' responses in those interactions contribute to inequalities in school.

This focus on the origins and consequences of children's class-based problem-solving strategies is important, but it leaves other questions unanswered—questions about how much children's class-based strategies matter and whether they change over time, questions about gender and race, and questions about social context and the extent to which students learn from their peers. This chapter turns to those lingering questions, weaving together my own data with evidence from prior research.

DO THESE DIFFERENCES REALLY MATTER?

As discussed in Chapter 6, teachers often said "yes" to middle-class students, even when they had reason to deny students' requests. How much did those "yeses" really matter? And for whom did they matter most?

In most situations at Maplewood Elementary, students who sought support—especially those who did so assertively and persistently—received the assistance, accommodations, and attention they desired. They got to share their stories. They got to express more creativity with their projects. They got to sit closer to the board. They got to take off their coats at recess. They got help dealing with bullies. They got extensions on assignments. They got extra hints on tests. They got teachers to check their work for them before turning it in.

Individually, the benefits were small, but together they had major ramifications. As Table 7.1 shows, middle-class students received higher grades (on average) than their working-class peers. This study cannot definitively link differences in grade point average (GPA) to differences in students' requests for support. However, if students were able to get more support from teachers and if they were able to use that support to improve their performance on tests and assignments, it certainly seems possible that social class differences in students' support-seeking could contribute to inequalities in student outcomes. Consistent with that possibility, research shows a strong correlation between students' (self-reported) help-seeking and higher achievement in school (Gall 1985; Newman 2000; Ryan, Hicks, and Midgley 1997; Stanton-Salazar 1997; Stanton-Salazar and Dornbusch 1995).

Support from teachers may also have been particularly beneficial for students who were struggling academically, socially, or emotionally. As Table 7.1 also shows, requests for assistance were most common among average/lower-achieving middle-class students and least common among working-class students in that same achievement category. Within the average/lower achievement category, the GPAs of middle-class students were higher than those of their working-class counterparts (3.41 vs. 2.96, respectively). Again, I cannot state for certain that differences in help-seeking contributed directly to differences in GPA. However, it seems possible that support from teachers may have allowed average- or lower-ability middle-class students to perform higher than otherwise expected. Such patterns

Table 7.1 AVERAGE REQUESTS FOR ASSISTANCE PER STUDENT PER DAY, BY SOCIAL CLASS AND ACHIEVEMENT[a]

Social Class	Achievement[b]	No. of Students	Average GPA	Average Requests per Day
Middle class	Higher achieving	18	3.93	7.3
	Average/lower achieving	24	3.41	8.1
Working class	Higher achieving	2	3.90	2.0
	Average/lower achieving	12	2.96	0.7

[a]Averages are calculated using the count data described in Chapter 3. This table breaks down the daily averages reported in Table 3.1 by social class and student achievement level. Averages include only white students.
[b]Higher achieving students are those with grade point averages (GPAs) more than half a standard deviation above the mean (>3.74). Lower-achieving students are those with GPAs that fall below that threshold (<3.74). GPAs are calculated using marking period grades in math, language arts, social studies, and science during grades 3–5. The overall grade distribution was relatively small, with most students receiving A's and B's (mean GPA, 3.46). Thus, I opted to divide the students into two groups rather than consider differences across narrower ranges of achievement.

would be consistent with research showing that average- and lower-ability youth often have the most to gain from privilege.[1] Research on tracking and ability grouping, for example, shows that even with actual ability controlled, more privileged students are disproportionately assigned to higher-ability groups in elementary school (Dauber, Alexander, and Entwisle 1996; Oakes 2005; Tach and Farkas 2006). Such placement exposes students to the kind of higher-quality instruction that bolsters subsequent achievement (Eder 1981; Gamoran 1986; Pallas et al. 1994). If help-seeking and other forms of self-advocacy act as signals to teachers of a student's aptitude and engagement with learning, then those requests might help explain both disproportionate placement decisions and the benefits that middle-class students, especially marginal middle-class students, reap from them.

In summary, these patterns support the idea that micro profits—the kinds of situational advantages middle-class students secure through their requests—could have a macro payoff. They might even contribute to persistent class-based inequalities in school achievement and attainment. As the next section explains, those profits also did not diminish over time. Rather, they seemed to compound as students progressed through school.

DO THESE DIFFERENCES PERSIST OVER TIME?

Another lingering question concerns the extent to which patterns of influence and deference persist as students move through school. It is known from work on higher education that first-generation college students often experience a cultural mismatch between their own beliefs, behaviors, and orientations and those valued by colleges (Lee and Kramer 2013; Stephens et al. 2012).[2] Jack (2016), for example, highlights social class differences in students' comfort interacting with faculty in elite colleges. Similarly, research on post-college transitions shows that upwardly mobile adults often experience cultural discomfort and even cultural discrimination in elite work environments (Lubrano 2004; Rivera 2010; Stuber 2005).

Consistent with such findings, my observations at Fair Hills Middle School suggested that class-based problem-solving strategies persisted as children got older and transitioned across different levels of schooling. As they moved from third to seventh grade,[3] the middle-class students seemed increasingly adept at voicing their needs and negotiating for assistance, accommodations, and attention. The working-class students instead seemed to grow more reserved with teachers than they were in the past. Those differences were readily apparent one afternoon in Mr. Warner's seventh-grade social studies class. The students had just finished a unit on sociology. Half of their final grade for the unit would be based on a group project on "institutions." Each group spent 2 weeks researching and preparing presentations about a particular institution (schools, family, government, etc.). On presentation day, however, a number of students realized that members of their groups were not in class because of a rehearsal for the upcoming band and orchestra concert:

> Gina Giordano and a number of other middle-class students get up from their seats and dash over to Mr. Warner, crowding around his desk. With worried expressions on their faces, they breathlessly explain that some of their group members are missing. Tugging anxiously at her long, curly hair, Gina even asks if her group can "go tomorrow" instead. Mr. Warner leans back in his chair and lets out a long breath. Ultimately, he decides that he needs to "stay on schedule." Tyler Matthews, another middle-class, white student with a round face and a mop of sandy-colored hair, hears this and moans loudly, complaining: "But it's not fair! We practiced all together!" and "We might not get a good grade!" Mr. Warner tries to reassure the students, but they continue to press him. Sensing the tension in the air, Mr. Warner asks the class: "Do you guys want five minutes to go over your stuff?" The students let out grateful exclamations of "Yes!" and "Yeah!" The room immediately begins to buzz with activity as the students cluster together with their group members to prepare.

As the students worked, and amid all the noise and movement, working-class, white student Shawn Marrone was standing quietly at his desk, a worried frown on his long, thin face:

> Shawn raises his hand and asks quietly: "Mr. Warner?" With all of the commotion, Mr. Warner does not hear Shawn or notice his raised hand. Instead, Mr. Warner is fielding questions from a group of middle-class students gathered around him. The students are asking (off-topic) questions about an upcoming field trip. As Shawn continues to wait with his hand raised, other students call out, asking: "What kind of shoes do we need?" and "What bus am I on?" and "What group am I in?" Gina Giordano joins the conversation, as well. She asks Mr. Warner to explain how the teachers assigned students to groups for the trip. As the field trip discussion continues, Shawn sighs and puts his hand down.

During that class period, Shawn never got his question answered. Middle-class students like Gina, on the other hand, got more time to work on their projects and also got answers to off-topic questions about the upcoming field trip. As those differences suggest, class-based patterns of support-seeking persisted from elementary middle school. Gina and the other middle-class students were very comfortable asking for assistance and accommodations and attention. Working-class students such as Shawn, however, continued to be more hesitant in making requests and backed down easily if teachers did not immediately notice and respond.

These class-based patterns seemed to persist, at least in part, because of the structure of different levels of schooling. In older grades, class sizes were larger: Third-grade classes typically had approximately 20 students, whereas many seventh-grade classes had closer to 30 students. In middle school, students also had a different teacher for each subject. Each teacher taught more than 100 students, and students spent only 45 minutes a day with each of their teachers. The curriculum also got more intense as students moved through school, with an increased emphasis on new material and less time in class for practice, review, and sharing of work. Given those constraints, teachers in older grades relied more on students to voice their own needs. Like Mr. Warner, they spent more time at their desks, waiting for students to approach them rather than circle around and monitor students for signs of struggle. That lack of outreach, coupled with the lack of time teachers spent with each student, may have led working-class students in older grades to feel more detached from (and thus even less inclined to seek support from) their teachers.

Compared to the elementary school teachers, however, the middle school teachers did seem somewhat more comfortable denying students' requests. One morning in Ms. Lupin's science class, the seventh graders were getting ready to go to the science lab to prep for a dissection project:

> Ms. Lupin calls out loudly, directing the students to pack up their notebooks and head across the hall. Meanwhile, Tyler Matthews (middle-class, white) is working on the computer. When Tyler does not immediately get up from his seat, Ms. Lupin glares at him and barks: "Tyler! Time to pack up." Rather than comply, Tyler protests: "But I'm not done!" Ms. Lupin lets out a breathy laugh, retorting skeptically: "Whadda you *mean* you're not done?" Tyler tries to give some sort of rambling explanation about how he is working on something for his lab journal, but Ms. Lupin just poo-poos him and tells him to "hurry up."

Later on in the period, Ms. Lupin caught another middle-class, white student, Oliver, with an "invisible ink" pen. Although Oliver tried to protest that he "wasn't doing anything wrong," Ms. Lupin took away the pen anyway. Middle school teachers generally had a more no-nonsense attitude compared to their elementary counterparts. They seemed to say "no" somewhat more often and were also gruffer with students, both in reprimanding them for misbehavior and in everyday, playful banter. That gruffness seemed particularly common in teachers' interactions with middle school boys, although I did witness gruff treatment of girls as well, such as when Ms. Lupin openly chastised a group of girls for talking during an in-class video and when she took a girl's notebook after hearing rumors that there was a disparaging remark about another student written inside.

Middle school teachers' willingness to deny students' requests could have helped to level the playing field, but ultimately it did not. That was because middle school teachers' increased gruffness also seemed to make it more difficult for working-class students to feel comfortable voicing their needs. By seventh grade, working-class students worried even more than they did in elementary school about upsetting or disrespecting teachers with their requests, and they seemed largely justified in those concerns. In a follow-up interview conducted during the summer after seventh grade, Jesse Compton (working-class, white) talked about the differences between elementary and middle school teachers, noting, "Elementary they stay nice the whole year. Middle school they get tough after half the year and they don't give you as much help." Jesse also believed that it was more difficult in middle school to talk to his teachers and more difficult to rely on them for support. He explained,

> It's so much pressure. And I'm trying as hard as I can. And my mom keeps telling me over and over again: "You've gotta pick up your grades." And I do, and then all of a sudden my grades go down and I'm thinking: "How did this happen?" Cuz like, the teachers will say: "You all did really well on this test." But then I didn't. And I was mad, but I didn't wanna say anything, because they'll just say you did it wrong.

In elementary school, Jesse would race down the hall so that he could be the first student in class each morning, and his teachers would often use that extra time to talk with Jesse and ask him about what was going on at home. In middle school, Jesse was almost always the first person in class each period, but he usually just sat by himself. He seemed to be waiting for teachers to approach him, but at least when I was there, they never did. Instead, middle school teachers typically spent the brief moments between periods setting up for the next lesson. As a result, and like other working-class students, seventh-grade Jesse seemed adrift. He wanted to connect with his teachers, but it was increasingly difficult for him to do so.

In middle school, then, working-class students seemed to be at an even larger disadvantage than they were in elementary school. Compared to their middle-class peers, working-class students were less comfortable seeking support for themselves and had less practice doing so. Thus, even when they could have asked for assistance or accommodations or attention, and even when doing so could have had real benefits, working-class students often opted not to do so. Jesse, for example, lost a language arts packet that he was supposed to complete for homework. Rather than ask Ms. Cartwright for a new one, Jesse just accepted a "0" for the assignment. A few weeks later, however, Jesse's mother found the packet when she was cleaning, and she encouraged Jesse to complete it anyway. Jesse did complete the assignment. He then put the completed packet on Ms. Cartwright's desk, leaving it for her without explanation. The next day, Ms. Cartwright gave the packet back to Jesse ungraded:

> Ms. Cartwright drops the packet on Jesse's desk. Firmly, and a bit incredulously, Ms. Cartwright explains: "It's a little too late for that now. I mean, that [assignment] was like a month ago!" Jesse does not look up. He nods slowly, but he keeps his shoulders hunched forward and his head low. As Ms. Cartwright heads back to her desk, Jesse sighs heavily. Sitting a few feet away, I give Jesse a reassuring smile. Jesse glances up at me, his face and shoulders heavy with resignation. He murmurs quietly, almost sadly: "It wasn't to get a better grade. It was to make me a better person."

I asked Jesse about that comment later, and he explained that his mother encouraged him to complete the packet not because she thought the teacher would grant him a reprieve and reverse the "0" grade but, rather, because she believed that it was the right thing to do—to work hard and take responsibility for his actions. Like Jesse, working-class students knew that teachers could help them or even change their grades, but they rarely sought such support for themselves. Instead, and as in elementary school, they tried to deal with problems on their own.

These persistent differences in student behavior are important because they align with larger patterns of inequality. It is known that achievement gaps between more and less privileged students widen as students move from elementary to secondary school (Gutman and Midgley 2000; Jimerson, Egeland, and Teo 1999; Rumberger and Palardy 2005). Although more research is needed to connect class-based patterns of support-seeking to students' academic outcomes, it seems possible that those problem-solving strategies could help explain the widening gaps. They might also help explain class-based gaps in disciplinary sanctions. Those sanctions are even more detrimental for students at the secondary level than at the elementary level (Bertrand and Pan 2011), making it important to understand the consequences of social class differences in accommodation-seeking over time.

DO CLASS CULTURES REALLY MATTER?

Some readers may question whether differences in students' problem-solving strategies are really the product of distinct class cultures. However, alternative explanations for such differences are largely incomplete.

Educational psychologists, for example, link classroom behavior to students' "goal orientations" (Dweck 1986). From that perspective, mastery-focused students should readily seek support from teachers, whereas performance-focused students should avoid doing so for fear of being perceived as "stupid" (Butler 1998; Karabenick 1998; Newman 2000; Newman and Goldin 1990). It is known, however, that middle-class families focus more than working-class families on grades and academic performance (Brantlinger 2003; Nelson 2010). Thus, differences in student motivation seem incapable of fully explaining social class differences in students' help-seeking.

Resistance theory offers another potential explanation for social class differences in student problem solving. From that perspective, working-class students reject school (and defy school authorities) because they perceive an incompatibility between their class identities and the kinds of behaviors valued and rewarded in school (Giroux 1983; MacLeod 1995; McGrew 2011; Willis 1977). As demonstrated at Maplewood, however, the working-class students wanted to do well in school. Although they were less focused on grades than were their middle-class peers, working-class students relished praise from their teachers, and they avoided challenging teachers or even creating the appearance of disrespect. The working-class students at Maplewood also appreciated help and support.[4] When asked in interviews (after both fifth grade and seventh grade) to describe a "good" teacher, one of the most common adjectives they used was "helpful." If anything, it was the middle-class students who more often appeared resistant to teachers' authority (see also McFarland 2001). Given such findings, it seems unlikely that resistance to school or teachers' authority can explain the differences in student–teacher interaction that I observed at Maplewood.

Instead, it seems likely that those differences resulted in large part from the class-based, cultural coaching that children received at home. As discussed previously, parents' messages had a deep and powerful impact on children. They shaped children's beliefs about the nature of success and the behaviors needed to achieve it. In the classroom, particularly when teachers' expectations were vague or varying, those class-based beliefs became a safety net, offering an alternative way through or around the kinds of tricky situations that students often encountered in school.

DOES GENDER MATTER?

Class is clearly not the only thing that matters in the classroom. It is known, for example, that girls typically outperform boys in school. Since the 1950s, girls have earned higher grades than boys, and that female advantage now extends to educational attainment as well (Buchmann, DiPrete, and McDaniel 2008; DiPrete and Buchmann 2013). There is also evidence that those advantages may be the result of gender differences in student behavior or at least gender differences in teachers' responses to student behavior (DiPrete and Jennings 2012; Owens 2016). On average, teachers rate girls' behavior more favorably, subject them to less frequent and less harsh punishment, and set higher expectations for their achievement in school (Bertrand and Pan 2011; Jones and Myhill 2004; Morris 2005).

Given those patterns, some might wonder: Does gender shape how students deal with challenges at school? Does it affect the messages parents teach their children at home? Does it affect how students activate strategies of influence or deference in the classroom? Does it affect how teachers respond to those efforts?

Although this study was not explicitly designed to assess how gender mattered in students' efforts to deal with challenges in the classroom, my findings do offer tentative insights in that regard. Overall, I found that whereas gender did matter in some aspects of classroom life, it was less salient in others (see also Blaise 2007; Eder 1995; Messner 2000; Thorne 1993). Specifically, boys and girls (from the same social class background) received similar lessons from parents about managing challenges at school, acted on those lessons in similar (although not identical) ways, and received similar responses from teachers in doing so.

Given the important role that parents play in gender socialization (Eccles, Jacobs, and Harold 1990; Gunderson et al. 2012; Kane 2006; Martin 2005; Raley and Bianchi 2006), I was surprised to see that parents did not teach boys and girls different lessons about interacting with teachers and securing support in school. Almost all of the parents I interviewed had more than one child, and those parents described similar coaching incidents with all of their children, regardless of gender. In many cases, they also talked about coaching one child while others were present and using the experience of one child as a lesson for all. When I interviewed working-class father Mr. Graham, for example, his oldest son, Trevor, was a junior in high school. Although Trevor did well in school, he was much more interested in music and spent a great deal of time practicing with his band. Trevor was contemplating graduating early and forgoing college so that he could "go on tour" and try to "get a record deal." Mr. Graham described the numerous conversations he had with his children—including Trevor and his younger sisters, Jenny and Amelia—about the decision:

> Trevor's not ruling out college. Is he going straight to college? No. But he's not ruling it out, and he's not opposed to it. His mother and I have tried to explain to him—to all of them—about what they can do now to affect where they're at twenty years from now.

Like, my vantage point on education is I bit myself in the butt so far. So I see the value of if I would've done something different to this point, and I tell them that. I would be thrilled for my kids to take education beyond what their parents, you know, what we did. Like, they've experienced first-hand some of the family frustrations we've had, our home, or maybe you can't buy a different vehicle when you need it. So they've had a sense of the financial . . . I'm not gonna say *hardship*, cuz we're not poor, but *frustrations*. We're trying to get them to understand that education, how that can benefit them down the road. Like, so with Trevor, even if it takes him ten years, take it! Just do it!

Mr. Graham wanted to support his children and give them the freedom to make their own decisions. Like other working-class parents, however, he (and his ex-wife) hoped that their children, regardless of gender, would not repeat the mistakes they believed they had made in their own lives. Certainly, there may have been gender differences in other lessons that parents taught to children (Gunderson et al. 2012; Martin 2005). With respect to problem-solving, however, those differences seemed minimal.

Gender also did not seem particularly consequential in children's efforts to get the assistance, accommodations, and attention they desired. Middle-class boys and girls, for example, asked similar questions and did so in similar ways (e.g., calling out rather than raising their hands and being persistent in the face of pushback). Girls and boys also made similar types of requests, asking to work with partners, to get extensions on assignments, to have extra recesses and other special privileges, and to avoid punishment when they forgot their homework or got in trouble for being off task or for not following the rules. Boys and girls also tried to get attention for similar things. Girls bragged about their soccer trophies. Boys showed the teacher how they learned to dance the Charleston in gym class. Both groups loved to share the stories they had written and the pictures they had drawn and the experiences they had with their friends and their families at home.

Despite those similarities, there were some subtle gender differences in problem-solving. With respect to assistance-seeking, for example, my count data suggested that although boys and girls made similar numbers of requests overall, boys made somewhat more frequent requests for information, often by connecting their own knowledge and interests to the topic at hand (e.g., "Are there any houses around here that were part of the Underground Railroad?"). Girls, on the other hand, made slightly more requests for clarification (e.g., "Are we supposed to circle the predicate or underline it?" or "I don't get what we're supposed to write here") (Table 7.2). Similarly, with respect to attention-seeking, although both boys and girls used self-deprecation ("I'm so bad at this!") to elicit reassurance from the teacher ("You're doing fine!"), those comments seemed somewhat more common among girls than among boys (especially in the

Table 7.2 STUDENTS' REQUESTS FOR HELP FROM TEACHERS, BY GENDER AND 60-MINUTE SUBJECT PERIOD[a]

	Math (Test/Quiz)		Language Arts (Writing Activity)		Science (In-Class Project)		Flex Time (Various Activities)		Total	
	Male	Female	Male	Female	Male	Female	Male	Female	Male	Female
Students present	27	25	25	25	26	28	27	28	26	27
Types of Requests										
Assistance[b]										
Requests per student (total requests)	0.74 (20)	0.76 (19)	0.24 (6)	0.40 (10)	0.38 (10)	0.14 (4)	0.26 (7)	0.21 (6)	1.62 (43)	1.47 (39)
Clarification[c]										
Requests per student (total requests)	0.73 (19)	1.00 (25)	0.64 (16)	0.80 (20)	0.69 (18)	0.61 (17)	0.48 (13)	0.64 (18)	2.49 (66)	3.02 (80)
Checking of work[d]										
Requests per student (total requests)	0.41 (11)	0.48 (12)	0.24 (6)	0.28 (7)	0.12 (3)	0.25 (7)	0.44 (12)	0.25 (7)	1.21 (32)	1.25 (33)
Information[e]										
Requests per student (total requests)	0.07 (2)	0.08 (2)	0.28 (7)	0.16 (4)	0.23 (6)	0.11 (3)	0.19 (5)	0.11 (3)	0.75 (20)	0.45 (12)
Total requests per student (total requests)	1.93 (52)	2.32 (58)	1.40 (35)	1.64 (41)	1.42 (37)	1.11 (31)	1.37 (37)	1.21 (34)	6.08 (161)	6.19 (164)

[a]Within each subject period, requests are aggregated across the four classrooms in fifth grade. Counts include only white students.
[b]Assistance: Direct ("Can you help me?") and indirect ("I don't get this") requests for interactive support for problems students are having with projects, activities, assignments, and physical aspects of the classroom environment.
[c]Clarification: Direct ("What does this mean?") and indirect ("This doesn't make sense") questions about general classroom instructions; directions for specific activities; and questions on tests, worksheets, and assignments.
[d]Checking of work: Direct ("Can you check this?") and indirect ("Is this right?") requests for teachers to look over or judge the accuracy of students' actions during classroom activities and their completed work on assignments, projects, and tests/quizzes.
[e]Information: Requests for teachers to provide additional knowledge or instruction (e.g., "Did they find water on the moon?" and "How do you use a protractor to draw 420 degrees?").

older grades). Those subtle differences could be taken to suggest that girls were somewhat less confident in their knowledge and abilities or at least were less comfortable demonstrating their expertise. Such conclusions would be consistent with what existing research indicates about gender and academic self-efficacy. It is known, for example, that despite outperforming boys on most measures, girls are more modest in assessing their academic capabilities and that those differences become more pronounced as children move from elementary to middle school (Pajares 2002; Wigfield, Eccles, and Pintrich 1996).

The girls at Maplewood, however, were not shrinking violets. Whereas the boys often focused their attention-seeking efforts on being funny, many of the girls tried to get noticed for their leadership skills. During group work, girls would often volunteer to take charge and to be the spokesperson for their group. Many of the middle-class girls, especially those who were heavily involved in sports such as soccer and basketball, were also intensely competitive. Lisa, for example, was the fastest student in the grade, handily beating the boys in gym class races, and she was widely celebrated for her athletic talents. Like their male counterparts, many of the middle-class girls were also competitive with respect to academics, eagerly comparing test scores with classmates to determine who had the highest grade. Although exploring those patterns is beyond the scope of this book, they may help explain why there were not more gender differences in students' problem-solving strategies, especially when compared to the differences that existed with respect to social class.

Teachers' responses to students' requests (or the lack thereof) were also similar across genders, albeit with key exceptions. Many teachers explicitly promoted gender equality, even going so far as to call students "kiddos" rather than "boys and girls." In keeping with those ideals, teachers generally treated boys' and girls' requests in similar ways. During math classes, for example, it was common for teachers to circle around while students were working on practice problems. As they did so, teachers often fielded requests for help and clarification, and I often heard them repeating the same hints or instructions almost verbatim as they moved from student to student. After answering the same question enough times, teachers would usually make an announcement to the class as a whole. Similarly, with regard to opportunities for sharing stories and answering questions in class, many of the teachers would make a point of alternating boy–girl to give everyone an "equal" chance to contribute.

However, there were ways that gender mattered in teachers' responses to strategies of influence and deference. Boys, for example, received somewhat more unsolicited support from teachers (Table 7.3). Those differences may have reflected the fact that more boys than girls had Individualized

Table 7.3 TEACHERS' OFFERS OF UNSOLICITED SUPPORT, BY GENDER AND
60-MINUTE SUBJECT PERIOD[a]

	Math (Test/Quiz)		Language Arts (Writing Activity)		Science (In-Class Project)		Flex Time (Various Activities)		Total	
	Male	Female	Male	Female	Male	Female	Male	Female	Male	Female
Students present	27	25	25	25	26	28	27	28	26	27
Requests per student (total requests)	0.41 (11)	0.28 (7)	0.28 (7)	0.12 (3)	0.12 (3)	0.21 (6)	0.44 (12)	0.18 (5)	1.25 (33)	0.79 (21)

[a]Within each subject period, offers of unsolicited support are aggregated across the four classrooms in fifth grade. Counts include only white students.

Education Plans (IEPs), a pattern consistent with national research on special education (Hibel, Farkas, and Morgan 2010). Knowing that those students had diagnosed learning disabilities may have prompted teachers to
check on those students more often.

Teachers were also somewhat gruffer with boys, although that high level
of gruffness seemed to be largely reserved for a group of boys (including
six middle-class and two working-class boys) who teachers openly labeled
"troublemakers." Teachers seemed to monitor those boys particularly
closely, and when they saw evidence of off-task or disruptive behavior,
they often responded with harsher words and reprimands. One morning in
math class, for example, both Ms. Hudson and her classroom aide repeatedly chastised Cody (working-class, mixed-race) and Kyle (middle-class,
white) for talking during the lesson. Although other students made noise
or carried on side conversations, and although Ms. Hudson occasionally
reminded the whole class to "quiet down" or "stay focused," only Cody and
Kyle were singled out by name. Similarly, when Ms. Hudson started going
over a set of practice problems on the board, she looked up at Cody (as if to
check if he was on task) and noticed that he was using a paper clip to bore a
hole in an eraser. Ms. Hudson immediately stopped and instructed Cody to
put the eraser on her desk. Cody did not protest. Instead, he got up slowly,
his face red with embarrassment, and slunk up to Ms. Hudson's desk, where
he deposited the eraser neatly before returning to his seat.

It is difficult to determine whether such treatment resulted from actual
or perceived gender differences in students' behaviors. I can state, however,
that even with teachers' heightened skepticism, the middle-class boys in the
"troublemaker" group still were generally successful in persuading teachers
to grant them the assistance, accommodations, and attention they desired.
One afternoon, for example, Gina, Lizbeth, and Christian (all middle-class,

white students) went to Ms. Hudson to ask for permission to use the computers to edit their essays rather than editing by hand. Ms. Hudson let them all use the computers, but she made Christian use the last available computer in her classroom while allowing Gina and Lizbeth to go across the hall to ask Mr. Potter if they could use computers in his classroom instead. Christian still got what he wanted (using the computer), even if he had to stay close by (presumably so that Ms. Hudson could keep an eye on him). Even more important, and as demonstrated with Christian's outburst in Chapter 1, male, middle-class "troublemakers" often managed to escape actual consequences for their misbehavior. The working-class "troublemakers" (Zach and Cody), on the other hand, often faced sanctions for misbehavior and rarely got the extra support they needed or desired.

Overall, these patterns suggest that although gender clearly matters in the classroom, boys and girls manage classroom challenges in similar ways and with similar (but not identical) consequences. These patterns may seem surprising, but they do align with prior research. It is known, for example, that although boys and girls often differ in their classroom behavior (Younger, Warrington, and Williams 1999)[5] and achievement (Buchmann and DiPrete 2013), those differences are typically less pronounced in schools—such as Maplewood—that actively celebrate learning and support those efforts with ample resources (Legewie and DiPrete 2012). Consistent with those patterns, I found that boys and girls at Maplewood performed similarly on standardized tests (averaging 224 and 221, respectively, on one fifth-grade math assessment) and received similar grades overall (average GPA in fifth grade, 3.38 and 3.44, respectively). The boys at Maplewood also did not actively reject school or pride themselves on exerting limited effort. Instead, and like the girls, the boys at Maplewood actively celebrated their own achievements and those of their friends.[6]

DOES RACE MATTER?

Given the importance of race and ethnicity in education more generally (Carter and Welner 2013; Kao and Thompson 2003), readers might wonder whether race and ethnicity might also impact the strategies children activate when managing challenges at school.

Race and ethnicity clearly matter in children's interactions with teachers. Teachers, especially white teachers, rate black students' behavior less favorably than they do that of white students (Downey and Pribesh 2004),[7] and they often underestimate the academic capabilities of black students (Oates 2003). Those teacher perceptions also have real consequences. Black students are more likely to be assigned to lower academic tracks (Gamoran and Mare 1989; Lucas and Berends 2002; Oakes 2005; Rist 2000), and they face more serious consequences for disciplinary infractions (Kupchik 2009; Morris 2005). Looking beyond black–white differences, the evidence is more mixed, but research does find that teacher race/ethnicity and student race/ethnicity interact to shape teachers' perceptions and treatment of students at school (Farkas 2003; McGrady and Reynolds 2013).

Race and ethnicity also matter in the kinds of socialization messages that children hear from their parents at home. Minority students are more likely to face both subtle and overt discrimination (Carter 2003; Delpit 2006; Lee and Rice 2007; Lewis 2003; Lewis and Diamond 2015; Morris 2005).[8] As a result, minority parents often try to help their children by instilling racial/ethnic pride and by preparing them for the possibility of bias (Hughes et al. 2006; McHale et al. 2006).[9]

Given such findings, it seems possible that class-based patterns of influence and deference could vary along racial and ethnic lines. To investigate those possibilities in a qualitative study, the researcher would need to be able to isolate the importance of race and ethnicity from that of other factors such as social class in shaping what students learn from their parents about interacting with teachers and dealing with challenges, how students internalize and act on those messages, how teachers respond to those efforts, and how those efforts contribute to inequalities. Because of the logistical challenges of studying both race and class in a single school setting, I opted to focus this study on white students and on the importance of social class in shaping children's efforts to deal with challenges at school. However, there were a number of minority students in my sample, and I can speak tentatively to the preliminary insights that can be drawn from their experiences in school.

Overall, my observations revealed that class-based patterns of influence and deference were present not only in the white population at Maplewood but also in the minority populations.[10] Like their white counterparts, for example, middle-class Asian American children (and the one middle-class mixed-race student) regularly activated strategies of influence at school. One afternoon in Ms. Phillips's class, the fourth graders were supposed to be working independently on various activities during "flex time." Ms. Phillips had to step out for a brief meeting with the principal, so a substitute came in to watch the class. The substitute, Ms. Jacobs, gave the students a list of approved activities and explained that they could each spend up to 8 minutes at the computer station, where they could work on finishing and printing the bibliography for their social studies projects. Brian (middle-class, mixed-race) and Kal (middle-class, Asian American), were the first to get on the computers. Fifteen minutes later, they were still there. Rather than work-ing on their bibliographies, however, the boys were chatting about "text speak" instead:

> Brian and Kal are at the computers talking, and Ms. Jacobs goes over to investi-gate, asking the boys why they are not working on their projects. Brian turns toward Ms. Jacobs and moans dejectedly: "My website disappeared!" Ms. Jacobs tries to reas-sure him, saying that he "probably hit the X by accident," but Brian protests, insisting that "it just disappeared on its own." Ms. Jacobs seems somewhat flustered and annoyed by this response, retorting: "Well, why don't you go do something else if you can't get it together on the computer?" Hearing this, Kal giggles, smiling at Brian. Ms. Jacobs sees this and begins to sputter, angrily telling Brian and Kal that they need to sign off of the computers as they have "been back here way more than 8 minutes."

The boys, however, immediately protested:

> Before Ms. Jacobs can finish, Kal jumps in, explaining that he finished his bibliography, but "just started working" on his math practice on the school website. Ms. Jacobs, how-ever, shakes her head, explaining that they only get "eight minutes total." Kal, however, protests again, saying breathlessly: "But no one else is waiting!" Brian hears this and begins to nod vigorously, echoing Kal's complaint and adding that he wants to work on his math practice, too. Ms. Jacobs thinks about this for a long moment, pursing her lips tight together. Then she nods, conceding that the boys can continue to work on the computers so long as no one else needs them.

Like their middle-class, white peers, Brian and Kal were comfortable seeking assistance, accommodations, and attention from teachers, and they were persistent in making those requests. Near the end of fifth grade, after Kal repeatedly got up and went over to Mr. Fischer to ask questions about a test, Mr. Fischer rocked back in his chair and laughed, saying: "I think that's enough questions. You're done." When Kal protested, Mr. Fischer continued, saying: "Like, you're cut off. You ask more questions than any kid I've ever had in fifth grade." Not all Asian American students were as vociferous as Kal in voicing needs and approaching teachers with requests. In general, however, middle-class minority students were simi-lar to their middle-class white peers in terms of their overall approach to support-seeking at school.

Working-class Latino students, on the other hand, were similar to their working-class white peers in that they regularly practiced strategies of def-erence at school. Gabe, for example, was well-liked by his teachers and his peers. He was even chosen as one of the recipients of the "School Spirit Medal" in fifth grade. Like other working-class Latino students and like other working-class students in general, Gabe rarely asked for assistance, accommodations, or attention from his teachers. One morning in fifth grade, Gabe was unpacking his backpack when he noticed that his hand was bleeding. Gabe had cut his hand at home the night before, and his mother had taken him to the emergency room to get stitches. Now, the cut was bleeding again:

> Gabe has a cluster of stitches on his palm, and they are not covered. There are drops of blood on the floor near Gabe's backpack, and the cut appears to be oozing blood. Gabe pulls on the sleeve of his black, hooded sweatshirt, tugging it over his hand and gripping it tight as if to try to stop the bleeding. He grimaces hard, but does not say anything. Meanwhile, Mandy (middle-class, white), whose cubby is next to Gabe's, notices the blood on the floor. "Is it bleeding?" Mandy asks, intrigued. Gabe pulls back the sweatshirt sleeve a bit to reveal the oozing wound. Mandy shrieks. She jumps back, horrified, and calls out loudly: "Gabe needs a Band-Aid!" Gabe's face flushes red and he quickly covers the wound again with his sweatshirt. Mandy, meanwhile, has already gone up to Ms. Dunham to request a Band-Aid on Gabe's behalf.[11]

Gabe could have asked for a Band-Aid himself. He could even have asked for permission to go to the nurse. Instead, he and other working-class students, like their white working-class peers, opted to try to deal with problems on their own.

Despite the similarities between white and non-white students of similar class backgrounds, and as discussed in the Introduction, there was evidence that class-based patterns in student–teacher interactions might vary for native-born and non-native-born children. Within the grade at Maplewood, for example, there were two middle-class Asian American boys who had recently immigrated with their families. Both boys knew at least some English before arriving in the United States, but they both spoke with thick accents and were very shy in interactions with both teachers and peers. Unlike their white middle-class peers, these two boys, Roger and Rajeev, rarely tried to advocate for themselves in the classroom. If you recall Mr. Potter's outburst in Chapter 6, for example, Roger was the only middle-class student in the room who did not ask for help with the practice problems, and Mr. Potter praised him for working so diligently on his own. More research is needed to understand these variations, but it seems possible that comfort and culture might both play a role.[11]

Given that my sample included only two mixed-race African American students (one middle-class and one working-class), more research is also needed to understand how requests from teachers might relate to larger patterns of black–white inequality. However, there is reason to suspect that black and white students from similar backgrounds might interact with teachers in similar ways. Lareau (2011), for example, found that middle-class black and white students both displayed high levels of entitlement in interactions with doctors and coaches. Similarly, Tyson (2002) found that black middle-class elementary school students were generally very enthusiastic about school, even engaging in the same kinds of "ability shows" (displaying their talents and knowledge for teachers and peers) that I frequently observed among middle-class white students at Maplewood. Furthermore, Hardie's (2015) interviews with high school girls revealed that both black and white working-class students had few ties to professional adults and "appeared hesitant to ask for career advice" (253). Middle-class black and white girls, on the other hand, had much broader networks on which to rely for advice about college and careers, and both groups reported being encouraged by their parents to seek help or information from those ties. The black middle-class girls did have somewhat smaller networks compared to those of the white middle-class girls, and they did show "signs of privilege and constraint" (253) in interactions with mentors, but Hardie suggests that those differences likely reflected, at least in part, the fact that the black middle-class girls were more upwardly mobile. As previously demonstrated with the white middle-class Healey family at Maplewood, that kind of mobility could have a tempering effect on the acquisition of class-based culture.

Such findings should not discount the importance of race in education. Institutional racism (Lewis 2003; Lewis and Diamond 2015), teacher biases (Kozlowski 2015; Oakes 2005; Ready and Wright 2011; Riegle-Crumb and Humphries 2012; Rist 2000), and unequal resources (Duncan and Magnuson 2004; Reardon 2011) all play a key role in maintaining racial and ethnic inequalities in school. However, the tentative insights offered here, particularly when coupled with prior research, do support the idea that class may be particularly salient in some aspects of classroom life. It seems, for example, that middle-class (or working-class) students from different racial and ethnic backgrounds might make similar requests from teachers and use those requests to manage challenges in similar ways.

DOES CONTEXT MATTER?

Closely related to the issue of racial variations in classroom behavior are questions about how school composition might shape children's efforts to manage classroom challenges. As noted in the Introduction, I chose Maplewood because of its demographic makeup. Specifically, focusing on one socioeconomically diverse, public school allowed me to compare how middle-class and working-class white students interacted in the same setting and with the same teachers and peers. Those strategic comparisons helped "isolate" the importance of social class in shaping students' experiences and interactions in school.

Yet, some readers might wonder: How does context matter here? Would working-class students experience similar disadvantages in predominantly working-class schools? School composition is closely linked to school culture and student outcomes (Barr and Dreeben 1983; Bryk, Lee, and Holland 1993; Thrupp, Lauder, and Robinson 2002). Thus, it seems possible that with fewer middle-class students in a classroom, teachers would automatically give more assistance, accommodations, and attention to working-class students. In addition, with fewer middle-class students in a classroom, working-class students might be more inclined to voice their own needs.[12] Those are real possibilities, and future research should certainly investigate these patterns in other settings.

There are, however, a number of reasons to suspect that class-based inequalities in student-teacher interactions are actually smaller at more privileged schools such as Maplewood. First, working-class students in predominantly middle-class schools might receive more encouragement to seek support and thus feel more comfortable doing so than they would at predominantly working-class schools. As discussed in the previous chapters, teachers at Maplewood openly encouraged support-seeking and rarely denied students' requests outright. Given what is known about middle-class parents' influence on school culture (Cucchiara 2013; Horvat, Weininger, and Lareau 2003; Lewis and Diamond 2015),[13] it seems likely that such a culture of support would be stronger in more privileged than in less privileged schools. That culture of support may have also made working-class students more comfortable voicing their needs than they would have been otherwise. As noted in previous chapters, working-class students often waited to make requests until after their middle-class peers had successfully done the same. In those cases, teachers' positive responses to middle-class requests likely signaled to working-class students that their own requests would not result in reprimand. Thus, by creating a culture in which support-seeking is (at least generally) encouraged and rewarded, more privileged schools might make it easier for working-class students to get more of the support they need.

Second, working-class students in predominantly middle-class schools might also receive more unsolicited support from teachers than they would in predominantly working-class schools. Some of that unsolicited support might result from proximity to middle-class students' requests. At Maplewood, for example, working-class students benefitted when middle-class requests prompted teachers to give additional assistance or accommodations to the class as a whole (i.e., by answering one student's question loud enough for everyone to hear or by giving everyone an extension on an assignment because one student asked for more time). If requests in general are less common in predominantly working-class schools, then working-class students in those schools would have fewer opportunities to benefit from inadvertent support.

Working-class students in predominantly middle-class schools might also receive more unsolicited support if privileged environments make teachers more sensitive to working-class students' needs. Consistent with that possibility, research shows that teachers in less privileged schools are more likely to underestimate the academic performance and potential of less privileged students than are teachers in more privileged schools (Ready and Wright 2011). If teachers in predominantly middle-class schools expect more from working-class students, they might be more inclined to reach out to those students with offers of support, especially if those students are not seeking support on their own. Furthermore, and given the number of requests for clarification that the Maplewood teachers received from middle-class students, teachers in more privileged schools might also be more inclined to recognize that their lessons and their assignments are not always clear. That recognition, in turn, might prompt teachers to check in more with students and offer assistance to those who might be struggling to understand.

Third, working-class students in predominantly middle-class schools might actually be more comfortable seeking support around middle-class peers than they would be in a classroom of working-class students. In interviews, some of the working-class students expressed concerns about being called "stupid" or "lazy" if they asked for support from their teachers. However, working-class students were primarily worried about criticism from other working-class peers. In an interview conducted during the summer after fifth grade, Jesse (working-class, white) recalled an incident with Sadie (also working-class, white):

> Like in math, I was stuck on this really hard division problem, and I got mixed up. And when Ms. Dunham came over I told her, and she was like: "Wait a minute, let me use a calculator." Because she didn't know it either. And then Sadie—I don't like Sadie—she said, "Jesse, why are you so stupid? I already got that problem." She's not really nice to me. She thinks she's all cool.

Like other working-class students, Jesse worried about being judged for seeking support, but he perceived other working-class students (such as Sadie) as the primary source of threat. In the classroom, I rarely saw students criticize each other for making requests from teachers, and the only such criticism I witnessed came from working-class students. Given working-class students' skepticism of support-seeking more generally, these patterns are not entirely surprising. However, if such patterns hold across contexts, then it would seem that working-class students in less privileged schools might be more reluctant to seek support than they would be when surrounded by more privileged peers.

DO CHILDREN LEARN FROM EACH OTHER?

Socioeconomically diverse school settings would also seem to give students the best chance at learning from each other. As discussed in the preceding chapters, working-class students would often gauge the appropriateness of support-seeking by observing teachers' responses to middle-class students' requests. When teachers responded willingly to those requests, working-class students were more comfortable voicing their own needs. When teachers instead responded gruffly or reluctantly, working-class students were quick to avoid making similar requests.

Beyond that kind of cue-taking, working-class students also appeared to learn from their middle-class peers in more explicit ways. At times, for example, middle-class students would directly instruct working-class students to "go ask" the teacher. During art class, students were working on collages. When Amelia (working-class, white) was ready to start cutting pictures from magazines, she realized that all the scissors at her table were being used. Amelia turned to Anna (middle-class, white), who was sitting next to her, to ask if she could borrow the scissors Anna was using when she was done. Rather than agree to share, Anna nonchalantly told Amelia to "go ask Ms. Cantore" for more scissors. Amelia was reluctant at first, but she eventually got up and (successfully) asked Ms. Cantore for help finding more scissors for her table. In such instances, it seemed that prompting from middle-class students could lead working-class students to set aside the class-based lessons they learned at home.[14]

Consistent with that possibility, many of the working-class parents lamented the "bad habits" their children picked up from peers at school. Recall from Chapter 2 how working-class mothers Ms. Campitello and Ms. Webb believed their children "whined" too much. In interviews, those mothers stressed that their children "didn't learn that at home." Ms. Campitello in particular seemed to believe that the teachers and peers at Maplewood were very different from those whom her children had encountered when they previously attended a predominantly working-class school. Such patterns could indicate that, at least to some extent, the behaviors of the middle-class students "rubbed off" on their working-class peers.

It is also important to note, however, that there were real limits on the frequency of cross-class learning and its impact on students' overall patterns of behavior. The working-class students, for example, were generally aware of their middle-class peers' requests, but they did not always link those behaviors to the benefits they could produce. This was shown with Jesse in the opening example of the book. He watched Ellen ask for help, and he saw Ms. Dunham working with Ellen, but he assumed that Ellen got the question right because she was "smart," and not because of the support she received. On the other hand, working-class student Jared, who was very high achieving and had all middle-class friends, did seem more aware of the potential benefits of support-seeking. However, as discussed in Chapter 3, when Jared got up and stood behind Aidan and Mr. Potter to watch as they worked through a confusing math problem, even he was reluctant to openly seek support on his own behalf.

Essentially, working-class students maintained a high level of skepticism about the kinds of support-seeking they saw in the classroom, and in some cases they actively tried to avoid emulating their middle-class peers. In social studies, Mr. Fischer had his fifth graders play a game with M&Ms to help them learn about government, laws, and taxation. During the game, a number of middle-class students started whining when they had to give up some of their M&Ms as "tax." Mr. Fischer, however, had instituted a "no whining" policy, with an M&M penalty for those who broke the rules. As the whining continued, some students began to run out of M&Ms, and one student named Brian (middle-class, mixed-race) was ultimately put in "jail." I interviewed Amelia Graham (working-class, white) during the summer after fifth grade, and she recalled the incident with disbelief:

> There were different laws. Some we got to make up, but one that Mr. F told us was that if you whine about something, you have to give up some M&Ms. His whole thing was about no whining. And if you ran out of M&Ms, you went to fake jail, which was under the table. And it's funny, because, you know Brian, right? He ran out of M&Ms, because he just kept whining and saying stuff. And when he was under the table, he said: "Please don't take away my bread and water!" And I thought that was funny, but I didn't get it. Because why would you whine so much if you're just going to lose all your M&Ms and end up in jail?

Working-class students often seemed aware of the requests and complaints that their middle-class peers made. In some cases, they even recognized the benefits associated with making requests. However, like Amelia in this example, and as described with Jared in Chapter 3 in his criticism of Julie for trying to use "half the ten," working-class students still viewed such behaviors as disrespectful or even ridiculous.

There were also real limits on the extent to which middle-class children learned from their working-class peers. In those cross-class interactions, middle-class students could have learned to be more patient, more polite, and more persistent in working through problems on their own before turning to others for support. Like their working-class peers, however, middle-class students were highly skeptical of behaviors that did not match their own class-based styles. In an interview during the summer after fifth grade, Aidan (middle-class, white) talked about the advantages and disadvantages of different problem-solving strategies. He noted,

> Sometimes they [the teachers] want you to raise your hand, but I think it's better to go up. If you raise your hand, it distracts other kids because the teacher has to come over and talk to you. If you go up, it's just easier because it doesn't draw attention for the other kids. It doesn't distract the other kids. And it's just annoying when the teacher has to get up and go around to all these kids. And so I think most kids just learn that you're supposed to go up if you have a question.

I went on to ask Aidan why some kids might raise their hands anyway or even opt not to ask when they had questions. He hesitated a moment, and then shrugged, explaining,

> Some kids just aren't comfortable asking for help. I don't know why. I guess they just don't like asking. I'm kind of like that. I'm willing to ask if I need to. But I don't really like asking for help if I can figure it out myself, and I'm not totally dependent on the teachers to help me. Like, some kids, every test they go up five times asking about the questions. I think it annoys the teachers a little. And in middle school, I think the teachers will want you to figure it out yourself more. They're still going to offer help, but they won't want you to go up 100 times every test.

Middle-class students generally recognized that there were a variety of strategies students could use in dealing with challenges at school. Like Aidan, a few of the middle-class students even sensed that their own behaviors, if taken to the extreme, could have drawbacks. Even in those cases, however, middle-class students were reluctant to adopt a more working-class approach to problem-solving at school.

That reluctance likely reflected the fact that close friendships rarely crossed class lines. In fourth grade, I asked students to complete surveys listing their five best friends. Throughout fourth and fifth grade, I also regularly tracked where and with whom student sat in the lunchroom. In keeping with research on homophily in friendships more generally (McPherson, Smith-Lovin, and Cook 2001; Smith, McPherson, and Smith-Lovin 2014), those data revealed that children's friendships were often segregated by social class.[15] That segregation, however, seemed to be more about opportunity than about overt preference. The overwhelming majority of students lived in class-segregated neighborhoods and rode different buses (which made it more difficult to travel to friends' houses for after-school play dates if those friends did not live nearby). Middle-class students also spent more of their after-school and weekend time in extracurricular activities, and their closest friends generally participated in those activities with them. With few opportunities to interact outside of school, students from different social class backgrounds rarely formed close bonds. As a result, their influence on each other's behaviors and orientations was likely limited.[16]

Students' reluctance to adopt the strategies of their other-class peers may also have stemmed from the deeply engrained nature of class cultures. Even students with cross-class friendships (e.g., Jared) still viewed their "own" behaviors as the best option. Such findings align with the idea that class cultures are habitual, taken for granted, and difficult to overcome (Bourdieu 1977, 1990).[17] Streib's (2005) research on cross-class marriages, for example, finds that upwardly mobile parents often cling to some aspects of the working-class parenting styles they experienced as children, even when doing so creates conflict with their spouse. Similarly, research on upward mobility more generally finds that adolescents and adults from working-class backgrounds often feel out of place in elite high schools, colleges, and work environments (Jack 2015; Lee and Kramer 2013; Lubrano 2004; Stuber 2005). Taken together, these findings highlight the difficulty involved in trying to learn new class-based behaviors, either through exposure to peers or through more formal training, a point to which I return in the Conclusion.

Conclusion

How does the middle-class secure advantages in school? As the preceding chapters have shown, the answer to that question is more nuanced than prior research has implied. Specifically, I find that the middle-class advantage is, at least in part, a *negotiated advantage*. Essentially, that means that the middle class secures advantages not just by complying with school expectations but also by requesting support and resources in excess of what is fair or required and by pressuring schools to grant those requests, even when they might prefer to say "no." As demonstrated in the classrooms at Maplewood Elementary, middle-class children were not content to follow the rules—they called out, interrupted, and persisted in their requests, even when teachers expected them not to do so. If anything, it was the working-class students who respected teachers' authority and worked hard to meet expectations. That deference had benefits—including avoiding reprimand and securing praise from teachers—but those benefits only went so far.[1] Instead, it was the middle-class students who secured the bulk of teachers' assistance, accommodations, and positive attention. Middle-class students also reaped the profits associated with that extra support, including correct answers on tests, more time to complete assignments, more opportunities for creativity, and more recognition for their ideas. Middle-class students secured those extra advantages by pressuring teachers—with the threat of wasted class time and with the possibility of parental challenges to teachers' personal and professional credibility—to grant their requests, even when teachers seemed inclined to say "no."

By highlighting the negotiations that produce the middle-class advantage, this book also reveals the interconnected roles that children, parents, and teachers play in the stratification process. This book traces social class differences in student behavior—especially students' problem-solving strategies—from their origins at home to their consequences in the classroom. We saw parents coaching children to see and react to the world in class-based ways. We saw children grappling with those lessons and choosing when and how to activate them on their own behalf. And we saw teachers responding to those actions and translating them into stratified profits. These findings build on the work of childhood scholars and their emphasis on children's agency—their active role in shaping their lives and experiences (Adler and Adler 1998; Corsaro 2005; Corsaro and Eder 1990; Eder 1995; Pugh 2009; Thorne 1993). These analyses also go further in showing both the contingent nature of children's agency and the role that agency can play in producing and reproducing inequalities. We see that children's actions are acquired, considered, carried out, and given consequences only through interactions with parents and teachers and peers. We also see that those actions and interactions contribute to inequalities in meaningful ways. This means, in turn, that children are not simply the passive recipients of inequalities that adults create for them. Rather, children—through their interactions with teachers, parents, and classmates—play a critical role in stratifying their own lives and experiences.[2]

CLASS BEYOND THE CLASSROOM

The findings presented in this book offer a number of potentially useful insights for scholars, educators, parents, and policymakers, especially those who care deeply about the inequalities that persist in our schools and our society today.

Implications for Research on Culture and Inequalities

The preceding chapters offer clear evidence of the link between culture and inequality. As others have argued, cultural skills and orientations act as a form of "capital" in institutional settings (Bourdieu 1990; DiMaggio 1982; Lareau 2000, 2011; Lareau and Weininger 2003). From that perspective, inequality results from a cultural matching process in which schools expect students to behave in middle-class ways and reward those who comply (DiMaggio and Markus 2010; Rivera 2010; Stephens et al. 2012). Schools, however, rarely make those expectations explicit (Contreras, Brint, and Matthews 2001; Farkas 1996; Halstead and Xiao 2010; Mehan 1980; Wren 1999).[3] That implicitness is problematic because it privileges middle-class students. Those students learn to follow similar expectations at home and thus have an advantage in school. These existing models of the relationship between culture and stratification are in some ways consistent with the patterns discussed in this book.

At the same time, the findings presented here also offer new insights regarding class, culture, and inequality. In particular, they suggest that the cultural processes that produce class-based inequalities are more complex than scholars typically recognize. We can see that in two ways.

First, we see that the middle-class advantage is not dependent on compliance with institutional expectations. Rather, particular behaviors can generate institutional rewards even when those behaviors directly contradict the rules and expectations in those settings. As shown in Chapters 3–5, middle-class students could secure advantages without adhering to teachers' stated instructions. Through their proactive, persistent, and sometimes pushy requests, middle-class students negotiated with teachers for assistance, accommodations, and attention. Those negotiations were also fruitful. Middle-class students generally persuaded teachers to provide the support they desired, even when that support exceeded what was fair or required. In doing so, middle-class students showed not only that they can create their own advantages but also that they can do so using strategies that have been previously associated with middle-class parents. Studies have shown, for example, that middle-class parents are often successful in pressuring educators to provide accommodations for their children, even when those demands create significant burdens on the school or disadvantage other students and families (Cucchiara 2013; Demerath 2009; Horvat, Weininger, and Lareau 2003; Lewis and Diamond 2015).

A second insight that these findings offer with respect to cultural processes and class-based inequalities involves the idea that institutional expectations are less fixed than existing research implies. Building on the work of Pierre Bourdieu (1984, 1996), scholars typically treat institutional expectations—or "fields"—as fixed and biased in favor of the middle class. Certainly, and consistent with those views, the expectations of teachers at Maplewood were far from neutral. As demonstrated in Chapter 2, however, teachers' expectations for student behavior also varied across different situations (see also McFarland 2001; Metz 1978; Pace 2003; Pace and Hemmings 2003).[4] There were times when teachers preferred middle-class strategies of influence (expecting students to acknowledge their struggles and call out with requests) and times when they preferred working-class strategies of deference (expecting students to work through difficult problems on their own or wait patiently with hands raised). Furthermore, as discussed in Chapter 6, teachers could be persuaded to change their expectations in the face of pushback (or potential pushback) from middle-class children and parents.

Taken together, these patterns suggest that class-based inequality results not from a fixed process but, rather, through ongoing negotiations between individuals and institutions.[5] Recognizing that dynamic process is important because it helps explain why inequalities persist despite social change (i.e., the seemingly constant emergence of new trends in parenting and in education policy and practice). Such inequalities persist, it seems, because dominant groups are constantly working to ensure that institutions meet their needs and maintain their privilege.

The ability of the middle class to challenge and change institutional standards is not, however, a function of culture alone. Rather, it also reflects a deep connection between culture, status, and power. Essentially, status translates culture into power and privilege. As Roscigno (2012) has argued,

> Those of lower status are constrained to playing by the rules much of the time, while those in higher positions might be able to create or use even seemingly neutral rules in self-beneficial ways. Consider how tax codes, exam criteria for college admissions, penalties surrounding "suite" versus "street crimes," and a bifurcated health care system benefit the already powerful while creating vulnerabilities and diminishing the power of others.

Chapter 4 clearly showed how the middle class—and even middle-class children—could create those unequal rules and applications. Chapter 6, in turn, showed the power those middle-class individuals held over institutions, with teachers and administrators reluctant to challenge middle-class families or deny them the advantages they desired.

In an era of school choice and accountability (Cookson 1994; Hallett 2010; Jennings 2010; Lauen 2007), educators' reluctance to challenge middle-class families is not surprising. School administrators and teachers may believe they cannot afford to ignore the demands of those who hold the purse strings—those who can afford to pay top-dollar for houses in "good" school districts, those who can easily send their children to private schools, and those who can persuade their friends to do the same (Cucchiara 2013; Horvat et al. 2003). As shown in this book, that power also trickles down to middle-class children, who can make their requests with the assurance that teachers might feel frustrated but forced to comply.

Essentially, it seems that status and power facilitate resistance to authority. Resistance is often treated as an aspect of working-class culture (MacLeod 1995; Willis 1977). In school, for example, working-class students are thought to resist teachers' authority (and their definitions of success) as a way to protect their dignity in the event of academic failure.[6]

As demonstrated at Maplewood, however, resistance to teachers' authority was not reserved for the working class. Rather, it was the middle-class students who most often challenged teachers' expectations. They called out, interrupted, and persisted in their requests for assistance, accommodations, and attention, even when those requests were in excess of what was fair or required, and even when teachers seemed inclined to say "no." Such findings are consistent with McFarland's (2001) research on student–teacher interactions in high school, in which he found that most efforts to undermine teachers' authority were undertaken by popular middle-class students (often boys). However, whereas McFarland found that those challenges were driven primarily by students' desire to impress or amuse their friends,[7] I found that middle-class students also used challenges to teacher authority as a way to secure real (and often unfair) advantages in school.

Implications for Research on Social Class and Parenting

The findings presented in this book also speak to research on class cultures and their impact on parenting. Consistent with prior research, my observations at Maplewood supported the idea that middle-class and working-class parents take different approaches to child-rearing (Brantlinger 2003; Hardie 2015; Lareau 2000, 2011; Nelson 2010). Simultaneously, however, my observations also suggested that class-based parenting patterns may be more nuanced and more context-dependent than scholars typically imply. The previous chapters provided that evidence of such complexity in three ways.

First, consistent with Streib's (2015) research on cross-class marriages, Chapter 1 showed how social mobility adds variation to class-based parenting styles. Upwardly mobile parents wavered more in their commitment to class-based parenting practices than did those with a stronger foothold in a particular class position. Ben Healey's parents, for example, heard teachers stressing that Ben needed to be more willing to seek help and support. They recognized that support-seeking could be important, and they sometimes conveyed those messages to Ben. By virtue of their own upbringings, however, the Healeys believed that Ben was mostly doing fine on his own. As a result, they coached Ben to use strategies of influence only infrequently and in a half-hearted way. Such findings are an important reminder that both class and class cultures are more varied than simple binaries imply. These findings also align with research on social mobility more generally, which shows that class-based habits and orientations are often resistant to change (Lee and Kramer 2013; Lubrano 2004) and that such stickiness extends to parenting practices as well (Streib 2015).

Competing priorities were a second key source of complexity in class-based parenting styles. All the parents of children attending Maplewood, regardless of class or mobility, wanted to support their children's academic success (Luster, Rhoades, and Haas 1989). At the same time, parents worried that too much support could undermine their children's development of good character (i.e., respect, responsibility, and work ethic). Middle-class and working-class parents alike struggled with how to balance those seemingly competing priorities.[8] Ultimately, middle-class parents prioritized good grades (see also Lareau 2011; Nelson 2010), and working-class parents prioritized good character (see also Edwards 2004). Both groups, however, made those choices with reservations. Such findings reveal that class-based parenting practices are not an automatic cultural response. Nor are they the result of some parents simply caring more about education, as scholars and policymakers sometimes imply. Rather, social class differences in parenting styles appear to be a dynamic and thoughtful outgrowth of parents' beliefs—rooted in their own circumstances and experiences (Kohn 1969; Lewis-McCoy 2014; Streib 2015)—about which goals to prioritize and how best to achieve them.[9]

A third source of variation in class-based parenting practices resulted from the context-dependency of parents' goals and strategies for achieving them. Middle-class families are often described as being more hands-on in their parenting (Cucchiara 2013; Hardie 2015; Lareau 2011; Nelson 2010). That was generally true at Maplewood as well, at least with respect to parents' interactions with the school. Regarding parents' coaching at home, however, both groups took a hands-on approach, but in different ways. Working-class parents' efforts to teach good character, for example, were much more calculated than might be assumed using an "accomplishment of natural growth" (Lareau 2011) model of working-class parenting (see also Edwards 2004). As illustrated by Ms. Webb and the Chap Stick incident, working-class parents even crafted elaborate punishments to teach their children hard lessons about the importance of respect, work ethic, and responsibility. Middle-class parents, on the other hand, took a slightly more hands-off approach to character development than might be anticipated from a "concerted cultivation" (Lareau 2011) model of middle-class parenting. Ms. Shore, for example, offered excuses for Christian's acting out in school rather than confronting it head-on, and she also blamed Mr. Fischer's excessive "negativity" for her older son's "bad year" in fifth grade rather than acknowledging that Trevor's actions might have warranted the punishment he received. Taken together, these patterns reveal that parenting styles may be more complex and context-dependent than scholars typically imply.

Implications for Research on Noncognitive Skills

With respect to non-cognitive skills, this study can help explain why particular behaviors matter for student outcomes and why the benefits of noncognitive skills are often stratified along social class lines. Prior research on noncognitive skills has linked student behavior to student achievement and attainment (Carneiro and Heckman 2003; Heckman and Rubinstein 2001; Jennings and DiPrete 2010; McLeod and Kaiser 2004; Tach and Farkas 2006). Evidence also suggests that those beneficial behaviors are more common among more privileged than among less privileged students. The findings in this book are in some ways consistent with those patterns. It was shown, for example, that middle-class and working-class students differed not only in their behaviors (e.g., seeking assistance vs. not seeking assistance) but also in the orientations that guided those behaviors (e.g., influence vs. deference) and in the styles they used in demonstrating them (e.g., proactive/persistent vs. patient/polite). Going beyond what prior research on non-cognitive skills has explored, the findings in this book also help to explain why non-cognitive skills vary along social class lines. As shown in Chapter 1, those behaviors, styles, and orientations emerged in response to the training children received at home. Those different strategies then prompted teachers to reward students with stratified profits at school. Chapter 3, for example, revealed that middle-class students were able to use their help-seeking strategies—especially their proactive and persistent efforts—to get fuller and more immediate assistance from teachers. That assistance also allowed middle-class students to complete their work more quickly and more accurately. Furthermore, as Chapter 7 explained, those stratified micro profits may also cumulate to produce larger patterns of inequality, possibly even helping explain persistent social class differences in student achievement.

These findings have clear implications for research on noncognitive skills. Most important, they suggest that such skills are not inherently beneficial. Rather, the value of particular behaviors depends on how students activate them and how teachers respond. That was especially true with regard to problem-solving. The profits associated with strategies of influence and deference were not fixed; rather, they depended on the institutional response those strategies elicited in a given moment. For example, children's efforts to proactively seek support were only beneficial when teachers granted those requests. When teachers said "no," those support-seeking efforts did not yield benefits. Furthermore, when teachers' frustrations finally erupted, those same behaviors could even result in reprimand. Prior research has recognized the critical (though arguably inadvertent) role that institutions play in translating individual behaviors into meaningful rewards (Bourdieu 1977; Bowles and Gintis 1976; Lareau 2000). This book goes a step further in showing that those reward processes are not fixed. Rather, the payoff of particular noncognitive skills can vary across different situations or settings.

The value of a given problem-solving strategy depended not only on when it was activated but also on how it was activated. In the classroom, what children did—seeking assistance, accommodations, or attention—mattered, but how they did it—proactively versus patiently, persistently versus politely—mattered as much or more. Such findings align with evidence of social class differences in "habitus" (or demeanor)[10] and also with arguments that habitus plays a critical role in the stratification process (Bodovski 2010; Dumais 2006; Horvat and Davis 2011). With respect to noncognitive skills, such findings indicate the need for more nuance in measuring and, as I discuss in more detail later, teaching those skills.

Variation in the rewards associated with particular behaviors is important not just from a theoretical perspective but also from a practical one. As I explain in the next section, those variations complicate policy efforts aimed at alleviating inequalities. They do so, for example, by encouraging a certain skepticism toward programs that attempt to fill the class-based gap in non-cognitive skills by teaching less privileged students to act more like their more privileged peers.

ALLEVIATING INEQUALITIES AT SCHOOL, AT HOME, AND IN SOCIETY

Before turning to questions of policy and practice, it is important to bear in mind that this book is neither an evaluation of particular teaching strategies nor an indictment of educators and their efforts. As Chapters 2 and 6 made clear, large class sizes, time constraints, accountability pressures, and high levels of need made it difficult for teachers to assess and respond to their students' individual needs. Given those challenges, teachers should not be blamed for class-based inequalities in problem-solving or in the rewards associated with those efforts. Teachers, however, can play a role in leveling the playing field. Along those lines, my work at Maplewood suggests that there may be steps teachers, schools, families, and policymakers can take to help tackle class-based inequalities.

Implications for Educators and Families

First, I urge teachers and schools to recognize social class—like race and ethnicity and nationality—as a powerful cultural force. Sensitivity to class cultures may help teachers connect with working-class students; recognize their struggles; and offer them assistance, accommodations, and attention, even when they cannot or do not seek it for themselves. As education scholars have argued in their work on minority students, sensitivity to diversity and inequalities may help teachers avoid subconsciously perpetuating privilege (Delpit 2006).

Second, educators can make their expectations explicit. As shown in Chapter 2, ambiguity in teachers' expectations led students to rely more heavily on the class-based strategies they learned at home. When teachers' expectations were explicit (and consistently enforced), it was easier for all students to comply. Mandy (middle-class, white), for example, talked in an interview after fifth grade about how going over directions could help students avoid confusion in the first place:

> Before a test, Ms. Dunham would like, go over the problems with us. She would like, read them aloud. And then she would say, "Okay, so, during this problem, I think it would be better if you gave a longer explanation, so put down three sentences near the top of your question." So you know how much to write. Instead of just saying, "Here you go. Here's your test. Have fun." And that was actually very helpful, because [if] there's something where they don't explain it, you're like: "Okay, but how much should I write? Or, what topic?" Or something like that. But if they go over it, it's clearer.

When teachers provided detailed instructions up front, students were better able to avoid confusion. However, some struggle was inevitable—directions were not always clear, mishaps occurred, and problems arose. In those cases, clear expectations helped students feel more confident about whether and how to seek support. As Jared (working-class, white) stated in Chapter 2,

> Most of the time, [teachers] explain too much, and you can't follow it all. So, I get lost, and I would just ask the person next to me. But, half the time, the teachers don't want us talking. So it's hard. Like, I don't know if I should go up and talk [to the teacher], or if I should ask the person next to me. So, sometimes I go to the teacher and say "I don't get this." But she might say: "Ask your partner" or "Ask your neighbor." So, I don't know if she'll get mad, or if she wants me to do that.

As discussed in Chapter 2, ambiguous and inconsistent expectations around support-seeking left working-class students worrying that any requests might result in reprimand. When teachers instead offered clear and consistent instructions for dealing with problems that arose, students seemed to feel more confident seeking support.

Teachers can also offer unsolicited support. Even when working-class students knew that support-seeking was encouraged, and even when they recognized its benefits, they could still be wary of the potential drawbacks. As a result, working-class students often went without support, even when they really needed it. For teachers, one of the best ways to bridge that gap is to offer unsolicited support. As Zach (working-class, white) explained to me in an interview after seventh grade, he was particularly grateful when teachers "came to me and told me what I got wrong and how I could do better." Such unsolicited support made it easier for working-class students to talk with their teachers about the challenges they faced because they could be certain that those exchanges would not result in reprimand.

In order to provide that unsolicited support, teachers should also look for and learn to recognize signs of struggle. On a practical level, that means circling around the classroom, looking over students' shoulders, and checking in one-on-one. As Julie (middle-class, white) explained in an interview during the summer after fifth grade,

> Teachers shouldn't grade papers during tests. They should be looking to see if kids need help. Maybe if it's a really easy quiz. But they shouldn't do it during a big test. Like, they should at least look around the classroom every couple of minutes to check.

Although time pressures might make it tempting for teachers to use tests and independent learning activities as an opportunity to catch up on grading or lesson plans, those are often the times when students struggle most. In those moments, appearing engaged and interested can make a real difference, especially for working-class students who might interpret an open laptop or a pile of paperwork as a "Do Not Disturb" sign.

On a more interpersonal level, it seems important for teachers to recognize what struggle looks like and how that appearance might vary. They can look for tapping pencils, slumped shoulders, and furrowed brows. Even putting a hand down does not necessarily mean that a student solved the problem on her own or no longer wants to share. Instead, putting a hand down—like falling off task—could mean that a student is so frustrated that she can no longer continue on. As illustrated by Carter and Sadie in Chapter 3, teachers sometimes mistook working-class students' frustrations for distraction or off-task behavior. Because working-class students were reluctant to challenge teachers' misperceptions, those situations often ended in reprimand. Furthermore, as described with Zach and the Smart Board in Chapter 4, when working-class students did end up off task, it was often because they had tried and failed to voice their needs. To avoid such pitfalls, I urge teachers not to jump to conclusions about students' behaviors. Instead, teachers can look carefully for subtle signs of struggle (including "distracted" and "off-task" behavior) and ask those students if they need support.

In addition, I recommend that, whenever possible, teachers provide assistance and accommodations to the class as a whole and not just to students who request them. One morning in Ms. Dunham's math class, for example, many of the students were struggling with a set of practice problems that required them to use the "distributive property" to do "mental math with big numbers." For example, if the problem was 4 × 53, then the correct answer would be written as follows:

$$4 \times 53 = (4 \times 50) + (4 \times 3)$$
$$4 \times 53 = 200 + 12$$
$$4 \times 53 = 212$$

Ms. Dunham had spent the past 20 minutes explaining and diagramming distributed property problems on the Smart Board, but many of the middle-class students in the class were still calling out for help and complaining that they did not know what to do:

Ms. Dunham is circling around frantically, going from student to student and offering assistance to those who are calling out and raising their hands. Finally, Ms. Dunham gives up. She stops, holding up her hands. Calling out loudly over the cacophony of complaints, Ms. Dunham announces: "If you're still struggling, meet me up on the green carpet." Ms. Dunham repeats the announcement as she makes her way up to the Smart Board.

Hearing that announcement, more than half of the class got up from their seats and found spots on the carpet at the front of the room. Before Ms. Dunham called the students up to the rug, none of the working-class students—Sadie, Jesse, Gabe, and Jeremy—asked for help. After the announcement, all four of the working-class students moved up to the front of the room to listen as Ms. Dunham went over the practice problems one by one. In that situation, Ms. Dunham responded to an individual question by providing support to the class as a whole. Had she not done so, the working-class students might not have gotten the help they needed to understand the problems and the math concept on which they were based. Thus, by using individual questions to gauge and respond to the level of understanding in the class as a whole, teachers avoided a slew of similar requests and also helped ensure that students got the support they needed, even if they were not comfortable seeking it themselves.

Teachers clearly play an important role in supporting students who are struggling, but they also need to be willing and able to say "no" to students' requests. As demonstrated in Chapters 3–5, middle-class students' requests for assistance, accommodations, and attention were sometimes aimed at meeting real needs. In other cases, however, those requests exceeded what was fair or required. That included requests for extensions on assignments, extra help with tests, and extra attention in class. Saying "no" to those requests could help teachers better level the playing field by preventing middle-class students from negotiating unfair advantages over their working-class peers. As discussed in Chapter 6, however, saying "no" is not an easy task. Teachers who say "no" risk pushback from middle-class students and parents—pushback that can result in wasted class time, a loss of resources, and even a loss of personal and professional credibility. Thus, teachers need to be supported in saying "no"—supported by administrators and by the community as a whole.

Relatedly, I urge parents—particularly those from more privileged backgrounds—to think beyond their individual interests and teach their children to do the same. Middle-class families can look to their working-class peers and learn that there is value in hard work, respect, and responsibility.[11] They can recognize that there are limits on teachers' time and attention and that individual actions can impact the amount of support others receive. Those who are skeptical should bear in mind that self-denial might even be self-serving. In an interview during the summer after fifth grade, I asked Amelia (working-class, white) what teachers and parents can do to support students in school. Her answer was as follows:

> Well, maybe like, give advice, and help them when they need help, but try to let them figure out some things on their own so you don't just tell them everything to do, because then, that wouldn't help them learn a lot.

Middle-class parents are often reluctant to let their students struggle. However, as Amelia points out so astutely, a balance of influence and deference, self-advocacy and self-denial, could be better for everyone in the long term.

Of course, that kind of parenting is not easy. I find that it is a struggle with my own children to practice what I preach. My almost-3-year-old daughter came home from day care one day and told me that a teacher had "grabbed" and "yelled at" her and "called Mommy on her cell phone." At first, I was shocked and angry. I frantically checked my phone—no missed calls. Part of me wanted to e-mail the teacher and demand an explanation, but I forced myself to do a little more digging first. After asking my daughter a few more questions, I was able to piece together that she had (like the girls discussed in Chapter 5) taken off her coat on the playground. The teacher believed that it was too cold to be going without coats and asked my daughter to put her coat back on. My daughter refused, saying "Mommy said I don't have to" (I had allowed her to go without a coat at the playground the prior afternoon) and then proceeded to run away. Eventually, the teacher was able to persuade my daughter to put her coat back on after pretending to call me on her cell phone. After figuring out what really (or at least probably) happened, I decided not to contact the teacher. Instead, I told my daughter that she needs to listen to her teachers—that the rules are there to keep her safe and make things fair for everyone.

I hope this book will encourage at least some parents to think beyond their own families and acknowledge how their actions and their children's actions can contribute to inequalities. However, I have real doubts about the willingness of most middle-class families to give up their negotiated advantage. Ultimately, then, it seems that schools must serve as the backstop. They have to set and enforce clear expectations. They have to avoid privileging those who opt for influence over deference and stand firm against efforts to secure resources and support in excess of what is fair or required.

Implications for Policies and Inequalities

The patterns I observed at Maplewood are relevant not only for individual teachers and families, but also for activists and policymakers interested in tackling class-based inequalities on a larger scale. In particular, my findings raise questions about policies and programs that aim to alleviate inequalities by teaching working-class students to act more like their middle-class peers.

Given what is known about noncognitive skills and their importance for learning and achievement, educators and policymakers have become increasingly interested in closing the skill gap between privileged students and their less privileged peers. Knowledge Is Power Program (KIPP) charter schools, for example, teach underprivileged students to sit up, listen, ask and answer questions, nod, and track the speaker (SLANT). There is also evidence that those skill-building efforts can bolster the learning and achievement of less privileged students (Horvat and Davis 2011). Similarly, a number of programs for at-risk youths have used cognitive–behavioral therapy to change habitual behaviors, reduce criminal recidivism, and increase engagement in school (Heller et al. 2013; Kahneman 2011).

This study is not designed to assess the efficacy of KIPP schools or other programs aimed at teaching noncognitive skills. However, my observations do highlight a number of challenges that such training programs will likely face in equalizing students' experiences and outcomes.

One potential challenge is the difficulty involved in changing cultural habits. As discussed in Chapter 7, class-based skills and orientations are extremely resistant to change. Even when working-class students saw middle-class students asking for assistance, accommodations, or attention, and even when they saw that those efforts were successful, they rarely activated similar strategies for their own gain. As illustrated by the interviews in Chapter 2, working-class students knew that they could ask for support and that they could call out or approach the teacher with questions, but they remained skeptical of the benefits of doing so and focused instead on the potential drawbacks. Such findings are consistent with research on upward mobility, which reveals that class-based habits and orientations are "sticky" (Lubrano 2004; Rivera 2010; Streib 2015). For less privileged students, changing class cultures is easiest when they are immersed in elite total institutions (e.g., private preparatory high schools) where they eat, sleep, and socialize with highly privileged peers (Cookson and Persell 1985; Jack 2014, 2016; Khan 2011). If cultural transformation requires that kind of deep immersion, it seems unlikely that shallower, more top-down efforts to teach the habits of privilege would yield the same results.

Another potential limitation of skill-training programs is their focus on rules and compliance. KIPP schools and other programs serving less privileged students often expect students to follow rigid codes of conduct and to suffer the consequences if they fail to comply.[12] The explicitness of those rules could be beneficial in some ways—for example, it might alleviate ambiguities that lead students to rely on class-based notions of appropriate behavior. However, the rigidity of those rules (when coupled with the reluctance of less privileged students to push back) could contribute to class-based inequalities in other ways. At Maplewood, middle-class students secured advantages not just by complying with rules and expectations but also by skirting or challenging those expectations to better meet their individual needs. Giving less privileged students the confidence and skills to successfully negotiate advantages is likely to be much more difficult than teaching them to follow simple guidelines such as SLANT. Teachers also have little incentive to encourage less privileged students to negotiate advantages. As discussed in Chapter 6, constant demands and challenges make life difficult for teachers. In many cases, they say "yes" to middle-class students' requests because they feel pressured to do so, not because they want to reward or encourage those efforts.

On a deeper level, then, these findings suggest that efforts to reduce achievement gaps by closing the skill gap are too one-sided. Programs such as KIPP focus on what less privileged students lack and try to fill the gaps between those students and their more privileged peers. In doing so, those programs and policies ignore the subtle but powerful ways that middle-class students (and their families) maintain a relative advantage. As demonstrated in this book, middle-class students used their requests for assistance, accommodations, and attention to negotiate advantages that went well beyond what teachers and schools intended to provide (and often well beyond what was fair). Policies and programs that focus only on less privileged students also ignore the pressure that teachers face to say "yes" to requests and the role that those "yeses" play in perpetuating middle-class advantages (see also Lewis and Diamond 2015).

SUMMARY

If we really want a more level playing field for students, we need middle-class families to be mindful of the consequences of wielding their privilege, and we need teachers to say "no" to unnecessary requests. Unfortunately, saying "no" will not be easy. Teachers who deny privileges to middle-class children will have to stand firm in the face of persistent demands and possible backlash. But, saying "no" is incredibly important; without it, middle-class students and their families will always remain a step ahead.

Maybe ironically, that step ahead will be one that is achieved not through hard work but, rather, through help from others. Our culture is quick to valorize up-by-their-own-bootstraps accounts of success and even quicker to demonize those who rely too heavily on others for support.[13] In reality, however, and as this book has shown, success is rarely won alone. Rather, the privileged in our society negotiate advantages by asking for assistance, accommodations, and attention (often in excess of what is fair or required) and by persuading others to grant those requests. The less privileged are the ones who try to go it alone. As a result, they have a steeper hill to climb and less support in navigating the obstacles they face. Despite those efforts, however, the less privileged are rarely celebrated for their respect, resourcefulness, and responsibility. Instead, society blames them for being failures or, at the very least, for being slower to achieve what others (with support) accomplish more quickly.

Our view of success is deeply distorted. We need to be clear-eyed about how middle-class families wring advantages from schools. We need to be clear-eyed about how educators enable that behavior or at least how they are pressured to comply. We need to be clear-eyed in recognizing that working-class children struggle to manage on their own. Negotiated advantages are real and consequential, and they need to be part of our understanding of inequality in schools and in society as a whole.

Methodology

As a graduate student neck-deep in fieldwork, I frequently found myself feeling lost or anxious or frustrated, sure that the whole project would fall apart in the end. In those moments, Annette Lareau's (2000) methodological appendix in *Home Advantage* was an invaluable companion. Beyond its lessons in good practice, it reassured me that side steps and missteps and even steps backward were a normal part of ethnographic research, and it gave me the confidence to move forward. I hope that this methodological appendix will offer similar reassurances while also helping readers understand the difficult decisions (and trade-offs) inherent in fieldwork.

A PLACE TO START

Ethnographic projects often start with a question—a problem to be solved. A good research question is like an anchor in the storm of ethnographic data. It keeps the researcher from spinning wildly off in a new direction each time an interesting bit of data passes by. A good research question is also like a roadmap for a long journey. It helps the researcher to see which path to take to reach the destination and which alternate paths are available should roadblocks come up along the way.

Given the benefits of having a research question, I strongly encourage my graduate students not to start a project without one. However, as Kristin Luker (2010) explains in her book, *Salsa Dancing into the Social Sciences*, initial research questions may not be fully formed or perfectly articulated. Instead, projects often emerge gradually out of a vague set of research interests. That was certainly the case for me.

My own interests lay at the intersection of social class and schooling, and they stemmed, at least in part, from my own experiences with social class. My parents both grew up in working-class families in Baltimore, Maryland, and they both viewed college as the ticket out of a disappearing reality. However, although both of my parents went to (and eventually graduated from) college, their experience was far from "traditional." They were both first-generation and commuter students, living at home with their parents and working long hours to pay their own way through school. My dad, who worked as a package sorter for UPS, still recounts with pride how he could sort more than 100 boxes per minute, grabbing them as they came down one conveyor belt and tossing them onto others depending on their destination.

My parents also married relatively young—my mom was 19 years old, and my dad was 21 years old. It was 1982, and my dad had just graduated from college with a degree in computer science. The best job he could find was hours away from home and family. For my mom, following him meant changing schools and leaving behind everything she knew. I was born not long after my parents left Baltimore. My mom was working as a typist and going to school at night. Despite not having child care or family nearby, she initially tried to return to both just days after I was born (she was afraid of losing her temp job and failing her classes). My dad would race home after work to watch me while my mom went either to work or to school.

Money was tight and a near-constant source of stress. I remember lying awake in my bed at night, covering my ears as my parents shouted about bills, convinced they were getting a divorce. I remember my mom's panicked voice when she told my dad there was no money left in the bank account. We ate mostly hot dogs, grilled cheese sandwiches, and pasta with butter—the low-cost staples my parents could cook and afford. My parents even sealed off part of our house to reduce heating costs.

My parents stayed together, but as our family grew, things got tighter—literally and figuratively. My sister was born when I was 5 years old, and my brother was born 2 years later. The three kids shared one bedroom, and there was only one bathroom for the whole family. It was normal for one person to be showering while another was brushing her teeth and a third was using the toilet. We had no concept of privacy.

As time went on, however, our situation changed. When I was in elementary school, my dad got a better job with a higher salary, and his company even paid for him to get a master's degree. My mom started running a day care out of our home, watching the children of the affluent "career women" who lived on the other side of town. She also went back to school.

By the time I finished eighth grade, my mom had completed her bachelor's and her master's degrees, and my dad had worked his way up to a six-figure salary. With money in the bank, my parents decided to leave our working-class neighborhood. Halfway through my freshman year of high school, we moved across town to a new house with six bedrooms, four bathrooms, and an in-ground pool. My parents started hanging out with our new neighbors—doctors and lawyers and corporate managers—and going to jazz concerts and wine-and-cheese parties.

For my parents, mobility was the plan all along. They expected to be able to work hard, scrimp and save, and pull themselves up from their working-class roots. For me, mobility was disorienting. I felt more at home with friends from our old neighborhood—hanging out and playing outside—than I ever did with kids in our new neighborhood. I liked Velveeta and Pop-Tarts. My clothes were mostly from Kmart or consignment shops.[1] I had never been on an airplane.

That feeling of being out of place in a world of class distinctions carried with me to college, where sociology gave me a language and a set of conceptual tools to use in making sense of my family's experiences. Research on the link between education and outcomes helped me understand the mobility that my parents had achieved. Bourdieu's ideas of habitus and cultural capital gave clarity to the disorienting feeling of interacting across social class lines.

And yet, I continued to find myself searching for a deeper understanding of class cultures. In particular, I wanted to know how class cultures come to be so deeply ingrained in our bodies and hearts and minds—how children (and not just adults) become members of a particular social class. I wanted to know how children come to activate those class cultures and how, in doing so, they shape their own opportunities and outcomes. I had the sense—from my own upbringing and from the experiences that I observed in my peers—that children play an active role in making sense of (and perpetuating) class inequalities. And I wanted to know how and why.

SETTING MY SITE

In graduate school, those broad questions gave way to a more specific focus on social class and peer interactions, especially how cross-class friendships might help alleviate inequalities. The suburban, public schools I attended as a child had students from diverse class backgrounds. Some of my friends lived in large, fancy houses, whereas others lived in cramped apartments on the other side of town. I was always somewhere in between, and my own transitional experience with social class brought those differences into sharp relief. As an undergraduate, I had also read studies comparing middle-class students in middle-class schools to working-class students in working-class schools, and I was curious about how those students might learn from each other if they had the chance to interact together in the same classrooms.[2]

I started the data collection for this project during the spring semester of my second year in graduate school. I was taking Melissa Wilde's Research Methods class, and one of the course requirements was to conduct a small set of interviews and observations. With the seed of the idea for my dissertation research quickly growing in my head, I wanted to jump right in.

Given my interest in social class and friendship, I knew I had to choose a research site where I could see middle-class and working-class students learning together in the same classrooms. But which school should I choose? Urban or suburban? Public or private? White or non-white? Familiar or far away? I knew there was much riding on that decision, and I fretted about which school to choose.

Ultimately, I opted for a systematic approach. Using the "school search" feature on the website of the National Center for Education Statistics (http://nces.ed.gov), I began identifying schools that might provide the necessary class diversity. I then began to narrow that list based on school type, geography, and social connections. In terms of school type, I decided to include only neighborhood public schools, not charter or magnet schools. Charter and magnet schools often have more socioeconomic diversity than traditional public schools (Kahlenberg and Potter 2012), but choosing one of these schools as a research site would have been problematic for two reasons. First, the diversity in such schools, particularly in the urban areas where such schools are typically located, usually breaks down along racial and ethnic lines (Cucchiara 2013; Holme 2002), making it difficult to isolate the importance of social class in the classroom. Second, parents have to actively choose to enroll their children in such schools. As a result, those parents might be different in many ways from the vast majority of parents who send their children to their local public school (Goldring and Phillips 2008; Yang and Kayaardi 2004).

In terms of geography, I opted to narrow my list to include only schools that were in (or at least near) my normal orbit. At the start of my fieldwork, and in addition to taking and teaching classes as a graduate student, I was also commuting 300 miles each week to visit my partner. Given the amount of time I would be spending in the field and writing field notes, I could not afford to spend more time commuting to a far-off site.

Although I might have been able to choose a research site and go in "blind," I opted to prioritize schools to which I had a personal connection. As Annette Lareau (2000) stresses in her appendix to *Home Advantage*, connections matter, and they can help you get in the door. That emphasis on connections also aligns with research highlighting the rewards that can often be gained through social ties (Coleman 1988; Granovetter 1973).

Fortunately, one school fit the bill. It had a good mix of students from middle-class and working-class backgrounds (and that mix did not divide along racial or ethnic lines). It was within my normal orbit. And I had a relative who worked in the district. It was not the "perfect" school—the demographic balance could have been more even; it could have had middle-class and working-class students from both white and minority families—but given its other advantages, it would have to do.

With my list narrowed to one, I set about trying to persuade the Fair Hills School District to let me in the door. I started with an e-mail to the superintendent, referencing my connection to the district and outlining the basics of the project. In hindsight, it likely would have been better to just show up at the district office, chat with the administrative staff, and ask for a meeting. The approval process might have been quicker and less formal that way.

Ultimately, and after a series of back-and-forth e-mails, I found myself in a meeting with the district superintendent, the Maplewood Elementary principal, and another high-ranking district official. After giving a brief presentation about the project, I spent almost an hour answering questions. There were questions about my graduate work, about my career plans, and of course about the project. What would I be doing in the classrooms? What was I looking for? What did I think I might find? What did I plan to do with those findings? I tried to answer their questions honestly but without belaboring the details. Given the climate of accountability that was pervading public schools at that time, I sensed that their real concern was about the potential for embarrassment. I assured them that I was there to learn and not to judge. I explained that although I planned to publish at least some of what I found, I would try my best to maintain the anonymity of those involved. With their questions answered and those reassurances in hand, the three district officials signed a letter giving me the go-ahead to start the project.

I then took that signed letter to the institutional review board (IRB) at the University of Pennsylvania. Historically, ethnographers have struggled against the constraints of a regulatory system designed primarily for medical research (Bosk and De Vries 2004; Lincoln and Tierney 2004). For me, the IRB review process was both challenging and useful. The process was challenging in that it is difficult with ethnography to know precisely what the research would reveal or how it would proceed in the field. On that point, my advice is that ethnographers should frame their studies as broadly as possible while also familiarizing themselves with the IRB amendment process and using it as needed (amendment reviews are generally much quicker and easier than initial reviews).[3]

At the same time, I found that preparing the IRB protocols forced me to recognize and plan for the potential ethical and logistical hurdles involved in observing children and conducting fieldwork more generally. It helped me to develop a "standard line" to use in introducing myself and describing the project.[4] It gave me a way to explain why I could not reveal to my subjects who else I was interviewing or what I had seen so and so do at school or what so and so had said (questions I encountered more frequently than I anticipated). The plan that I created for the IRB review essentially became my guidebook. It outlined procedures for obtaining consent from parents and teachers; procedures for explaining the study to the students and obtaining their assent; and procedures for collecting, analyzing, and storing the data in such a way that risks to privacy and confidentiality would be minimized. Having those steps laid out, up front, was deeply reassuring, particularly in the whirlwind that is the first few weeks and months of data collection with a new project.

WHO ARE YOU AND WHAT ARE YOU DOING HERE?

With IRB approval in place, my next task was to invite the teachers and the families at Maplewood to take part in the project. I started with the teachers, knowing that their buy-in would be tremendously important both logistically and for putting the parents and students at ease with my presence in the school. Maplewood's principal first introduced me to the teachers at a school-wide faculty meeting. Palms sweating, I talked for a few minutes about myself, the project, and what it would entail. I explained that I was interested in learning about children's interactions in school. I also distributed information packets and consent forms. I then met with the third-, fourth-, and fifth-grade teachers in small groups (because it would be their classrooms in which I would spend the most time) to talk through their lingering questions and concerns. Those conversations felt friendly, which helped put me at ease. Mostly, the teachers wanted to know that I was not there to evaluate them or their students and that I would try not get in the way. To my great relief, they all agreed to allow me in their classrooms.

After meeting with the teachers, I held an information session for parents of students in the target cohort at Maplewood. Again, I was nervous as I spoke about myself, my project, and what it would entail. More than half of the parents attended and received consent documents and parent surveys to complete. For the remaining families, I sent packets home with the students and included self-addressed, stamped envelopes to use in returning the materials. Food is a fantastic motivator, so to encourage families to return the forms (regardless of whether they said "yes" or "no" to participating), I told the teachers I would have a "pizza party" for the class that returned the most forms. The teachers regularly reminded the students to bring back their forms, and the winning class got pizza, cupcakes, and juice. Two of the classes tied for first, and all four of the classes got so "into" the competition that I decided to make cupcakes for the remaining two classes as well. Ultimately, after weeks of stress and waiting and numerous reminder messages sent home, 80 (out of approximately 100) families agreed to participate in the study and also completed the background surveys.[5]

In hindsight, I wish I would have requested IRB permission for "passive consent," at least for the observation portion of the study.[6] Doing so would have allowed me to include students in the project unless they or their parents specifically decided to opt out. As I explain later, I used passive consent procedures in subsequent waves of the study, and it made the process faster and less complicated. Not using the passive consent procedures for the initial observations was a more conservative approach because it ensured that all participants were fully aware of the project and willing to take part, but it also had real drawbacks. Specifically, it meant that I could not write field notes involving students who did not agree to participate in observations, which made it difficult to document interactions between groups of students. Those difficulties were one reason why I ultimately opted not to focus on friendships and peer interactions.

Despite the stress and hassle involved, the consent process, especially the pizza competition between classes, did help increase response rates on the survey, which was critical for determining students' social class backgrounds. The pizza and cupcake celebrations also gave me the opportunity to introduce myself to the students and tell them about the project. The students had dozens of questions. Mostly, they wanted to know about me. How old was I? (mid-twenties) Was I married? (not at the time, but I did get married halfway through the project, which prompted many more questions) Did I have kids? (not at the time, but I hoped to) What were my favorite sports teams? (the Eagles, the Broncos, and the Orioles) Where did I go to college? (Brown University) Was I training to be a teacher? (sort of, but for college, not elementary school)[7] More important, however, the students were concerned about whether I would "tell on" them if I saw them misbehaving. I assured them that I would not do so, unless in situations in which someone's life was in jeopardy.

That question of trust was a persistent theme in my interactions with the students. They wanted to know if I was with them or against them. After reading *Harriet the Spy* in fourth grade, for example, a few of the boys started asking me if I was "a spy." That prompted many sleepless nights on my part, as I worried about students going home and reporting that there was a "spy" in their classroom that day. The students would also regularly ask me how long I would be "hanging around." I tried to show my allegiance in small ways—through the backpack[8] I carried and by not "telling on" them, even if they misbehaved in front of me. Over time, the students grew more comfortable with my presence. If they saw me in the hallway, they would call out with big hellos and ask eagerly if I was observing in their class that day. Some students would even invite me to sit with them at lunch, tell me stories about their weekends, or proudly show me their projects in class.

My relationship with the teachers also evolved to gain more trust over time. During the first few weeks of each school year, most teachers dealt with me warily. They were very polite and welcoming, but they were also business-like in showing me where to sit and talking me through the various logistics of the school day. Gradually, however, especially after I sat down with the teachers for one-on-one interviews, those more formal walls began to erode. During most of my observations, the teacher and I were the only adults in the room. When something particularly funny or exasperating happened, the teachers would sometimes catch my eye, and we would briefly share an eye roll or a knowing smile. Occasionally, the teachers would also pull me aside to vent about frustrating students or e-mails from parents or new district policies, and those informal conversations became a particularly rich source of data—far richer than the formal interviews I conducted with the teachers in school.

A NEW DIRECTION

When I entered the field, I quickly found myself frustrated with my research question and the challenges I faced in answering it. Almost from day one, it was apparent that studying how social class mattered in students' friendships and peer interactions (and especially how students learned from each other) would be much more difficult than I had presumed. Those difficulties were, in part, logistical. In busy, noisy classrooms, it was often impossible to "eavesdrop" on students' conversations, and getting close enough to hear one whispered exchange meant ignoring the countless others going on throughout the room. Conversations between teachers and students were typically easier to hear (and I could check in with teachers after the fact to verify what I had heard) and happened one at a time (at least in most cases), making it much easier to get a sense of the overall patterns.[9]

The difficulties in studying cross-class interactions also resulted from the fact that students' friendships were highly stratified along social class lines. These elementary-aged students did not seem to be particularly aware of social class differences. All of the students dressed similarly (simple T-shirts, jeans, and sweatshirts were the norm, and name brands were rarely overtly displayed, at least in elementary school). Maplewood also tried to prevent status distinctions by banning toys and electronics that might otherwise have distinguished students' and their social class status. Yet, friends typically lived in the same neighborhoods, rode the same busses (making it easier to go to friends' houses in the afternoons), and participated in the same after-school activities, all of which were heavily segregated by social class.[10]

As a result of that friendship segregation, I mostly saw cross-class interaction during in-class activities in which students were working in small groups. Those interactions were certainly very interesting to observe, and as discussed in Chapter 7, there were indeed moments when students from different social class backgrounds learned from each other. However, those moments of cross-class learning were also rare enough that I was reluctant to retain them as the focus of my analysis.

At the same time, I was also observing that social class mattered even more in a different set of interactions—those between students and teachers. Those patterns became particularly apparent as students moved from third to fourth grade. During that time, parents' class-based advice about managing challenges at school really seemed to "sink in" for students, particularly those who were initially somewhat reluctant to heed the lessons they learned at home. Documenting those patterns in my field notes left me feeling re-energized about the project after months of frustrations and fears.

Embracing that renewed enthusiasm, I decided (albeit not without hesitation and long talks with my advisors) to refocus my analysis on student–teacher interactions, particularly students' requests for assistance, accommodations, and attention. That shift in my question began approximately 6 months into the fieldwork, during my third year in graduate school. In that sense, starting the project early was a blessing because it allowed time for my question to evolve in response to the patterns that emerged in the field.

However, changing my question was not without challenges. As originally planned, the project involved in-school observations during third, fourth, and fifth grade; interviews with the third-, fourth-, and fifth-grade teachers; and the collection of data from students' school records. As I contemplated shifting my research question, it became apparent that I would need more data to answer the new subquestions that had emerged: How did students learn to behave in such different ways? How did they perceive requests for assistance, accommodations, or attention? How did they decide to activate those strategies in school?

In order to better answer those questions, I expanded the study to include interviews with students and parents. I opted to conduct those interviews during the summer after the students finished fifth grade and before they started sixth grade at Fair Hills Middle School. I wanted students to offer honest assessments of their teachers and their classmates, and it seemed they would be more comfortable doing so after graduating from Maplewood and outside of the confines of the school year. Those interviews took place during the summer between my fourth and fifth years in graduate school, and, at least at the time, I thought that would be the end of the data collection for the project.

I spent my fifth year in graduate school analyzing data and working and reworking the various chapters of my dissertation. By the summer of 2011, I had submitted the first chapter of the dissertation for publication as an article, and I was gearing up to go on the job market in the fall. By January 2012, halfway through my sixth and final year in graduate school, I had published the first article from the Maplewood project, I had gotten my dream job, I was finishing my dissertation, I was undergoing fertility treatments (my partner and I had been trying to have a baby since we got married in 2009), and I was preparing to buy a house and move halfway across the country. It was all pretty hectic.

That same winter, I met with my advisor to talk about next steps. Annette asked if I was planning to continue following the Maplewood students over time. I felt the color drain from my face and I felt sort of sick to my stomach. I knew that I wanted to continue with more follow-up research, but before that moment I had not fully considered the time and effort it would take to go back into the field. It would mean more time away from my partner (we had just started living together full-time, after 7 years living in separate states). It would mean another round of IRBs and permissions and trust-building. It would mean more hours writing field notes and chasing down interview subjects and doing all of the other ethnographic grunt work. It all seemed daunting. However, as Annette reminded me, I was also moving away—10 hours by car from my field site—and distance would only make going back more difficult. She stressed that if I really wanted to do follow-up research, I should not wait. Knowing that I already had two papers written from my dissertation, Annette also suggested that we take advantage of an option (rarely used by qualitative researchers in my department) to complete the doctoral requirement with three papers (plus an introduction and conclusion). At that point, I had been planning to rework the existing papers into a book-type manuscript, so switching to a three-article format would give me more time for data collection. Ultimately, then, I decided to go back into the field.

Following my conversation with Annette—and a few heated discussions with my partner, who believed that I was already too stressed with work—I began the process of expanding the project to include follow-up research with the students in middle school. The goal with the follow-up study was to understand how students' interactions with friends, classmates, and teachers changed over time and how they varied from elementary to middle school. During the spring of the 2011–2012 school year, and after obtaining permission from the IRB, the school district, the parents, and the students, I spent 8 weeks observing in the seventh-grade classrooms at Fair Hills Middle School.

That consent process was complicated by the fact that Maplewood was one of a number of elementary schools that fed into Fair Hills Middle School. As a result, the students from Maplewood were mixed in classes with students who were not originally part of the project. Although the follow-up study focused on the students I had also observed in elementary school, I sent notification letters and opt-out forms to all of the parents in the grade. All of the original participants agreed to take part in the follow-up (although three families had moved away), and only a handful of the "new" students opted out (meaning that I would not take notes on anything their children did or said).

Unfortunately, two of the "new" families decided that they did not want me observing in their children's classrooms at all, and they contacted the principal (and in one case, cc'd me) to complain about the study. The parent who e-mailed me was upset by the passive consent procedure and concerned about the steps that would be taken to ensure that those who opted out would not be included in any aspect of the project. Although I am reluctant to include the actual text of the e-mail here (for fear of further reprisal), the tone of the e-mail was clearly angry—with numerous ALL CAPS phrases, talk of invasion of privacy, and firm demands. Receiving that e-mail (and the subsequent phone call from the principal) terrified me, and I contemplated abandoning the project right there. Fortunately, the principal—who was used to dealing with parents—reassured me that we could work through the problem. With the principal as go-between, I offered to meet with the concerned parents to discuss the project, but they refused. In the end, and after more than 2 weeks of back-and-forth negotiations (and sleepless nights on my end), they agreed to drop the issue if I agreed not to observe in any classrooms in which those two students were present. Unfortunately, that meant that there were also a handful of students from the original study whom I was unable to observe (because all of their classes were with one of those two excluded students).

The harsh words (and even veiled threats) from the two disgruntled families left me, the Fair Hills principal, and the district administration ill at ease. The school and the district had been supportive of the project from the start. After that incident, however, they made it clear that I would not be permitted to conduct any additional observations in the schools. That decision was disappointing but also a bit of a relief—I did not want to deal with those parents again. Thus, although I hope to continue following up with the students through interviews over time, I do not anticipate going back to observe in high school.

However, despite the challenges I faced in conducting the follow-up research, I was able to observe most of the original students in seventh grade at Fair Hills. I also interviewed 10 seventh-grade teachers, asking about their students, their teaching, and the kinds of interactions they typically observed in their classrooms. During the summer of 2012, I also completed follow-up interviews with 13 students whom I had previously interviewed after fifth grade. All of the students remembered me and seemed eager to tell me about how their lives had changed since I had last seen them in elementary school. They also seemed eager to eat the brownies I brought with me as thank-you gifts.

WON'T YOU BE MY MENTOR?

In hindsight, starting the project in my second year of graduate school and rushing into the research design, the IRB approval, and the whole process of fieldwork (without a formal ethnography course under my belt) was not the best idea. If I had taken more time at the front end, I might have anticipated some of the difficulties in studying social class and friendship. Waiting until I had taken more ethnography classes might also have improved the quality of the data that I collected during my initial foray into the field. Because it took a while to get good at writing field notes and conducting interviews, the data from the students' fourth- and fifth-grade years are far more usable than the data I collected while they were in third grade. However, my professors at Penn (especially Melissa Wilde, who taught the Research Methods class, and Charles Bosk, the graduate chair at the time) were instrumental in helping me navigate the logistics and get the project off the ground.

As I entered my third year in graduate school, and despite still taking a full load of classes and being a teaching assistant for others, I dove into full-time fieldwork. I also worked to build my ethnographic toolkit, taking methods classes with noted ethnographers in the Sociology Department (David Grazian)[11] and in the Graduate School of Education (Stanton Wortham).[12] With that training, my field notes improved dramatically, capturing not just a running log of what was going on but also the meaning of those interactions as they unfolded. I learned to notice and describe facial expressions, body language, and tone of voice. I also learned how to manage the data

I was collecting and how to move dialectically back and forth between data and theory to analyze what I had found.

The start of my third year in graduate school also marked Annette Lareau's arrival at Penn and ultimately the beginning of a relationship with a new advisor. Prior to that point, Grace Kao, whose work includes research on racial and ethnic diversity in students' friendships, had been my primary advisor, and a tremendous one at that. She was (and still is) always full of hard-hitting, deeply insightful advice. At the same time, Grace was not an ethnographer, and as my focus shifted away from friendship, her connection to my research at Maplewood seemed less clear. And so I began to wonder: Should I ask Annette to be my advisor instead? Would she say yes, given that she had not been involved in the project from the start? Given the overlap between my work and Annette's work, it seemed important for me to seek her out as a mentor or, at the very least, meet with her to talk about the project. And yet, I was worried. I worried that Annette would not like me and that she would think my project was silly or underdeveloped or overly critical of her own work.

I remember our first meeting vividly. It was before the school year began, and Annette's office was not yet ready, so we planned to meet at a coffee shop across the street from the Penn sociology building. Before heading to meet her, I anxiously checked and rechecked the back cover of my copy of *Unequal Childhoods* (Lareau 2011), trying to familiarize myself with Annette's face so that I would be able to spot her in the crowd. Sitting at a table (a full 15 minutes early), I went over my project "pitch" again and again in my head. Of course, when the time came, I felt like I bumbled every word, but Annette was incredibly gracious and eager to learn more about the project and what I was finding in the field.

We began meeting regularly to talk about fieldwork and, to my great relief and delight, Annette agreed to sign on as the primary advisor for the project. I also audited the year-long ethnography class she taught during my fourth year in graduate school. Although a third ethnography class was not necessary, it gave me the chance to get regular feedback on fieldnotes, transcripts, and memos from Annette and from other graduate students doing fieldwork. Those weekly class meetings kept me accountable and motivated me to go back into the field looking for more. More observations. More interviews. As much data as I could muster. In those classes and in my regular meetings with Annette, I learned the art of reflection, periodically pulling back from the fieldwork to write memos, search for patterns, and interrogate those patterns in relation to existing literature and theories. I also learned grace—how to accept criticism and how to criticize others in a way that moves my own work (and, ideally, the field as a whole) a step forward.

CLIMBING MOUNT DATA

Conducting ethnographic research is like climbing a mountain of data that you build as you go. And with more than 4 years of data collection from the start of the project to its completion, it felt like a mountain indeed. There were observations of teachers and students. There were interviews with students, parents (usually mothers, but in some cases fathers), and teachers. There were surveys and school records and follow-up research in middle school. Table A.1 provides an overview of the data collected and the number of participants involved in each part of the project.

Table A.1 PARTICIPANTS BY ROLE AND TYPE OF PARTICIPATION

Elementary Observations

Students[a]	55 middle-class	25 working-class
Teachers[b]	17	

Elementary Interviews

Total families[c]	12 middle-class	9 working-class
Students	12 middle-class	9 working-class
Parents	15 middle-class	9 working-class
Teachers	12	

Background Surveys

Total families	44 middle-class	23 working-class

School Records[d]

Total students	40 middle-class	14 working-class

Middle School Observations

Students[e]	47 middle-class	18 working-class
Teachers	10	

Middle School Interviews

Students	6 middle-class	7 working-class
Teachers	10	

[a] I solicited parents' consent for all students in the target cohort at Maplewood ($N = \sim 100$). A total of 80 families agreed to participate; 67 completed demographic surveys. The remaining families (~ 20) opted out of the study or never returned either the surveys or the consent forms despite repeated attempts at contact.

[b] At Maplewood, I observed the third-, fourth-, and fifth-grade teachers and the five teachers of "enrichment" classes (gym, art, music, library, and Spanish). At Fair Hills Middle School, 10 of the seventh-grade teachers participated in observations. The teachers also participated in interviews, and some teachers were interviewed more than once.

[c] I interviewed parents and children from the same families, selecting from those who were participating in observations at Maplewood. I contacted all 14 of the white, working-class families and a randomly selected group of 15 of the 29 white, middle-class families. Of the 29 families contacted, 2 families were never reached despite repeated attempts, and 5 families were unable to complete interviews because of scheduling conflicts. In 3 families (all middle-class), mothers and fathers took part in a joint interview. In the remaining parent interviews, only one parent took part. Most of those one-parent interviews involved mothers (I asked to speak with the child's primary caregiver), but the sample did include two divorced fathers raising their children alone (both working-class). Although most parent interview participants were married, six parents were not (three working-class and three middle-class).

[d] Some parents agreed to allow their children to participate in observations but did not grant me access to their children's school records. Because I reviewed the records at the end of the students' fifth-grade school year, I was also unable to collect information for students who moved away prior to that point.

[e] This includes only students who were also in the original cohort at Maplewood.

Collecting all that data was physically and mentally exhausting. I spent hundreds of hours observing and thousands of hours writing field notes and analytic memos. I conducted 85 interviews, listening to all of them multiple times (often while I was commuting) and transcribing more than half of them myself. The surveys and school records that I collected for students in elementary school were not originally digitized. I spent a solid week holed up in a conference room at Maplewood, carefully combing through stacks of paper files and inputting the relevant information (grades, teacher comments, standardized test scores, etc.) into spreadsheets.

It was an ambitious project—maybe too ambitious. Between fieldwork, grad school, and commuting, I rarely had time for more than 5 or 6 hours of sleep each night. That is less than I get now with a baby and a toddler. I drank 2 liters of Diet Mountain Dew every day, and there were more than a few times when I almost fell asleep at the wheel. I never thought about giving up or even pulling back—I have trouble saying "no" or giving less than 110%—but I wonder whether I could do the project again.

And that is in part because collecting the data was only half the battle. Analyzing all that data, like climbing to the top of any mountain, also had its challenges. First, I had to keep the mountain from crumbling under me, and that meant keeping the data as organized and secure as possible. I cannot stress enough the importance of a good file system—and keeping double and triple copies of everything. Cloud storage (e.g., Box and Dropbox) is an excellent option, but ethnography almost inevitably involves paper files as well. I nearly had a heart attack one time when, while stopped at a station on my train ride home, a sheet of notebook paper with my field jottings flew out of my hands and out the door of the train, landing on the tracks below. It would not have been the end of the world to lose that one piece of paper (although it would have required a report to the IRB), but I must have looked so horrified that the conductor took pity on me, alerted the engineer, and let me climb down to retrieve the paper.

Another major challenge was figuring out what to do with all of that data. How would I find the patterns? How would I look for disconfirming evidence? Like most contemporary ethnographers, I diligently went through the process of coding my field notes and interview transcripts with Atlas.ti. Unfortunately, I quickly realized that even with the best bells and whistles, qualitative data software could not really "do the analysis" for me. Instead, most of the actual analysis happened while I was re-reading, thinking about (often while running or driving), writing about (often in analytic memos), or talking about the data. I cannot stress enough how valuable it is to share blinded field notes and memos with friends, colleagues, and advisors and to have the chance to talk them through what you have found. In those thoughts and memos and conversations, the patterns began to crystalize.

Atlas.ti, in turn, became a useful tool for tracking those emerging patterns in the data and quickly finding the excerpts I needed when I was ready to write about what I had found. I also took to using data matrices[13]—in my case, spreadsheets with references to instances in field notes or interview transcripts, organized by participant characteristics (social class, race/ethnicity, gender, etc.)—as a way to search for disconfirming evidence and to check alternative explanations.

The process of collecting and analyzing all that data often felt overwhelming. I rarely got enough sleep, and I worried constantly about next steps. Did I have enough data? What was my research question? How should I frame the argument? Will these findings ever be published? In hindsight, however, and despite those challenges, it is difficult to think of anything that I would have or could have done differently and still achieve the same depth and breadth of data. Less commuting probably would have helped with the exhaustion, but it also gave me time to think and reflect on my fieldwork without distractions. Unfortunately, building and climbing a mountain of data is just not an easy process.

On the plus side, however, building and climbing that mountain of data has allowed me to answer my research questions and discover others to answer as well. When I got to Indiana University, I began working with two of my colleagues (Weihua An and graduate student Will McConnell) to turn my lunchroom observations (which included diagrams of where students sat) into network data, and we are working on a paper examining stratification patterns in students' peer interactions over time. In my virtual desk drawer, I also have half-written drafts of papers on gender and teaching styles and helicopter parenting. I guess if you are going to climb a mountain, you might as well have a few good stories to show for it in the end. And, of course, having built and climbed one mountain of data, I feel much more prepared to do it again.

As I hope this appendix has made clear, ethnography is difficult and often exhausting work. Managing people and trust and emotions is far more complicated and unpredictable than managing numbers on a screen. There are countless decisions to be made, and those decisions often have trade-offs—such as time spent with partners and family and friends—that are much larger than the project itself. I do not regret the decisions I made, and I am tremendously grateful for the successes I have found because of them. Nevertheless, I might build a smaller mountain next time, or I might not do it alone.

NOTES

INTRODUCTION

1. All names are pseudonyms, including the name of the school. Some identifying details have been changed to protect the anonymity of the participants.

2. We know from research on noncognitive skills that certain behavioral traits and competencies—such as effort, motivation, help-seeking, and organizational skills—are also closely correlated with student outcomes (Carneiro and Heckman 2003; Farkas 2003; Heckman and Rubinstein 2001). We also know that those skills are unevenly distributed, with more privileged students outperforming less privileged students on measures of cognitive and noncognitive skills (Jennings and DiPrete 2010; Lubienski 2000; McLeod and Kaiser 2004; Tach and Farkas 2006). Less clear, however, is why noncognitive skills vary along social class lines and why different skills and strategies generate such unequal rewards.

3. Although cultural capital research typically focuses on cultural matching and compliance with institutional expectations, scholars have defined and operationalized the concept in myriad ways. That includes Bourdieu, whose own use of the term was not always consistent (Lamont and Lareau 1988). Building on Bourdieu's *Distinction* (1984), for example, scholars such as DiMaggio (1982) treat cultural capital (defined as consumption of "high" culture) as a signal of elite status. Those scholars argue that cultural capital can be used to exert power and monopolize resources, but they say little about how that process actually works. We do not see, for example, how individuals activate signals of elite status or how institutions respond to those signals in allocating opportunities and rewards.

4. Lareau (2000), for example, argues that schools have standardized expectations regarding the appropriate amount and type of parental involvement in schooling and that middle-class parents are better able to meet those standards.

5. Such preferences are consistent with an emphasis on "grit," the idea that independence and perseverance are valuable for success in school and in life (Duckworth et al. 2007).

6. Lareau (2011) does describe a middle-class child asking questions at the doctor's office (at his mother's urging) and getting the information he desires. In that case, however, it is unclear whether the child's questions generated support in excess of what the doctor intended to provide (the doctor asked if the child had questions).

7. Research on teacher bias predates work on implicit bias, but the two are closely related. Implicit bias describes the subconscious ways that stereotypes impact people's perceptions and treatment of others, particularly others from less privileged groups (Greenwald et al. 2002). Although scholars who study teacher bias often imply that those biases are subconscious, their studies are rarely designed to distinguish implicit from explicit biases. Thus, I opt to use the term "teacher bias" rather than "implicit bias" in discussing what that research has found.

8. This is true both at the individual level and at the school level, where research shows that instructional practices are closely linked to socioeconomic composition (Anyon 1981; Camburn and Han 2011; Gamoran et al. 2000).

9. Qualitative research suggests that implicit bias may extend to parents as well. Schools often treat less privileged parents as second-class citizens, and that treatment seems (at least in some cases) to affect how parents perceive schools and their role in them (Cucchiara 2013; Lareau and Horvat 1999; Lewis-McCoy 2014).

10. Dumais (2006) finds that teachers evaluate low-SES students (but not high-SES) more positively when those students participate in cultural activities. Dumais, however, does not actually observe how those activities (or other aspects of children's behavior) guide teachers in responding to students in school.

11. However, scholars have questioned the extent to which middle-class parents' interventions actually boost student achievement (Domina 2005; McNeal 1999; Robinson and Harris 2014).

12. Contemporary studies also define student resistance in a somewhat different way. Whereas student resistance was historically viewed as a response to the cultural alienation experienced by working-class and minority students (Bettie 2014; Fordham and Ogbu 1986; MacLeod 1995; Willis 1977), McFarland (2001) views challenges to teacher authority as a response to peer pressure and teacher-centered instruction (663). Similarly, Pace and Hemmings (2006) argue that identities alone are too "multifaceted and fluid" (19) to fully explain behaviors like resistance.

13. Although studies have found evidence of middle-class parents challenging institutions to secure advantages for their children (Brantlinger 2003; Horvat et al. 2003; Lareau 2011; Lewis and Diamond 2015), it is unclear whether those behaviors should be viewed as cultural capital and whether middle-class children activate similar strategies with similar success.

14. Such "opportunity hoarding" by the middle class has important parallels to the idea of "negotiated advantage." Tilly (2003) defines opportunity hoarding as a situation in which a group on one side of some categorical boundary "excludes people on the opposite side of the boundary from use of the value-producing resource, captures the returns, and devotes some of the returns to reproducing the boundary" (34). The concept has been widely used in education, usually to describe privileged parents' efforts to limit access to key resources such as high-track classes (Kelly and Price 2011) and higher education credentials (Wright 2009).

15. Writing good field notes takes time—often three or four hours for every hour in the field—and even good field notes can only document a portion of everything that an ethnographer observes.

16. For notable exceptions, see Streib (2011) and Willis (1981).

17. Research shows, for example, that teacher bias against less privileged students is more pronounced in schools with higher percentages of poor and minority students (Ready and Wright 2011). See also Diamond, Randolph, and Spillane (2004).

18. Minority students are now the majority in American public schools (National Center for Education Statistics 2013).

19. Racial inequalities in teacher perceptions of students persist even after controlling for other factors that might contribute to such biases (McGrady and Reynolds 2013; Riegle-Crumb and Humphries 2012).

20. Charter and magnet schools are often more socioeconomically diverse than traditional public schools (Kahlenberg and Potter 2012), but choosing one of these schools as a research site would have been problematic because that diversity usually breaks down along racial and ethnic lines (Cucchiara 2013; Holme 2002), making it difficult to isolate the importance of social class in the classroom. Parents also choose to enroll their children

in such schools, meaning that they are likely different in many ways from the vast majority of parents who send their children to their local public school (Goldring and Phillips 2008; Yang and Kayaardi 2004).

21. Although schools are often highly segregated, Maplewood is in many ways typical of the kinds of schools that most white students attend. As Saporito and Sohoni (2007) have shown, white students generally attend schools with low poverty rates.

22. Middle- and upper-middle-class families differed primarily in terms of access to costly goods and services such as new-model iPhones, private tutoring, and trips to Disney World. Poor and working-class differences were also rooted in finance, with poor families struggling more to make ends meet and often relying on charities and public assistance to help meet basic needs.

23. According to 2010 Census data, the median household income in Fair Hills (the community surrounding Maplewood) was roughly $90,000.

24. Home value estimates are based on public records data (for participants' home addresses) collected from Zillow.com in 2011. The median home value in Fair Hills at that time was approximately $420,000.

25. Some research (Bennett et al. 2012) has suggested that differences in parents' financial resources are the primary driver of social class differences in parenting styles. These findings, however, have been determined to explain only one aspect of parenting—children's enrollment in extracurricular activities—and not broader social class differences in family life (e.g., differences in parents' use of negotiation vs. directives to guide children's behavior).

26. A few families participated in the study but did not complete the parent survey. In those cases, I determined students' social class backgrounds from conversations with teachers.

27. Choosing one class to observe would have allowed me to spend more time with the students and teacher in that class, but it would have severely limited the number of working-class students and teachers in the observation sample. It also would have made it difficult to observe the same students over time. Over time observations were important, in turn, because they allowed me to see how a particular student interacted with multiple teachers.

28. In some cases, parents granted me permission to observe their children but not to collect information from their academic records. In those cases, I was able to get a rough sense of students' achievement levels from students' math placement, from conversations with teachers, and from my observations of the students in class.

29. I did not interview the five enrichment (gym, art, library, music, and Spanish) teachers who also participated in the study.

30. All four fourth-grade teachers were interviewed twice—once in the fall and once in the spring. Third-, fifth-, and seventh-grade teachers were interviewed only once. All teacher interviews took place in classrooms, and they usually lasted 60–90 minutes.

31. For other examples of count data, see Rist (2000) and Nelson and Schutz (2007).

32. In each classroom, I counted help-seeking during a science period involving in-class projects, a language arts period involving independent writing activities, a math period involving a test or quiz, and a flex-time period in which students were working individually on various projects.

33. Although it would have been ideal to conduct similar counts for other types of behaviors (e.g., accommodation- and attention-seeking), the large number of students and the fast-paced nature of classroom interaction made it difficult to track multiple behaviors simultaneously. Adding additional count periods would have reduced the quality of the ethnographic data collected. I wrote field notes about the periods that I observed while counting, but they were generally less rich in detail and dialogue. Adding observations for count sessions would also have been difficult because working-class students were often

absent (see also Balfanz and Byrnes 2012), and I conducted counts only during periods in which all working-class students were present.

34. When classrooms were particularly noisy or when students were crowded around the teacher, it could be difficult to determine the precise number or nature of requests. In those situations, I prioritized documenting working-class students' requests. I did so by moving closer to hear and by asking teachers to describe exchanges after the fact. Thus, although my counts accurately document working-class students' requests, they may underestimate middle-class requests.

35. See Hallett (2010) for a discussion of the challenges that accountability pressures create for teachers. See also Valli and Buese (2007) for a discussion of how accountability pressure has changed the teacher's role.

36. I created an Excel workbook for each pattern. The file on help-seeking, for example, had sheets for hand-raising, calling out, approaching the teacher, unsolicited assistance, and not seeking help. Within each sheet, I listed students' names in the leftmost column, grouping them by social class, gender, and math level (a rough proxy for academic ability). In the cells to the right of each name, I included references to each instance of such behavior (e.g., each time Julie asked for help by raising her hand). This visual arrangement of the data made patterns readily apparent. It also allowed me to consider alternative explanations for such patterns (e.g., whether it was really gender or academic ability driving what I saw) and made it easy to identify any students who did not seem to fit the overall patterns.

37. Certainly, these patterns may have been different in a more racially diverse school. Exploring such possibilities is difficult, however, given that most schools are highly segregated by race (Logan et al. 2012).

CHAPTER 1

1. This is particularly apparent in research on parents' gender socialization (Eccles, Jacobs, and Harold 1990; Gunderson et al. 2012; Kane 2006; Martin 2005; Raley and Bianchi 2006) and racial socialization efforts (Crouter et al. 2008; Demo and Hughes 1990; Hughes et al. 2006; Lareau 2011; Lewis 2003), which are generally shown to be more deliberate processes.

2. Some research (Bennett, Lutz, and Jayaram 2012) has questioned the importance of class-based parenting logics, suggesting instead that parents' financial resources are the primary driver of social class differences in parenting styles. Those findings, however, have only been found to explain one aspect of parenting—children's enrollment in extracurricular activities—and not broader social class differences in family life (e.g., differences in parents' use of negotiation vs. directives to guide children's behavior).

3. In some families, mothers and fathers both played a role in coaching children to manage problems at school. More often, however, it seemed to be mothers who took the lead. Such findings are consistent with existing research on gender and parenting, which suggests that fathers often play a supporting role (Heard 2007; Lareau 2000; Reay 1995).

4. Like other working-class parents, Ms. Compton believed that if her children relied too much on others, it would undermine their development of respect and responsibility and might result in reprimand. However, Ms. Compton also admitted to me in an interview that it was a struggle for her to help Jesse with homework. She described, close to tears, how overwhelmed she felt by frequent, complex assignments and by her own work schedule, which prevented her from being home in the afternoons. Those challenges also seemed to play a role in prompting Ms. Compton to encourage Jesse to tackle problems on his own.

5. Jared Carson, for example, was the only working-class boy in the top-level math class. Jared's closest friends—Jason, Aidan, Ben, and Steve—were all from middle-class families. On surveys, a few other working-class students listed middle-class classmates as friends,

but Jared was the only working-class student to regularly interact with middle-class peers both in and out of school.

6. In teaching those strategies, parents demonstrated some of the class-based parenting styles found in prior research. Consistent with Lareau's (2011) model of "concerted cultivation," the middle-class parents reasoned with their children about the importance of self-advocacy (e.g., "This is a place where you go every day. You talk to this teacher every day. He's invested in your interests. He likes you. You couldn't be any safer unless you were at my house. It's okay to ask questions in that setting."). Similarly, and consistent with the "accomplishment of natural growth," working-class parents used directives in emphasizing the importance of good character (e.g., "Don't give your teachers a hard time.").

7. For a discussion of alternative models of cultural capital, see Lamont and Lareau (1988).

8. Although prior research has shown that middle-class parents often intervene at school to secure advantages for their children, including advantages that the school may have been reluctant to provide (Brantlinger 2003; Horvat et al. 2003; Lareau 2011; Lewis and Diamond 2015), it is unclear whether those behaviors should be viewed as cultural capital. Nor do we know whether middle-class children activate similar behaviors to secure advantages on their own behalf.

9. These patterns are important in revealing that parents, regardless of social class, do not operate on autopilot. Parenting is often assumed to be a sort of instinctual process—a natural outgrowth of either parents' values or the resources available to them (Bourdieu 1990; Duncan and Magnuson 2003; Edin and Lein 1997; Kohn 1969). What I found, instead, was that parents were very deliberate, at least in deciding how to deal with problems at school and teaching their children to do the same. They worried and fretted and ultimately chose parenting strategies that they believed best matched their primary goals. In doing so, they engaged in a parenting process that was much more active and strategic than existing research tends to imply.

CHAPTER 2

1. For a discussion of alternative models of cultural capital, see Lamont and Lareau (1988).

2. The No Child Left Behind Act of 2001 required annual assessments of all students in grades 3–8 (US Department of Education 2010). Those assessments were designed and administered at the State level. Because students' scores on those assessments had real consequences for teachers and schools, considerable class time was often devoted to helping students prepare for those tests (Abrams, Pedulla, and Madaus 2003; Hallett 2010; Spillane et al. 2002).

3. Of the 12 teachers observed and interviewed at Maplewood, 4 were raised in working-class families.

4. Ms. Corsaro, a middle-class mother and former teacher, explained, "Having been a teacher, I know when I made stuff up, it was clear to me, because I knew what I meant. But I could see how kids could sometimes misinterpret something. And so I would have been very receptive to [students asking for clarification], and I think I'm very aware of that. And all of the teachers I've encountered at Maplewood for sure would have been. I worked with teachers who would have been like, 'Figure it out yourself.' But kids feel frustrated when they say that. Because they're doing the right thing by asking. I think most teachers would be receptive to it. I think most teachers would look at it [a request for clarification] and realize what the kids are asking."

5. Many of the teachers seemed to view their higher-achieving students as lacking in "problem-solving skills." As Mr. Fischer explained in an interview, "They speed right through. They don't check their work. Some of them, a few of the kids that test lower actually do a lot better in that regard, which is kind of interesting. Because they work harder and they're reflective of their work. Some of the kids, like Alan [a middle-class, Asian

American student] and Jason [a middle-class, white student] test off the scales, but on a performance kind of thing they fall short because they don't check their work and use their problem-solving strategies."

6. Even when teachers did not want to grant students' requests, they rarely said "no" outright. Instead, teachers often opted for a more subtle approach, using sarcasm to dissuade students from making further requests.

7. Working-class students were very cautious about voicing their needs. Rather than push through moments of ambiguity, they typically reserved their requests for moments when a positive response seemed likely. That included moments when teachers offered unsolicited support (i.e., going up to a student and saying, "You okay? Need some help?" or "That's a great story! Do you want to share?") and moments when teachers specifically called for questions or volunteers. Because teachers were busy, however, offers of unsolicited support were relatively rare. As a result, and as discussed in more detail in Chapters 3–5, working-class students were often left struggling on their own.

8. We know from research on teacher authority and classroom interaction that flexible standards are useful for teachers in managing the various (and often competing) demands of classroom life (Buzzelli and Johnston 2002; Diehl and McFarland 2012; Metz 1978; Mullooly and Varenne 2006; Pace and Hemmings 2006; Swidler 1979). Essentially, avoiding fixed and firmly stated expectations allowed teachers to adapt to the situation at hand. For example, a teacher setting up a bulletin board at the front of the room while her students work on their individual book reports might prefer that students approach her directly with questions so that she would not have to stop working. During a math test, on the other hand, that same teacher might prefer that students either not ask questions at all or raise their hands and wait for her to come to them so that they would not disrupt other students.

9. Prior research has shown that middle-class parents are often successful in lobbying schools to provide additional (and often unfair) advantages to their children (Baker and Stevenson 1986; Lewis and Diamond 2015; Lewis-McCoy 2014; Useem 1992). It is unclear, however, whether those behaviors should be viewed as cultural capital. Prior research also has not shown whether middle-class children activate similar behaviors to secure advantages on their own behalf.

CHAPTER 3

1. Although these behaviors were distinct in many ways, they could serve overlapping purposes. For example, students sometimes used requests for help or prolonged negotiations over rules as a way to get attention from teachers as well.

2. For a discussion of alternative models of cultural capital, see Lamont and Lareau (1988).

3. Together, the observed periods (science, language arts, math, and flex-time) represent the bulk of a "typical" school day. I did not conduct explicit counts during other portions of the day (e.g., enrichment activities such as gym and library, lunch, recess, and before/after school), but my qualitative data revealed similar patterns in help-seeking during those times as well. Thus, my count data provide a conservative estimate of overall help-seeking frequency.

4. In my qualitative observations, requests from working-class students for information and checking of work were also extremely rare.

5. There were a handful of students in both social class groups who missed large amounts of class time due to illness and/or family vacations. Among the middle-class students, for example, Jason, Adam, Ben, and Tyler all missed more than 10 days in fifth grade. Among the working-class students, Shawn missed 22 days in fourth grade, and Sidney missed 15 days. There were also students in both groups with perfect or near-perfect attendance. On average, however, working-class students were absent more often than

their middle-class peers. White middle-class students missed, on average, 4.5 days per year, whereas white working-class students missed, on average, 6.5 days per year. This is consistent with existing research showing that absenteeism is often a problem for less privileged students and one that exacerbates class-based inequalities in school outcomes (Ready 2010).

6. It is known from prior research that support from adults and especially support from institutional authorities has powerful social and psychological consequences for students (Stanton-Salazar 1997, 2001).

7. Whereas working-class students tried to deal with problems on their own, middle-class students were quick to seek help with similar logistical challenges. On another day, for example, middle-class student Gina immediately scurried over to Ms. Nelson when her own pencil got stuck, lamenting dramatically "the sharpener ate my pencil!"

8. Interestingly, Gina went up to ask Ms. Nelson for help while her partner, Pedro (working-class, Latino), waited at his seat.

9. It is also known that those skills are unevenly distributed, with more privileged students outperforming less privileged students on measures of cognitive and noncognitive skills (Jennings and DiPrete 2010; Lubienski 2000; McLeod and Kaiser 2004; Tach and Farkas 2006).

10. Working-class students wanted to do well in school and were proud when they earned good grades, but they were less grade-focused compared to their middle-class peers. They also focused more on good character. Such findings are consistent with resistance theory in suggesting that working-class culture may elevate alternative models of success as a way to protect individual self-worth against the possibility of academic or socioeconomic failure (Bettie 2014; MacLeod 1995; Willis 1977).

CHAPTER 4

1. Lareau and Horvat (1999) found that schools generally did little to address middle-class black parents' concerns about racial discrimination. They argued that the lack of responsiveness resulted from a mismatch between parents' actions and teachers' expectations that parents would not openly criticize the school. Specifically, they noted that "the Masons framed the issues with contestation and anger, but the school had a standard that emphasized positive, polite interactions" (49).

2. Teachers typically allowed students to use the bathroom, get a drink, or sharpen pencils without asking for permission, but they had tacit expectations about when and how often it was appropriate to do so.

3. For a discussion of alternative models of cultural capital, see Lamont and Lareau (1988). For evidence of middle-class parents securing advantages by persuading institutions to meet their demands, see Baker and Stevenson (1986), Cucchiara (2013), Lewis and Diamond (2015), and Useem (1992).

CHAPTER 5

1. As noted in previous chapters, cultural capital theory typically views middle-class advantages as the result of a cultural matching process in which middle-class individuals are better able to comply with institutional expectations (Lamont and Lareau 1988; Lareau and Weininger 2003).

CHAPTER 6

1. Cucchiara (2013) finds that when white, middle-class families move into areas with predominantly black, low-income schools, their persistent demands on the schools pressure educators to make real reforms.

2. In three other cases, middle-class parents initially challenged and then ultimately deferred to teachers' placement decisions. In those cases, however, the parents agreed to the school's placement decision only after requesting (and being promised) that their children would receive extra assignments and more one-on-one support from teachers. The middle-class Ford family, for example, had their son Sammy tested by an outside expert after the school IQ test failed to qualify him for the gifted program. As Ms. Ford explained in an interview after fifth grade, "Sammy's got a mild learning disability. And because of that, when they do the IQ testing on him, he comes out as 98th percentile, 97th percentile, 34th percentile. Because his processing speed is so slow. So he's very bright, but he doesn't fit the firm definition of gifted." Initially, the Fords lobbied to have Sammy admitted under an alternate measure of intelligence that an outside expert viewed as more appropriate for Sammy's condition. When school district officials refused, the Fords agreed not to press the issue further if the principal and the teachers would provide "math challenge packets and other enrichment work" and "possibly do a test participation in some gifted groups."

3. Such findings are consistent with prior studies showing that middle-class parents are quick to voice their concerns about teachers to other parents. Horvat et al. (2003), for example, found that before she even got home from work, middle-class mother Mrs. Tallinger had already received numerous voicemails from other mothers informing her that her son Garrett had been mistreated by a teacher at school. Those parents also called school district officials and ultimately got the teacher suspended.

CHAPTER 7

1. The idea that support from teachers allows average- and lower-ability students to perform higher than expected would also be consistent with research showing that supportive relationships with teachers are particularly beneficial for less privileged and minority students, who often struggle more in school (Crosnoe, Erickson, and Dornbusch 2002; Crosnoe, Johnson, and Elder 2004; Stanton-Salazar 1997).

2. Less privileged students also experience cultural discomfort in interactions with peers (Armstrong and Hamilton 2013; Jack 2014; Khan 2011; Stuber 2011).

3. See the Appendix for more details regarding the follow-up research completed during the students' seventh-grade year at Fair Hills Middle School.

4. Stanton-Salazar (2001) also finds evidence of student appreciation for teacher support in his work with high school students from low-income, minority families.

5. Following what other studies have shown, the boys at Maplewood were often louder than the girls, and they got in more trouble for talking or goofing around with their friends.

6. Research on boys' school rejection focuses on older, less privileged students (Morris 2008; Willis 1981).

7. Downey and Pribesh (2004) conclude that racial differences in teachers' ratings are likely the result of biased perceptions and not black students' embrace of oppositional culture. However, research also shows that teachers vary in their level of bias against less privileged and minority students. Alexander, Entwisle, and Thompson (1987) find, for example, that teachers from high-status backgrounds exhibit more bias against those students than do teachers from lower-status backgrounds.

8. Whereas scholars such as Fordham and Ogbu (1986) have suggested that black students face peer pressure to avoid "acting white" (i.e., by doing well in school), other scholars have found little evidence to support such claims (Ainsworth-Darnell and Downey 1998; Carter 2005; Warikoo and Carter 2009).

9. White parents rarely discuss race and ethnicity with their children or do so in ways that fail to create real understanding of persistent racial inequalities (Lewis 2003; Tatum 2003).

10. Those class-based similarities across racial and ethnic groups could reflect the fact that students' friendships were more segregated by class than by race and ethnicity. The

working-class Latino students, for example, all had working-class white friends. They also lived in the same apartment complexes and mobile home neighborhoods as their working-class white peers. Middle-class Asian American students, on the other hand, all had middle-class white friends. They also lived in middle-class white neighborhoods and participated in extracurricular activities with their middle-class white peers.

11. Cross-cultural comparisons show that support-seeking is less common in more interdependent cultures and those with a stronger emphasis on deference to authority (Mojaverian and Kim 2013).

12. Some scholars believe that attending more privileged schools will undermine the self-esteem (and subsequent achievement) of less privileged students. Others provide evidence that the correlation between school climate, self-esteem, and subsequent achievement is limited, at best (Bachman and O'Malley 1986)

13. Cucchiara's (2013) research suggests, for example, that increasing the number of middle-class families in a school leads the school to develop a more middle-class culture that includes greater responsiveness to parental requests.

14. As I discuss elsewhere (Lareau and Calarco 2012), there was also evidence of working-class mothers learning from middle-class "cultural mentors." A few working-class mothers recalled middle-class mothers "coaching" them (often during little league games or other similar events) on how to intervene at school and make requests (e.g., to have a child tested for learning disabilities or to not have a child placed in a specific class). Although those working-class mothers told me that they appreciated the advice they received, and although the coaching seemed to help them achieve particular goals, it did not seem to lead to larger-scale changes in the working-class mothers' parenting styles.

15. See Calarco et al. (2014) for more details.

16. Although some scholars argue that peer cultures are more influential than individual friends in shaping student behavior (Bearman and Bruckner 1999), there is evidence that close friends may have a more direct impact (Alexander et al. 2001; Cherng, Calarco, and Kao 2013; Urberg 1992).

17. Bourdieu (1977, 1990) uses the concept of "habitus" to describe the tastes and worldviews that individuals internalize by virtue of their class status. Bourdieu tends to view habitus as deriving primarily from early life experiences and thus as difficult to change. As Lee and Kramer (2013) note, however, Bourdieu does recognize that habitus is not fixed; rather, it is constantly being either reinforced or transformed by exposure to new social environments, experiences, and influences.

CONCLUSION

1. Such findings are consistent with the notion that perseverance or "grit" is beneficial for students (Duckworth et al. 2007), but they also challenge the idea that grit automatically results in better outcomes at school. It is, however, somewhat unclear which problem-solving behaviors scholars like Duckworth et al. (2007) would count as "grit." On the one hand, working-class students' desire to tackle problems on their own (rather than seeking support) could be seen as "gritty." On the other hand, middle-class students' persistence in seeking the support they desire (rather than conceding when teachers say "no") could also be seen as a form of grit. Future research should investigate these distinctions.

2. Prior research has highlighted inequalities that emerge in and through peer group interactions. It is known, for example, that social class is linked to popularity and to social belonging (Eder 1995; Pugh 2009; Thorne 1993). Those studies, however, have not shown how peer-related inequalities contribute to larger patterns of stratification in school and in society.

3. Instead, those expectations are part of the "hidden curriculum" of schooling (Apple 1980; Jackson 1990).

4. This idea of varying expectations is consistent with research on teacher authority, which finds that classroom rules and procedures are far more malleable than they are often assumed to be (McFarland 2001; Metz 1978; Pace 2003; Pace and Hemmings 2003).

5. This idea is consistent with "inhabited institutionalism," which suggests that institutions exist and evolve through the actions of those who comprise them (Hallett 2010).

6. Consistent with that view, and as discussed in Chapter 1, working-class students did adopt alternative definitions of success, focusing more on good character than on good grades.

7. The middle-class students at Maplewood were also very focused on amusing and impressing their friends. As discussed in Chapter 5, middle-class students (and especially boys) tried to use jokes and snide remarks to elicit laughter and approval from peers. Compared to the high school students McFarland (2001) observed, however, the elementary-aged students at Maplewood seemed more focused on impressing and amusing their teachers as well. This may have been a function of age. Research suggests that whereas young children sometimes challenge the specifics of adult rules, older adolescents are more inclined to challenge the basis of adults' authority to make rules (Montemayor 1983).

8. Such findings indicate that parenting anxiety may not be reserved for the middle class, as prior research (e.g., Hays 1996; Nelson 2010) has suggested.

9. At their core, those parents' contrasting decisions about which goals to prioritize and how to achieve them are equally valid. Unfortunately, institutions value and reward those decisions in unequal ways that often privilege the middle class (Bourdieu 1996; Lareau and Weininger 2003).

10. Bourdieu (1984) defines habitus as the orientations, preferences, and demeanors that an individual acquires through his or her experience of holding a particular position (e.g., gender, race, and social class) in society. For evidence of social class differences in habitus, see Dumais (2006), Lee and Kramer (2013), and Lehmann (2014).

11. Consistent with such arguments, a number of high-profile books for parents and teachers (with provocative titles such as *The Price of Privilege* and *The Gift of Failure*) have highlighted the drawbacks of children's dependency on adults and called on parents to stop protecting their children from struggle and failure. See Lahey (2015), Levine (2008), and Lythcott-Haims (2015).

12. Scholars disagree about whether these "no excuses" schools are good for less privileged students. See Carter (2000) for a discussion of their strengths and Lack (2009) for a discussion of their drawbacks.

13. In the late 19th and early 20th centuries, novelists such as Horatio Alger (1895) popularized individual notions of success (Weiss 1969). Public opinion polls show that those beliefs have been tremendously persistent over time. See Cozzarelli, Wilkinson, and Tagler (2001), Hunt (1996), and Smith and Stone (1989).

APPENDIX

1. Even today, my mom scoffs at the idea of spending more than $5 on a shirt or $10 on a pair of pants.

2. Survey-based research has examined the impact of school composition (Crosnoe 2009; Rumberger and Palardy 2005) and cross-class friendships (Cherng, Calarco, and Kao 2013) on outcomes such as school achievement and attainment, but what was less clear, and what seemed ripe for ethnographic research, was precisely how those environments and interactions shaped students' outcomes over time.

3. In hindsight, it would have been easier to include everything in the IRB up front, but a willingness to amend was crucial for responding to the new and surprising patterns that emerged in the field.

4. I highly recommend that ethnographers talk about their studies as "projects" (and not "studies") when interacting with subjects. It is a much less loaded term and one that is much more relatable, especially in an educational context.

5. The remaining families either opted out of the study or never returned the surveys and/or consent documents despite repeated attempts at contact.

6. Even with passive consent for observations, I still would have had to obtain consent for surveys and interviews.

7. The students at Maplewood were used to being "observed," usually by teachers in training from nearby colleges.

8. Although I dressed more like a teacher (slacks and sweaters or, occasionally, jeans) than a student (girls typically wore leggings and hooded sweatshirts), I carried a giant backpack that often sparked questions and admiration from students ("How much can you hold in there?!").

9. Focusing on individual student–teacher interactions also avoided the consent issues noted previously because it was easier to exclude any interactions involving students who were not participating in the project.

10. Research shows that neighborhoods are often highly segregated by social class (Iceland and Wilkes 2006). Along those lines, scholars have investigated the effects of neighborhood poverty on students' school outcomes, but these effects are generally found to be smaller and less significant than those for family background (Quillian 2012; Sastry and Pebley 2010). Research also shows that friendships tend to exhibit high levels of social class homophily (Cherng et al. 2010; McPherson, Smith-Lovin, and Cook 2001).

11. David Grazian is an urban ethnographer who studies popular culture, mass media, and entertainment. His books include *Blue Chicago* (Chicago University Press, 2003), *On the Make* (Chicago University Press, 2008), and *American Zoo* (Princeton University Press, 2015).

12. Stanton Wortham is a linguistic anthropologist who focuses on issues related to identity in education. His notable publications include *Learning Identity* (Cambridge University Press, 2006), *Narratives in Action* (Teachers College Press, 2001), and "From Good Student to Outcast: The Emergence of a Classroom Identity" (*Ethos*, June 2004).

13. See Miles and Huberman (1994: 240).

REFERENCES

Abrams, Lisa M., Joseph J. Pedulla, and George F. Madaus. 2003. "Views from the Classroom: Teachers' Opinions of Statewide Testing Programs." *Theory into Practice* 42(1): 18–29.

Adler, Patricia A., and Peter Adler. 1998. *Peer Power: Preadolescent Culture and Identity*. New Brunswick, NJ: Rutgers University Press.

Ainsworth-Darnell, James W., and Douglas B. Downey. 1998. "Assessing the Oppositional Culture Explanation for Racial/Ethnic Differences in School Performance." *American Sociological Review* 63(4): 536–553.

Alexander, Karl L., Doris R. Entwisle, and Maxine S. Thompson. 1987. "School Performance, Status Relations, and the Structure of Sentiment: Bringing the Teacher Back In." *American Sociological Review* 52(5): 665–682.

Alexander, Cheryl, Marina Piazza, Debra Mekos, and Thomas Valente. 2001. "Peers, Schools, and Adolescent Cigarette Smoking." *Journal of Adolescent Health* 29(1): 22–30.

Alger, Horatio. 1895. *Ragged Dick: Or, Street Life in New York with the Boot-Blacks*. Philadelphia, PA: Henry T. Coates.

Amato, Paul R. 1994. "Father–Child Relations, Mother–Child Relations, and Offspring Psychological Well-Being in Early Adulthood." *Journal of Marriage and Family* 56(4): 1031–1042.

Anyon, Jean. 1980. "Social Class and the Hidden Curriculum of Work." *Journal of Education* 162(1):67–92.

Anyon, Jean. 1981. "Social Class and School Knowledge." *Curriculum Inquiry* 11(1): 3–42.

Apple, Michael W. 1980. "The Other Side of the Hidden Curriculum: Correspondence Theories and the Labor Process." *Interchange* 11(3): 4–22.

Armstrong, Elizabeth A., and Laura T. Hamilton. 2013. *Paying for the Party: How College Maintains Inequality*. Cambridge, MA: Harvard University Press.

Arnot, Madeleine, and Diane Reay. 2007. "A Sociology of Pedagogic Voice: Power, Inequality, and Pupil Consultation." *Discourse* 28(3): 311–325.

Bachman, Jerald G., and Patrick. M. O'Malley. 1986. "Self-Concepts, Self-Esteem, and Educational Experiences: The Frog Pond Revisited (Again)." *Journal of Personality and Social Psychology* 50(1): 35–46.

Baker, David P., and David L. Stevenson. 1986. "Mothers' Strategies for Children's School Achievement: Managing the Transition to High School." *Sociology of Education* 59(3): 156–166.

Baker, Jean A. 2006. "Contributions of Teacher–Child Relationships to Positive School Adjustment During Elementary School." *Journal of School Psychology* 44(3): 211–229.

Balfanz, Robert, and Vaughan Byrnes. 2012. *Chronic Absenteeism: Summarizing What We Know from National Available Data*. Baltimore, MD: Johns Hopkins University, Center for Social Organization of Schools. http://www.ccrscenter.org/products-resources/resource-database/chronic-absenteeism-summarizing-what-we-know-nationally

Ballenger, Cynthia. 1992. "Because You Like Us: The Language of Control." *Harvard Educational Review* 62(2): 199–208.

Barnard-Brak, Lucy, DeAnn Lechtenberger, and William Y. Lan. 2010. "Accommodation Strategies of College Students with Disabilities." *The Qualitative Report* 15(2): 411–429.

Barr, Rebecca, and Robert Dreeben. 1983. *How Schools Work*. Chicago, IL: University of Chicago Press.

Bearman, Peter S., and Hannah Bruckner. 1999. *Peer Effects on Adolescent Girls' Sexual Debut and Pregnancy Risk*. Washington, DC: Pregnancy Prevention for Youth Network.

Bennett, N., A. C. Lutz, and L. Jayaram. 2012. "Beyond the Schoolyard: The Role of Parenting Logics, Financial Resources, and Social Institutions in the Social Class Gap in Structured Activity Participation." *Sociology of Education* 85(2): 131–157.

Bernstein, Basil E. 1958. "Some Sociological Determinants of Perception: An Enquiry into Sub-cultural Differences." *British Journal of Sociology* 9(2): 159–174.

Bernstein, Basil E. 1990. *Class, Codes, and Control*. London, UK: Routledge.

Bertrand, Marianne, and Jessica Pan. 2011. "The Trouble with Boys: Social Influences and the Gender Gap in Disruptive Behavior." Working Paper 17541. Cambridge, MA: National Bureau of Economic Research.

Bettie, Julie. 2014. *Women Without Class: Girls, Race, and Identity*. Berkeley, CA: University of California Press.

Blaise, Mindy. 2007. "A Feminist Poststructuralist Study of Children 'Doing' Gender in an Urban Kindergarten Classroom." *Early Childhood Research Quarterly* 20(1): 85–108.

Bodovski, Katerina. 2010. "Parental Practices and Educational Achievement: Social Class, Race, and Habitus." *British Journal of Sociology of Education* 31(2): 139–156.

Boostrom, Robert. 1991. "Nature and Function of Classroom Rules." *Curriculum Inquiry* 21(2): 193–216.

Bosk, Charles L., and Raymond G. De Vries. 2004. "Bureaucracies of Mass Deception: Institutional Review Boards and the Ethics of Ethnographic Research." *Annals of the American Academy of Political and Social Science* 595(1): 249–263.

Bourdieu, Pierre. 1977. *Outline of a Theory of Practice*. Cambridge, UK: Cambridge University Press.

Bourdieu, Pierre. 1984. *Distinction: A Social Critique on the Judgement of Taste*. London, UK: Routledge.

Bourdieu, Pierre. 1990a. *In Other Words: Essays Towards a Reflexive Sociology*. Translated by Matthew Adamson. Stanford, CA: Stanford University Press.

Bourdieu, Pierre. 1990b. *The Logic of Practice*. Translated by R. Nice. Stanford, CA: Stanford University Press.

Bourdieu, Pierre. 1996. *The State Nobility: Elite Schools in the Field of Power*. Translated by Lauretta C. Clough. Stanford, CA: Stanford University Press.

Bourdieu, Pierre, and Jean-Claude Passeron. 1990. *Reproduction in Education, Society and Culture*. Thousand Oaks, CA: Sage.

Bowles, Samuel, and Herbert Gintis. 1976. *Schooling in Capitalist America*. New York, NY: Basic Books.

Brantlinger, Ellen. 2003. *Dividing Classes: How the Middle Class Negotiates and Rationalizes School Advantage*. New York, NY: Routledge.

Bronfenbrenner, Uri. 1958. "Socialization and Social Class Through Time and Space." In *Readings in Social Psychology*, edited by Eleanor E. Maccoby, Theodore M. Newcomb, and Eugene L. Hartley, pp. 400–425, 3rd ed. New York: Holt, Rinehart & Winston.

Brophy, Jere E., and Thomas L. Good. 1972. "Teacher Expectations: Beyond the Pygmalion Controversy." *Phi Delta Kappan* 54(4): 276–278.

Brophy, Jere E., and Thomas L. Good. 1974. *Teacher–Student Relationships: Causes and Consequences*. Oxford, UK: Oxford University Press.

Bryk, Anthony S., Valerie E. Lee, and Peter B. Holland. 1993. *Catholic Schools and the Common Good*. Cambridge, MA: Harvard University Press.

Buchmann, Claudia, and Thomas A. DiPrete. 2006. "The Growing Female Advantage in College Completion: The Role of Family Background and Academic Achievement." *American Sociological Review* 71(4): 515–541.

Buchmann, Claudia, and Thomas A. DiPrete. 2013. *The Rise of Women: The Growing Gender Gap in Education and What it Means for American Schools*. New York: Russell Sage.

Buchmann, Claudia, Thomas A. DiPrete, and Anne McDaniel. 2008. "Gender Inequalities in Education." *Annual Review of Sociology* 34: 319–337.

Butler, Ruth. 1998. "Determinants of Help Seeking: Relations Between Perceived Reasons for Classroom Help-Avoidance and Help-Seeking Behaviors in an Experimental Context." *Journal of Educational Psychology* 90(4): 630–643.

Buzzelli, Cary, and Bill Johnston. 2002. *The Moral Dimensions of Teaching*. New York, NY: Routledge.

Calarco, Jessica McCrory. 2011. "'I Need Help!' Social Class and Children's Help-Seeking in Elementary School." *American Sociological Review* 76(6): 862–882.

Calarco, Jessica McCrory. 2014a. "Coached for the Classroom: Parents' Cultural Transmission and Children's Reproduction of Educational Inequalities." *American Sociological Review* 79(5): 1015–1037.

Calarco, Jessica McCrory. 2014b. "The Inconsistent Curriculum: Cultural Toolkits and Student Interpretations of Ambiguous Expectations." *Social Psychology Quarterly* 77(2): 185–209.

Calarco, Jessica McCrory, Weihua An, and William R. McConnell. 2014. "Save Me a Seat: Segregation in Elementary Students' Lunchroom Seating Networks over Two Years." Paper presented at the 2014 Annual Meeting of the American Sociological Association. San Francisco, CA.

Camburn, Eric, and Seong Won Han. 2011. "Two Decades of Generalizable Evidence on U.S. Instruction from National Surveys." *Teachers College Record* 113(3): 561–610.

Campbell, Susan B. 1995. "Behavior Problems in Preschool Children: A Review of Recent Research." *Journal of Child Psychology and Psychiatry* 36(1): 113–149.

Carneiro, Pedro Manuel, and James J. Heckman. (2003). "Human Capital Policy." In *Inequality in America: What Role for Human Capital Policies?* edited by J. J. Heckman, A. B. Krueger, and B. M. Friedman, pp. 77–240. Cambridge, MA: MIT Press.

Carter, Prudence. 2003. "'Black' Cultural Capital, Status Positioning, and Schooling Conflicts for Low-Income African American Youth." *Social Problems* 50(1): 136–155.

Carter, Prudence. 2005. *Keepin' It Real: School Success Beyond Black and White*. New York, NY: Oxford University Press.

Carter, Prudence L., and Kevin G. Welner. 2013. *Closing the Opportunity Gap: What America Must Do to Give Every Child an Even Chance*. New York, NY: Oxford University Press.

Carter, Samuel Casey. 2000. *No Excuses: Lessons from 21 High-Performing, High-Poverty Schools*. Washington, DC: Heritage Foundation.

Cherng, Sebastian, Jessica McCrory Calarco, and Grace Kao. 2013. "Along for the Ride: Best Friends' Resources and Adolescents' College Completion." *American Educational Research Journal* 50(1): 76–106.

Chin, Tiffany, and Meredith Phillips. 2004. "Social Reproduction and Child-Rearing Practices: Social Class, Children's Agency, and the Summer Activity Gap." *Sociology of Education* 77(3): 185–210.

Coleman, James S. 1988. "Social Capital in the Creation of Human Capital." *American Journal of Sociology* 94: S95–S120.

Condron, Dennis J. 2009. "Social Class, School and Non-School Environments, and Black/White Inequalities in Children's Learning." *American Sociological Review* 74(5): 685–708.

Contreras, Mary F., Steven Brint, and Michael T. Matthews. 2001. "Socialization Messages in Primary Schools : An Organizational Analysis." *Sociology of Education* 74(3): 157–180.

Cookson, Peter W. 1994. *School Choice: The Struggle for the Soul of American Education*. New Haven, CT: Yale University Press.

Cookson, Peter W., and Caroline Hodges Persell. 1985. *Preparing for Power: America's Elite Boarding Schools*. New York, NY: Basic Books.

Cornelius-White, Jeffrey. 2007. "Learner-Centered Teacher–Student Relationships Are Effective: A Meta-Analysis." *Review of Educational Research* 77(1): 113–143.

Corsaro, William A. 2005. *The Sociology of Childhood*, 2nd ed. Thousand Oaks, CA: Pine Forge Press.

Corsaro, William A., and Donna Eder. 1990. "Children's Peer Cultures." *Annual Review of Sociology* 16: 197–220.

Cozzarelli, Catherine, Anna V. Wilkinson, and Michael J. Tagler. 2001. "Attitudes Toward the Poor and Attributions of Poverty." *Journal of Social Issues* 57(2): 207–227.

Crosnoe, Robert. 2009. "Low-Income Students and the Socioeconomic Composition of Public High Schools." *American Sociological Review* 74(5): 709–730.

Crosnoe, Robert, Kristan Glasgow Erickson, and Sanford M. Dornbusch. 2002. "Protective Functions of Family Relationships and School Factors on the Deviant Behavior of Adolescent Boys and Girls: Reducing the Impact of Risky Friendships." *Youth & Society* 33(4): 515–544.

Crosnoe, Robert, Monica Kirkpatrick Johnson, and Glen H. Elder. 2004. "Intergenerational Bonding in School: The Behavioral and Contextual Correlates of Student–Teacher Relationships." *Sociology of Education* 77(1): 60–81.

Crouter, Ann C., Megan E. Baril, Kelly D. Davis, and Susan M. McHale. 2008. "Processes Linking Social Class and Racial Socialization in African American Dual-Earner Families." *Journal of Marriage and Family* 70(5): 1311–1325.

Cucchiara, Maia Bloomfield. 2013. *Marketing Schools, Marketing Cities: Who Wins and Who Loses When Schools Become Urban Amenities*. Chicago, IL: University of Chicago Press.

Dauber, Susan L., Karl L. Alexander, and Doris R. Entwisle. 1996. "Tracking and Transitions Through the Middle Grades: Channeling Educational Trajectories." *Sociology of Education* 69(4): 290–307.

Davidson, Ann Locke. 1996. *Making and Molding Identity in Schools*. Albany, NY: State University of New York Press.

Delpit, Lisa D. 2006. *Other People's Children*. New York, NY: New Press.

Demerath, Peter. 2009. *Producing Success: The Culture of Personal Achievement in an American High School*. Chicago, IL: University of Chicago Press.

Demo, David H., and Michael Hughes. 1990. "Socialization and Racial Identity Among Black Americans." *Social Psychology Quarterly* 53(4): 364–374.

Diamond, John B., Antonia Randolph, and James P. Spillane. 2004. "Responsibility for Student Learning: The Importance of Race, Class, and Organizational Habitus." *Anthropology & Education Quarterly* 35(1): 75–98.

Diehl, David, and Daniel A. McFarland. 2012. "Classroom Ordering and the Situational Imperative of Routine and Ritual." *Sociology of Education* 85(4): 326–349.

DiMaggio, Paul. 1982. "Cultural Capital and School Success: The Impact of Status Culture Participation on the Grades of U.S. High School Students." *American Sociological Review* 47(2): 189–201.

DiMaggio, Paul. 1997. "Culture and Cognition." *Annual Review of Sociology* 23: 263–287.

DiMaggio, Paul, and Hazel R. Markus. 2010. "Culture and Social Psychology: Converging Perspectives." *Social Psychology Quarterly* 73(4): 347–352.

DiPrete, Thomas A., and Claudia Buchmann. 2013. *The Rise of Women: The Growing Gender Gap in Education and What It Means for American Schools*. New York: Russell Sage.

DiPrete, Thomas A., and Jennifer L. Jennings. 2012. "Social and Behavioral Skills and the Gender Gap in Early Educational Attainment." *Social Science Research* 41: 1–15.

Domina, Thurston. 2005. "Leveling the Home Advantage: Assessing the Effectiveness of Parental Involvement in Elementary School." *Sociology of Education* 78(3): 233–249.

Downey, Douglas B., and Shana Pribesh. 2004. "When Race Matters: Teachers' Evaluations of Students' Classroom Behavior." *Sociology of Education* 77(4): 267–282.

Duckworth, Angela L., Christopher Peterson, Michael D. Matthews, and Dennis Kelly. 2007. "Grit: Perseverance and Passion for Long-Term Goals." *Journal of Personality and Social Psychology* 92(6): 1087–1101.

Dumais, Susan A. 2006. "Early Childhood Cultural Capital, Parental Habitus, and Teachers' Perceptions." *Poetics* 34(2): 83–107.

Duncan, Greg J., and Jeanne Brooks-Gunn. 1997. *Consequences of Growing up Poor.* New York, NY: Russell Sage Foundation.

Duncan, Greg J., and Katherine A. Magnuson. 2003. "Off with Hollingshead: Socioeconomic Resources, Parenting, and Child Development." In *Socioeconomic Status, Parenting, and Child Development,* edited by Marc Bornstein and Robert H. Bradley, Chapter 3. Mahwah, NJ: Erlbaum.

Duncan, Greg J., and Katherine A. Magnuson. 2004. "Can Family Socioeconomic Resources Account for Racial and Ethnic Test Score Gaps?" *The Future of Children* 15(1), 35–54.

Duncan, Greg J., W. Jean Yeung, Jeanne Brooks-Gunn, and Judith R. Smith. 1998. "How Much Does Childhood Poverty Affect the Life Chances of Youth?" *American Sociological Review* 63(3): 406–423.

Dweck, Carol S. 1986. "Motivational Processes Affecting Learning." *American Psychologist* 41(10): 40–48.

Eccles, Jacquelynne S., Janis E. Jacobs, and Rena D. Harold. 1990. "Gender Role Stereotypes, Expectancy Effects, and Parents' Socialization of Gender Differences." *Journal of Social Issues* 46(2): 183–201.

Eder, Donna. 1981. "Ability Grouping as a Self-Fulfilling Prophecy: A Micro-Analysis of Teacher–Student Interaction." *Sociology of Education* 54(3): 151–162.

Eder, Donna. 1995. *School Talk: Gender and Adolescent Culture.* New Brunswick, NJ: Rutgers University Press.

Edin, Kathryn, and Laura Lein. 1997. *Making Ends Meet: How Single Mothers Survive Welfare and Low-Wage Work.* New York, NY: Russell Sage Foundation.

Edwards, Margie L. Kiter. 2004. "We're Decent People: Constructing and Managing Family Identity in Rural Working-Class Communities." *Journal of Marriage and Family* 66(2): 515–529.

Elder, Glen H. Jr. 1947. *Children of the Depression: Social Change and Life Experience.* Chicago, IL: University of Chicago Press.

Elias, Maurice J., and Norris M. Haynes. 2008. "Social Competence, Social Support, and Academic Achievement in Minority, Low-Income, and Urban Elementary School Children." *Social Psychology Quarterly* 23(4): 474–495.

Entwisle, Doris R., Karl L. Alexander, and Linda S. Olson. 2007. "Early Schooling: The Handicap of Being Poor and Male." *Sociology of Education* 80(2): 114–138.

Epstein, Joyce L. 1986. "Parents' Reactions to Teacher Practices of Parental Involvement." *Elementary School Journal* 86(3): 277–294.

Farkas. George. 1996. *Human Capital or Cultural Capital: Ethnicity and Poverty in an Urban School District.* New York, NY: de Gruyter.

Farkas, George. 2003. "Cognitive Skills and Noncognitive Traits and Behaviors in Stratification Processes." *Annual Review of Sociology* 29: 541–562.

Ferguson, Ronald F. 2003. "Teachers' Perceptions and Expectations and the Black–White Test Score Gap." *Education and Urban Society* 38(4): 460–507.

Fine, Gary Alan. 1987. *With the Boys: Little League Baseball and Preadolescent Culture*. Chicago, IL: University of Chicago Press.

Florio, Susan, and Jeffrey Shultz. 1979. "Social Competence at Home and at School." *Theory into Practice* 18(4): 234–243.

Foley, Douglas E. 1990. *Learning Capitalist Culture*. Philadelphia, PA: University of Pennsylvania Press.

Ford, Donna Y., and J. John Harris. 1996. "Perceptions and Attitudes of Black Students Toward School, Achievement, and Other Educational Variables." *Child Development* 67: 1141–1152.

Fordham, Signithia, and John U. Ogbu. 1986. "Black Students' School Success: Coping with the 'Burden of Acting White.'" *Urban Review* 18: 176–206.

Gall, Sharon Nelson-Le. 1985. "Help-Seeking Behavior in Learning." *Review of Research in Education* 12: 55–90.

Gamoran, Adam. 1986. "Instructional and Institutional Effects of Ability Grouping." *Sociology of Education* 59(4): 185–198.

Gamoran, Adam. 1992. "The Variable Effects of High School Tracking." *American Sociological Review* 57(6): 812–828.

Gamoran, Adam, and Robert D. Mare. 1989. "Secondary School Tracking and Educational Inequality: Compensation, Reinforcement, or Neutrality?" *American Journal of Sociology* 94(5): 1146–1183.

Gamoran, Adam, Walter G. Secada, and Cora B. Marrett. 2000. "The organizational context of teaching and learning: Changing theoretical perspectives." In *Handbook of Research in the Sociology of Education*, edited by Maureen T. Hallinan, pp. 37–63. New York, NY: Kluwer.

Gilberts, G. H., M. Agran, C. Hughes, and M. L. Wehmeyer. 2001. "The Effects of Peer-Delivered Self-Monitoring Strategies on the Participation of Students with Severe Disabilities in General Education Classrooms." *Journal of the Association for Persons with Severe Handicaps* 26: 25–36.

Giroux, Henry. 1983. "Theories of Reproduction and Resistance in the New Sociology of Education: A Critical Analysis." *Harvard Educational Review* 53(3): 257–293.

Goldring, Ellen B., and Kristie J. R. Phillips. 2008. "Parent Preferences and Parent Choices: The Public–Private Decision About School Choice." *Journal of Education Policy* 23(3): 209–230.

Goyette, Kimberly A. 2008. "College for Some to College for All: Social Background, Occupational Expectations, and Educational Expectations over Time." *Social Science Research* 37(2): 461–484.

Granovetter, Mark S. 1973. "The Strength of Weak Ties." *American Journal of Sociology* 78(6): 1360–1380.

Greenwald, Anthony G., Mahzarin R. Banaji, Laurie A. Rudman, Shelly D. Farnham, Brian A. Nosek, and Deborah S. Mellott. 2002. "A Unified Theory of Implicit Attitudes, Stereotypes, Self-Esteem, and Self-Concept." *Psychological Review* 109(1): 3–25.

Gregory, Anne, Russell J. Skiba, and Pedro A. Noguera. 2010. "The Achievement Gap and the Discipline Gap: Two Sides of the Same Coin?" *Educational Researcher* 39(1): 59–68.

Gunderson, Elizabeth A., Gerardo Ramirez, Susan C. Levine, and Sian L. Beilock. 2012. "The Role of Parents and Teachers in the Development of Gender-Related Math Attitudes." *Sex Roles* 66(3): 153–166.

Guo, Guang, and Kathleen Mullan Harris. 2000. "The Mechanisms Mediating the Effects of Poverty on Children's Intellectual Development." *Demography* 37(4): 431–447.

Gutman, Leslie Morrison, and Carol Midgley. 2000. "The Role of Protective Factors in Supporting the Academic Achievement of Poor African American Students." *Journal of Youth and Adolescence* 29(2): 223–248.

Hallett, Tim. 2010. "The Myth Incarnate: Recoupling Processes, Turmoil, and Inhabited Institutions in an Urban Elementary School." *American Sociological Review* 75(1): 52–74.

Halstead, Mark, and Jiamel Xiao. 2010. "Values Education and the Hidden Curriculum." In *International Research Handbook on Values Education and Student Well-Being*, edited by Terence Lovat, Ron Toomey, and Neville Clement, pp. 303–317. New York, NY: Springer.

Hammersley, Martyn, and Paul Atkinson. 1995. *Ethnography: Principles in Practice*. New York, NY: Routledge.

Hamre, Bridget K., and Robert C. Pianta. 2001. "Early Teacher–Child Relationships and the Trajectory of Children's School Outcomes Through Eighth Grade." *Child Development* 72(2): 625–638.

Hardie, Jessica Halliday. 2015. "The Best Laid Plans: Social Capital in the Development of Girls' Educational and Occupational Plans." *Social Problems* 62(2): 241–265.

Harris, Kathleen Mullan, Frank F. Furstenberg, and Jeremy K. Marmer. 1998. "Paternal Involvement with Adolescents in Intact Families: The Influence of Fathers over the Life Course." *Demography* 35(2): 201–216.

Harris, Kathleen Mullan, and Jeremy K. Marmer. 1996. "Poverty, Paternal Involvement, and Adolescent Well-Being." *Journal of Family Issues* 17(5): 614–640.

Hart, Betty, and Todd R. Risley. 1995. *Meaningful Differences in the Everyday Experience of Young American Children*. Baltimore, MD: Brookes.

Hart, Juliet E., and Julianne Brehm. 2013. "Promoting Self-Determination: A Model for Training Elementary Students to Self-Advocate for IEP Accommodations." *Teaching Exceptional Children* 45(5): 40–48.

Hatch, J. Amos. 1987. "Impression Management in Kindergarten Classrooms: An Analysis of Children's Face-Work in Peer Interactions." *Anthropology & Education Quarterly* 18(2): 100–115.

Hays, Sharon. 1996. *The Cultural Contradictions of Motherhood*. New Haven, CT: Yale University Press.

Heard, Holly E. 2007. "Fathers, Mothers, and Family Structure: Family Trajectories, Parent Gender, and Adolescent Schooling." *Journal of Marriage and Family* 69(2): 435–450.

Heath, Shirley Brice. 1983. *Ways with Words*. Cambridge, UK: Cambridge University Press.

Heath, Shirley Brice. 2012. *Words at Work and Play: Three Decades in Family and Community Life*. Cambridge, UK: Cambridge University Press.

Heckman, James J., and Yona Rubinstein. 2001. "The Importance of Noncognitive Skills: Lessons from the GED Testing Program." *American Economic Review* 91(2): 145–149.

Heckman, James J., Jora Stixrud, and Sergio Urzua. 2006. *The Effects of Cognitive and Noncognitive Abilities on Labor Market Outcomes and Social Behavior*. Working Paper No. 12006. Cambridge, MA: National Bureau of Economic Research.

Hedges, Larry V., and Stella W. Rowley. 1994. "Does Money Matter? A Meta-Analysis of Studies of the Effect of Differential School Inputs on Student Outcomes." *Educational Researcher* 23(3): 5–14.

Heller, Sara, Harold A. Pollack, Roseanna Ander, and Jens Ludwig. 2013. "Preventing Youth Violence and Dropout: A Randomized Field Experiment." NBER Working Paper Series, Working Paper No. 19014. Cambridge, MA: National Bureau of Economic Research.

Hemmings, Annette. 2003. "Fighting for Respect in Urban High Schools." *Teachers College Record* 105(3): 416–437.

Hibel, Jacob, George Farkas, and Paul L. Morgan. 2010. "Who Is Placed into Special Education?" *Sociology of Education* 83(4): 312–332.

Hitlin, Steven, and Jane Allyn Piliavin. 2004. "Values: Reviving a Dormant Concept." *Annual Review of Sociology* 30: 359–393.

Holme, Jennifer Jellison. 2002. "Buying Homes, Buying Schools: School Choice and the Social Construction of School Quality." *Harvard Educational Review* 72(2): 177–206.

Hoover-Dempsey, Kathleen V., and Howard M. Sandler. 1995. "Parental Involvement in Children's Education: Why Does It Make a Difference?" *Teachers College Record* 97(2): 310–331.

Horvat, Erin McNamara, and James Earl Davis. 2011. "Schools as Sites for Transformation: Exploring the Contribution of Habitus." *Youth & Society* 43(1): 142–170.

Horvat, Erin McNamara, Elliot B. Weininger, and Annette Lareau. 2003. "From Social Ties to Social Capital: Class Differences in the Relations Between Schools and Parent Networks." *American Educational Research Journal* 40(2): 319–351.

Hughes, Diana, James Rodriguez, Emilie P. Smith, and Deborah J. Johnson. 2006. "Parents' Ethnic–Racial Socialization Practices: A Review of Research and Directions for Future Study." *Developmental Psychology* 42(5): 747–770.

Hunt, Matthew O. 1996. "The Individual, Society, or Both? A Comparison of Black, Latino, and White Beliefs About the Causes of Poverty." *Social Forces* 75(1): 293–322.

Iceland, John, and Rima Wilkes. 2006. "Does Socioeconomic Status Matter? Race, Class, and Residential Segregation." *Social Problems* 53(2): 248–273.

Jack, Anthony Abraham. 2014. "Culture Shock Revisited: The Social and Cultural Contingencies to Class Marginality." *Sociological Forum* 29(2): 453–475.

Jack, Anthony Abraham. 2016. "(No) Harm in Asking: Class, Acquired Cultural Capital, and Academic Engagement at an Elite University." *Sociology of Education* 89(1): 1–19.

Jackson, Philip W. 1990. *Life in Classrooms*. New York, NY: Teachers College Press.

Jennings, Jennifer L. 2010. "School Choice or Schools' Choice? Managing in an Era of Accountability." *Sociology of Education* 83(3): 227–247.

Jennings, Jennifer L., and Thomas A. DiPrete. 2010. "Teacher Effects on Social and Behavioral Skills in Early Elementary School." *Sociology of Education* 83(2): 135–159.

Jimerson, Shane, Byron Egeland, and Adrian Teo. 1999. "A Longitudinal Study of Achievement Trajectories: Factors Associated with Change." *Journal of Educational Psychology* 92(1): 116–126.

Jones, Susan, and Debra Myhill. 2004. "'Troublesome Boys' and 'Compliant Girls': Gender Identity and Perceptions of Achievement and Underachievement." *British Journal of Sociology of Education* 25(5): 547–561.

Jussim, Lee, and Kent D. Harber (2005). "Teacher Expectations and Self-Fulfilling Prophecies: Knowns and Unknowns, Resolved and Unresolved Controversies." *Personality and Social Psychology Review* 9(2): 131–155.

Kahlenberg, Richard, and Halley Potter. 2012. *Diverse Charter Schools: Can Racial and Socioeconomic Integration Promote Better Outcomes for Students?* Washington, DC: Century Foundation.

Kahneman, Daniel. 2011. *Thinking Fast and Slow*. New York, NY: Farrar, Strauss & Giroux.

Kalleberg, Arne. 2011. *Good Jobs, Bad Jobs: The Rise of Polarized and Precarious Employment Systems in the United States, 1970s to 2000s*. New York, NY: Russell Sage Foundation.

Kane, Emily W. 2006. "'No Way My Boys Are Going to Be Like That!' Parents' Responses to Children's Gender Nonconformity." *Gender & Society* 20(2): 149–176.

Kao, Grace, and Jennifer S. Thompson. 2003. "Racial and Ethnic Stratification in Educational Achievement and Attainment." *Annual Review of Sociology* 29: 417–442.

Karabenick, Stuart A. 1998. *Strategic Help Seeking: Implications for Teaching and Learning*. Mahwah, NJ: Lawrence Erlbaum.

Karabenick, Stuart A., and John R. Knapp. 1991. "Relationship of Academic Help Seeking to the Use of Learning Strategies and Other Instrumental Achievement Behavior in College Students." *Journal of Educational Psychology* 83(2): 221–230.

Kelly, Sean, and Heather Price. 2011. "The Correlates of Tracking Policy: Opportunity Hoarding, Status Competition, or a Technical–Functional Explanation?" *American Educational Research Journal* 48(3): 560–585.

Kerin, Roger A., P. Rajan Varadarajan, and Robert A. Peterson. 1992. "First-Mover Advantage: A Synthesis, Conceptual Framework, and Research Propositions." *Journal of Marketing* 56(4): 33–52.

Khan, Shamus Rahman. 2011. *Privilege: The Making of an Adolescent Elite at St. Paul's School.* Princeton, NJ: Princeton University Press.

Kohn, Melvin L. 1969. *Class and Conformity.* Chicago, IL: University of Chicago Press.

Kozlowski, Karen Phelan. 2015. "Culture or Teacher Bias? Racial and Ethnic Variation in Student–Teacher Effort Assessment Match/Mismatch." *Race and Social Problems* 7(1): 43–59.

Kupchik, Aaron. 2009. "Things are Tough All Over: Race, Ethnicity, Class and School Discipline." *Punishment & Society* 11(3): 291–317.

Lack, Brian. 2009. "No Excuses: A Critique of the Knowledge Is Power Program (KIPP) Within Charter Schools in the USA." *Journal for Critical Education Policy* 7(2): 126–153.

Lacy, Karyn. 2015. "Race, Privilege and the Growing Class Divide." *Ethnic and Racial Studies* 38(8): 1246–1249.

Ladd, Gary W. 1990. "Having Friends, Keeping Friends, Making Friends, and Being Liked by Peers in the Classroom: Predictors of Children's Early School Adjustment?" *Child Development* 61(4): 1081–1100.

Lahey, Jessica. 2015. *The Gift of Failure: How the Best Parents Learn to Let Go So Their Children Can Succeed.* New York, NY: HarperCollins.

Lamont, Michèle. 1992. *Money, Morals, and Manners: The Culture of the French and American Upper-Middle Class.* Chicago, IL: University of Chicago Press.

Lamont, Michèle. 2009. *The Dignity of Working Men.* Cambridge, MA: Harvard University Press.

Lamont, Michèle, and Annette Lareau. 1988. "Cultural Capital: Allusions, Gaps and Glissandos in Recent Theoretical Developments." *Sociological Theory* 6(2): 153–168.

Lareau, Annette. 2000. *Home Advantage: Social Class and Parental Intervention in Elementary Education.* London, UK: Falmer.

Lareau, Annette. 2011. *Unequal Childhoods: Class, Race, and Family Life.* Berkeley, CA: University of California Press.

Lareau, Annette, and Jessica Calarco. 2012. "Class, Cultural Capital, and Institutions: The Case of Families and Schools." In *Facing Social Class*, edited by Susan T. Fiske and Hazel Rose Markus, pp. 61–85. New York, NY: Russell Sage Foundation.

Lareau, Annette, and Dalton Conley. 2008. *Social Class: How Does It Work?* New York, NY: Russell Sage Foundation.

Lareau, Annette, and Erin McNamara Horvat. 1999. "Moments of Social Inclusion and Exclusion: Race, Class, and Cultural Capital in Family–School Relationships." *Sociology of Education* 72(1): 37–53.

Lareau, Annette, and Elliot B. Weininger. 2003. "Cultural Capital in Educational Research: A Critical Assessment." *Theory and Society* 32(5–6): 567–606.

Lauen, Douglas Lee. 2007. "Contextual Explanations of School Choice." *Sociology of Education* 80(3): 179–209.

Lee, Elizabeth M., and Rory Kramer. 2013. "Out with the Old, in with the New? Habitus and Social Mobility at Selective Colleges." *Sociology of Education* 86(1): 18–35.

Lee, Jenny J., and Charles Rice. 2007. "Welcome to America? International Student Perceptions of Discrimination." *Higher Education* 53(30): 381–409.

Lee, Jung-Sook, and Natasha K. Bowen. 2006. "Parent Involvement, Cultural Capital, and the Achievement Gap Among Elementary School Children." *American Educational Research Journal* 43(2): 193–218.

Lee, Valerie E., and David T. Burkam. 2002. *Inequality at the Starting Gate: Social Background Differences in Achievement as Children Begin School.* Washington, DC: Economic Policy Institute.

Legewie, Joscha, and Thomas A. DiPrete. 2012. "School Context and the Gender Gap in Educational Achievement." *American Sociological Review* 77(3): 463–485.

Lehmann, Wolfgang. 2014. "Habitus Transformation and Hidden Injuries: Successful Working-Class University Students." *Sociology of Education* 87(1): 1–15.

Levine, Madeline. 2008. *The Price of Privilege: How Parental Pressure and Material Advantage Are Creating a Generation of Disconnected and Unhappy Kids.* New York, NY: HarperCollins.

Levinson, Bradley U. 2001. *We Are All Equal.* Durham, NC: Duke University Press.

Lewis, Amanda E. 2003. *Race in the Schoolyard: Reproducing the Color Line in School.* New Brunswick, NJ: Rutgers University Press.

Lewis, Amanda E., and John B. Diamond. 2015. *Despite the Best Intentions: Why Racial Inequality Thrives in Good Schools.* New York, NY: Oxford University Press.

Lewis-McCoy, R. L'Heureux. 2014. *Inequality in the Promised Land: Race, Resources, and Suburban Schooling.* Stanford, CA: Stanford University Press.

Lincoln, Yvonna S., and William G. Tierney. 2004. "Qualitative Research and Institutional Review Boards." *Qualitative Inquiry* 10(1): 219–234.

Logan, John R., Elisabeta Minca, and Sinem Adar. 2012. "The Geography of Inequality: Why Separate Means Unequal in American Public Schools." *Sociology of Education* 85(3): 287–301.

Lubienski, Sarah Theule. 2000. "A Clash of Social Class Cultures? Students' Experiences in a Discussion-Intensive Seventh-Grade Mathematics Classroom." *Elementary School Journal* 100(4): 377–403.

Lubrano, Alfred A. 2004. *Limbo: Blue-Collar Roots, White-Collar Dreams.* New York, NY: Wiley.

Lucas, Samuel R., and Mark Berends. 2002. "Sociodemographic Diversity, Correlated Achievement, and De Facto Tracking." *Sociology of Education* 75(4): 328–348.

Luker, Kristin. 2010. *Salsa Dancing into the Social Sciences: Research in an Age of Info-Glut.* Cambridge, MA: Harvard University Press.

Luster, Tom, Kelly Rhoades, and Bruce Haas. 1989. "The Relation Between Parental Values and Parenting Behavior: A Test of the Kohn Hypothesis." *Journal of Marriage and Family* 51: 139–147.

Lythcott-Haims, Julie. 2015. *How to Raise an Adult: Break Free of the Overparenting Trap and Prepare Your Kids for Success.* New York, NY: Holt.

MacLeod, Jay. 1995. *Ain't No Makin' It: Aspirations and Attainment in a Low-Income Neighborhood.* Boulder, CO: Westview.

Markus, Hazel R., and Shinobu Kitayama. 1991. "Culture and the Self: Implications for Cognition, Emotion, and Motivation." *Psychological Review* 98(2): 224–253.

Martin, Karin A. 2005. "William Wants a Doll. Can He Have One? Feminists, Child Care Advisors, and Gender-Neutral Child Rearing." *Gender & Society* 19(4): 456–479.

McFarland, Daniel A. 2001. "Student Resistance: How the Formal and Informal Organization of Classrooms Facilitate Everyday Forms of Student Defiance." *American Journal of Sociology* 107(3): 612–678.

McGrady, Patrick B., and John R. Reynolds. 2013. "Racial Mismatch in the Classroom: Beyond Black–White Differences." *Sociology of Education* 86(1): 3–17.

McGrew, Ken. 2011. "A Review of Class-Based Theories of Student Resistance in Education." *Review of Educational Research* 81(20): 234–266.

McHale, Susan M., Ann C. Crouter, Ji-Yeon Kim, Linda M. Burton, Kelly D. Davis, Aryn M. Dotterer, and Dena P. Swanson. 2006. "Mothers' and Fathers' Racial Socialization in African American Families: Implications for Youth." *Child Development* 77(5): 1387–1402.

McLeod, Jane D., and Karen Kaiser. 2004. "Childhood Emotional and Behavioral Problems and Educational Attainment." *American Sociological Review* 69(5): 636–658.

McLeod, Jane D., and Michael J. Shanahan. 1993. "Poverty, Parenting, and Children's Mental Health." *American Sociological Review* 58(3): 351–366.

McNeal, Ralph B., Jr. 1999. "Parental Involvement as Social Capital: Differential Effectiveness on Science Achievement, Truancy, and Dropping Out." *Social Forces* 78(1): 117–144.

McPherson, Chad Michael, and Michael Sauder. 2013. "Logics in Action: Managing Institutional Complexity in a Drug Court." *Administrative Science Quarterly* 58(2): 165–196.

McPherson, Miller, Lynn Smith-Lovin, and James M. Cook. 2001. "Birds of a Feather: Homophily in Social Networks." *Annual Review of Sociology* 27: 415–444.

McRobbie, Angela. 2000. "The Culture of Working-Class Girls." In *Feminism and Youth Culture*, 2nd ed., pp. 44–66. New York, NY: Routledge.

Mehan, Hugh. 1980. "The Competent Student." *Anthropology & Education Quarterly* 11(3): 131–152.

Messner, Michael A. 2000. "Barbie Girls Versus Sea Monsters: Children Constructing Gender." *Gender & Society* 14(6): 765–784.

Metz, Mary E. 1978. *Classrooms and Corridors*. Berkeley, CA: University of California Press.

Miles, Matthew B., and A. Michael Huberman. 1994. *Qualitative Data Analysis*, 2nd ed. Newbury Park, CA: Sage.

Milner, Murray, Jr. 2004. *Freaks, Geeks, and Cool Kids: American Teenagers, Schools, and the Culture of Consumption*. New York, NY: Routledge.

Mojaverian, Taraneh, and Heejung S. Kim. 2013. "Interpreting a Helping Hand: Cultural Variation in the Effectiveness of Solicited and Unsolicited Social Support." *Personality & Social Psychology Bulletin* 39(1): 88–99.

Montemayor, Richard. 1983. "Parents and Adolescents in Conflict." *Journal of Early Adolescence* 3(1-2): 83–103.

Morris, Edward W. 2005. "'Tuck in That Shirt!' Race, Class, Gender, and Discipline in an Urban School." *Sociological Perspectives* 48(1): 25–48.

Morris, Edward W. 2008. "'Rednecks,' 'Rutters,' and 'Rithmetic." *Gender & Society* 22(6): 728–751.

Mullooly, James, and Herve Varenne. 2006. "Playing with Pedagogical Authority." Chapter 3 in *Classroom Authority: Theory, Research, and Practice*, edited by Judith L. Pace and Annette Hemmings, pp. 63–88. Mahwah, NJ: Erlbaum.

National Center for Education Statistics. 2013. *Digest of Education Statistics: 2013*. Washington, DC: Institute of Education Sciences. https://nces.ed.gov/programs/digest/d13/tables/dt13_203.50.asp

Nelson, Margaret K. 2010. *Parenting out of Control: Anxious Parents in Uncertain Times*. New York, NY: New York University Press.

Nelson, Margaret K., and Rebecca Schutz. 2007. "Day Care Differences and the Reproduction of Social Class." *Journal of Contemporary Ethnography* 36(3): 281–317.

Newman, Richard S. 2000. "Social Influences on the Development of Children's Adaptive Help Seeking: The Role of Parents, Teachers, and Peers." *Developmental Review* 20(3): 350–404.

Newman, Richard S., and Laura Goldin. 1990. "Children's Reluctance to Seek Help with Schoolwork." *Journal of Educational Psychology* 82(1): 92–100.

Oakes, Jeannie. 2005. *Keeping Track: How Schools Structure Inequality*, 2nd ed. New Haven, CT: Yale University Press.

Oates, Gary L. St. C. 2003. "Teacher–Student Racial Congruence, Teacher Perceptions, and Test Performance." *Social Science Quarterly* 84(3): 508–525.

Owens, Jayanti. 2016. "Early Childhood Behavior Problems and the Gender Gap in Educational Attainment in the United States." *Sociology of Education* 89(3): 236–258.

Pace, Judith L. 2003. "Managing the Dilemmas of Professional and Bureaucratic Authority in a High School English Class." *Sociology of Education* 76(1): 37–52.

Pace, Judith L., and Annette Hemmings. 2006. "Understanding Classroom Authority as a Social Construction." Chapter 1 in *Classroom Authority*, edited by Judith L. Pace and Annette Hemmings, pp. 1–32. Mahwah, NJ: Erlbaum.

Pajares, Frank. 2002. "Gender and Perceived Self-Efficacy in Self-Regulated Learning." *Theory into Practice* 41(2): 116–125.

Pallas, Aaron M., Doris R. Entwisle, Karl L. Alexander, and M. Francis Stluka. 1994. "Ability-Group Effects: Instructional, Social, or Institutional?" *Sociology of Education* 67(1): 27–46.

Patrick, Helen, Lynley H. Anderman, Allison M. Ryan, Kimberley C. Edelin, & Carol Midgley. (2001). "Teachers' Communication of Goal Orientations in Four Fifth-Grade Classrooms." *Elementary School Journal* 102(1): 35–58.

Perry, Brea L., and Edward W. Morris. 2014. "Suspending Progress: Collateral Consequences of Exclusionary Punishment in Publish Schools." *American Sociological Review* 79(6): 1067–1087.

Pescosolido, Bernice. 1992. "Beyond Rational Choice: The Social Dynamics of How People Seek Help." *American Journal of Sociology* 97(4): 1096–1138.

Pianta, Robert C., Sheri L. Nimetz, and Elizabeth Bennett. 1997. "Mother-Child Relationships, Teacher-Child Relationships, and School Outcomes in Preschool and Kindergarten." *Early Childhood Research Quarterly* 12(3): 263–280.

Pugh, Allison J. 2009. *Longing and Belonging: Parents, Children, and Consumer Culture.* Berkeley, CA: University of California Press.

Quillian, Lincoln. 2012. "Does Segregation Create Winners and Losers? Residential Segregation and Inequality in Educational Attainment." *Social Problems* 61(3): 402–426.

Quinn, David M. 2015. "Kindergarten Black–White Test Score Gaps: Re-examining the Roles of Socioeconomic Status and School Quality with New Data." *Sociology of Education* 88(2): 120–139.

Raley, Sara, and Suzanne Bianchi. 2006. "Sons, Daughters, and Family Processes: Does Gender of Children Matter?" *Annual Review of Sociology* 32: 401–421.

Ready, Douglas D. 2010. "Socioeconomic Disadvantage, School Attendance, and Early Cognitive Development." *Sociology of Education* 83(4): 271–286.

Ready, Douglas D., and David L. Wright. 2011. "Accuracy and Inaccuracy in Teachers' Perceptions of Young Children's Cognitive Abilities: The Role of Child Background and Classroom Contexts." *American Educational Research Journal* 48(2): 335–360.

Reardon, Sean F. 2011. "The Widening Academic Achievement Gap Between the Rich and the Poor: New Evidence and Possible Explanations." In *Wither Opportunity? Rising Inequality, Schools, and Children's Life Chances*, edited by Greg J. Duncan and Richard J. Murnane, pp. 91–116. New York, NY: Russell Sage Foundation.

Reay, Diane. 1995. "A Silent Majority? Mothers in Parental Involvement." *Women's Studies International Forum* 18(3): 337–348.

Reay, Diane. 1998. *Class Work: Mothers' Involvement in Their Children's Primary Schooling.* London, UK: UCL Press.

Riegle-Crumb, Catherine, and Melissa Humphries. 2012. "Exploring Bias in Math Teachers' Perceptions of Students' Ability by Gender and Race/Ethnicity." *Gender & Society* 26(2): 290–322.

Rist, Ray C. 1970. "Student Social Class and Teacher Expectations: The Self-Fulfilling Prophecy in Ghetto Education." *Harvard Educational Review* 40: 72–73.

Rist, Ray C. 2000. "HER Classic: Student Social Class and Teacher Expectations— The Self-Fulfilling Prophecy in Ghetto Education." *Harvard Educational Review* 70(3): 257–301.

Rivera, Lauren. 2012. "Hiring as Cultural Matching: The Case of Elite Professional Service Firms." *American Sociological Review* 77: 999–1022.

Robinson, Keith, and Angel L. Harris. 2014. *The Broken Compass: Parental Involvement with Children's Education*. Cambridge, MA: Harvard University Press.

Roscigno, Vincent J. 2012. "Power, Sociologically Speaking." *The Society Pages* (Special Feature). Accessed April 27, 2016, from https://thesocietypages.org/specials/power

Roscigno, Vincent J., and James W. Ainsworth-Darnell. 1999. "Race, Cultural Capital, and Educational Resources: Persistent Inequalities and Achievement Returns." *Sociology of Education* 72(3): 158–178.

Rosenfeld, Lawrence B., Jack M. Richman, and Gary L. Bowen. 2000. "Social Support Networks and School Outcomes: The Centrality of the Teacher." *Child and Adolescent Social Work Journal* 17(3): 205–226.

Rosenthal, Robert, and Lenore Jacobson. 1968. "Pygmalion in the Classroom." *The Urban Review* 3(1):16–20.

Rubin, Lillian B. 1976. *Worlds of Pain: Life in the Working-Class Family*. New York, NY: Basic Books.

Rumberger, Russell W., and Gregory J. Palardy. 2005. "Does Segregation Still Matter? The Impact of Student Composition on Academic Achievement in High School." *Teachers College Record* 107(9): 1999–2045.

Ryan, Allison, Lynley Hicks, and Carol Midgley. 1997. "Social Goals, Academic Goals, and Avoiding Seeking Help in the Classroom." *Journal of Early Adolescence* 17(2): 152–171.

Saporito, Salvatore, and Deenesh Sohoni. 2007. "Mapping Educational Inequality: Concentrations of Poverty Among Poor and Minority Students in Public Schools." *Social Forces* 85(3): 1227–1253.

Sastry, Narayan, and Anne R. Pebley. 2010. "Family and Neighborhood Sources of Socioeconomic Inequality in Children's Achievement." *Demography* 47(3): 777–800.

Shifrer, Dara, Chandra Muller, and Rebecca Callahan. 2011. "Disproportionately and Learning Disabilities: Parsing Apart Race, Socioeconomic Status, and Language." *Journal of Learning Disabilities* 44(3): 246–257.

Sirin, Selcuk R. 2005. "Socioeconomic Status and Academic Achievement: A Meta-Analytic Review of Research." *Review of Educational Research* 75(3): 417–453.

Skiba, Russell J., Robert S. Michel, Abra Carroll Nardo, and Reece L. Peterson. 2002. "The Color of Discipline: Sources of Racial and Gender Disproportionality in School Punishment." *The Urban Review* 34(4): 317–342.

Smith, Jeffrey A., Miller McPherson, and Lynn Smith-Lovin. 2014. "Social Distance in the United States: Sex, Race, Religion, Age, and Education Homophily Among Confidants, 1985 to 2004." *American Sociological Review* 79(3): 432–456.

Smith, Kevin B., and Lorene H. Stone. 1989. "Rags, Riches, and Bootstraps." *The Sociological Quarterly* 30(1): 93–107.

Smith, Sheila Graham, Ron English, and Dae Vasek. 2002. "Student and Parent Involvement in the Transition Process for College Freshmen with Learning Disabilities." *College Student Journal* 36(4): 491–503.

Spencer, Thomas J., Joseph Biederman, and Erick Mick. 2007. "Attention-Deficit/Hyperactivity Disorder: Diagnosis, Lifespan, Comorbidities, and Neurobiology." *Journal of Pediatric Psychology* 32(6): 631–642.

Spillane, James P., John B. Diamond, Patricia Burch, Tim Hallett, Loyiso Jita, and Jennifer Zoltners. 2002. "Managing in the Middle: School Leaders and the Enactment of Accountability Policy." *Educational Policy* 16(5): 731–762.

Stanton-Salazar, Ricardo. 1997. "A Social Capital Framework for Understanding the Socialization of Racial Minority Children and Youth." *Harvard Educational Review* 67(1): 1–41.

Stanton-Salazar, Ricardo. 2001. *Manufacturing Hope and Despair: The School and Kin Support Networks of U.S.-Mexican Youth*. New York, NY: Teacher's College Press.

Stanton-Salazar, Ricardo, and Sanford M. Dornbusch. 1995. "Social Capital and the Reproduction of Inequality: Information Networks among Mexican-Origin High School Students." *Sociology of Education* 68(2): 116–135.

Stephens, Nicole M., Stephanie A. Fryberg, Hazel Rose Markus, Camille S. Johnson, and Rebecca Covarrubias. 2012. "Unseen Disadvantage: How American Universities' Focus on Independence Undermines the Academic Performance of First-Generation College Students." *Journal of Personality and Social Psychology* 102(6): 1178–1197.

Streib, Jessi. 2011. "Class Reproduction by Four Year Olds." *Qualitative Sociology* 34: 337–352.

Streib, Jessi. 2015. *The Power of the Past: Understanding Cross-Class Marriages*. New York, NY: Oxford University Press.

Stuber, Jenny M. 2005. "Asset and Liability? The Importance of Context in the Occupational Experiences of Upwardly Mobile White Adults." *Sociological Forum* 20(1): 139–166.

Stuber, Jenny M. 2011. *Inside the College Gates: How Class and Culture Matter in Higher Education*. Plymouth, UK: Lexington Books.

Sui-Chu, Esther Ho, and J. Douglas Willms. 1996. "Effects of Parental Involvement on Eighth-Grade Achievement." *Sociology of Education* 69(2): 126–141.

Swidler, Ann. 1979. *Organization Without Authority: Dilemmas of Social Control in Free Schools*. Cambridge, MA: Harvard University Press.

Tach, Laura Marie, and George Farkas. 2006. "Learning-Related Behaviors, Cognitive Skills, and Ability Grouping when School Begins." *Social Science Research* 35: 1048–1079.

Tatum, Beverly. 2003. *Why Are All the Black Kids Sitting Together in the Cafeteria? And Other Conversations About Race*. New York, NY: Basic Books.

Thornberg, Robert. 2007. "Inconsistencies in Everyday Patterns of School Rules." *Ethnology and Education* 2(3): 401–416.

Thorne, Barrie. 1993. *Gender Play: Girls and Boys in School*. New Brunswick, NJ: Rutgers University Press.

Thrupp, Martin, Hugh Lauder, and Tony Robinson. 2002. "School Composition and Peer Effects." *International Journal of Educational Research* 37(5): 483–504.

Tilly, Charles. 2003. "Changing Forms of Inequality." *Sociological Theory* 21(1): 31–36.

Torche, Florencia. 2011. "Is a College Degree Still the Great Equalizer? Intergenerational Mobility Across Levels of Schooling in the United States." *American Journal of Sociology* 117(3): 763–807.

Tough, Paul. 2012. *How Children Succeed: Grit, Curiosity, and the Hidden Power of Character*. New York, NY: Houghton Mifflin.

Tyson, Karolyn. 2002. "Weighing in: Elementary-Age Students and the Debate on Attitudes Toward School Among Black Students." *Social Forces* 80(4): 1157–1189.

Urberg, Kathryn A. 1992. "Locus of Peer Influence: Social Crowd and Best Friend." *Journal of Youth and Adolescence* 21(4): 439–450.

US Department of Education. 2010. Public Law Print of PL 107–110, the *No Child Left Behind Act of 2001*. http://www2.ed.gov/policy/elsec/leg/esea02/index.html

Useem, Elizabeth L. 1992. "Middle School Math Groups: Parents' Involvement in Children's Placement." *Sociology of Education* 65(4): 263–279.

Valentine, Gill. 1997. "'Oh Yes I Can.' 'Oh No You Can't': Children and Parents' Understandings of Kids' Competence to Negotiate Public Space Safely." *Antipode* 29(1): 65–89.

Valli, Linda, and Daria Buese. 2007. "The Changing Roles of Teachers in an Era of High-Stakes Accountability." *American Educational Research Journal* 44(3): 519–558.

Walpole, MaryBeth. 2003. "Socioeconomic Status and College: How SES Affects College Experiences and Outcomes." *Review of Higher Education* 27(1): 45–73.

Warikoo, Natasha, and Prudence Carter. 2009. "Cultural Explanations for Racial and Ethnic Stratification in Academic Achievement: A Call for a New and Improved Theory." *Review of Educational Research* 79(1): 366–394.

Weiss, Richard. 1969. *The American Myth of Success: From Horatio Alger to Norman Vincent Peale.* New York: Basic Books.

Wentzel, Kathryn R., and Kathryn Caldwell. 1997. "Friendships, Peer Acceptance, and Group Membership: Relations to Academic Achievement in Middle School." *Child Development* 68(6): 1198–1209.

Wigfield, Allan, Jacquelynne S. Eccles, and Paul R. Pintrich. 1996. "Development Between the Ages of 11 and 25." In *Handbook of Educational Psychology,* edited by D. C. Berliner and R. C. Calfee, pp. 148–185. New York, NY: Simon & Schuster.

Williams, Christine L. 2006. *Inside Toyland: Working, Shopping, and Social Inequality.* Berkeley, CA: University of California Press.

Willingham, Warren W., and Nancy S. Cole, eds. 1997. *Gender and Fair Assessment.* Hillsdale, NJ: Lawrence Erlbaum.

Willis, Paul E. 1977. *Learning to Labor: How Working-Class Kids Get Working-Class Jobs.* New York, NY: Columbia University Press.

Willis, Paul E. 1981. *Learning to Labor: How Working-Class Kids Get Working-Class Jobs.* New York: Columbia University Press.

Wren, David J. 1999. "School Culture: Exploring the Hidden Curriculum." *Adolescence* 34(135): 593–596.

Wright, Erik O. 2009. "Understanding Class: Towards an Integrated Analytical Approach." *New Left Review* 60: 101–116.

Yang, Philip Q., and Nihan Kayaardi. 2004. "Who Chooses Non-Public Schools for Their Children?" *Educational Studies* 30(3): 231–249.

Younger, Michael, Molly Warrington, and Jacquetta Williams. 1999. "The Gender Gap and Classroom Interactions: Reality and Rhetoric?" *British Journal of Sociology of Education* 20: 325–341.

Zelizer, Viviana. 2002. "Kids and Commerce." *Childhood* 9(4): 375–396.

INDEX